11TH EDITION

THE
SUPREME COURT

11TH EDITION

THE
SUPREME COURT

LAWRENCE BAUM
Ohio State University

Los Angeles | London | New Delhi
Singapore | Washington DC

Los Angeles | London | New Delhi
Singapore | Washington DC

FOR INFORMATION:

CQ Press

An Imprint of SAGE Publications, Inc.

2455 Teller Road

Thousand Oaks, California 91320

E-mail: order@sagepub.com

SAGE Publications Ltd.

1 Oliver's Yard

55 City Road

London, EC1Y 1SP

United Kingdom

SAGE Publications India Pvt. Ltd.

B 1/I 1 Mohan Cooperative Industrial Area

Mathura Road, New Delhi 110 044

India

SAGE Publications Asia-Pacific Pte. Ltd.

3 Church Street

#10-04 Samsung Hub

Singapore 049483

Photo Credits: 12: Chip Somodevilla/Getty Images. 19: © John A. Angelillo/Corbis. 34: © Win McNamee/Pool/CNP/Corbis. 57: Maria Bryk/Newseum. 62: AP Photo/J. Scott Applewhite. 73: Photo by Diego M. Radzinschi, 2012. 77: Alex Wong/Getty Images. 107: © Dana Verkouteren/AP/Corbis. 123: Diana Walker/Time Life Pictures/Getty Images. 135: © Benjamin J. Myers/Corbis. 144: Brendan Smialowski/Bloomberg via Getty Images. 162: © Owen Franken/Corbis. 169: © Chris Stewart/ San Francisco Chronicle/Corbis. 178: Photo by Diego M. Radzinschi, 2011. 189: © Mark Makela/In Pictures/Corbis. 196: Justin Sullivan/Getty Images. 210: © Wally McNamee/Corbis.

Printed in the United States of America

Library of Congress Cataloging-in-Publication Data

Baum, Lawrence.

The Supreme Court/Lawrence Baum.—Eleventh ed.

p. cm.
Includes bibliographical references and index.

ISBN 978-1-4522-2096-3 (pbk.)
1. United States. Supreme Court. 2. Constitutional law—United States. 3. Courts of last resort—United States. 4. Judicial review—United States. I. Title.

KF8742.B35 2013
347.73'26—dc23   2012017419

This book is printed on acid-free paper.

Acquisitions Editor: Charisse Kiino

Associate Editor: Nancy Loh

Production Editor: Laureen Gleason

Copy Editor: QuADS Prepress (P) Ltd.

Typesetter: C&M Digitals (P) Ltd.

Proofreader: Ellen Howard

Indexer: Lawrence Baum

Cover Designer: Candice Harman

Marketing Manager: Jonathan Mason

Permissions Editor: Adele Hutchinson

12 13 14 15 16 10 9 8 7 6 5 4 3 2 1

To my students

Contents

Tables, Figures, and Boxes

Tables

Figures

Boxes

Preface

The importance of the Supreme Court's role in American life was
abundantly clear in the first half of 2012. The Court ruled on major
issues that ranged from the power of a state to enact and enforce laws
against illegal immigration to limits on the use of GPS devices by law
enforcement agencies to track people. It accepted a case that was likely to
produce a definitive ruling on the use of affirmative action in admission
of students to colleges. And after three days of oral arguments in March
that attracted enormous attention, the Court in June ruled on the
constitutional challenges to the federal health care law sponsored by
President Obama. The Court's decision to uphold all but one provision
of the law did not produce a final resolution of the heated debate over the
law. But that decision allowed the law to continue in operation, and it
helped shape the course of the 2012 elections.

The Supreme Court's importance and the level of public interest in
the Court are not fully matched by understanding of the Court. It is a
complicated institution, one that is more difficult to comprehend than
the other branches of government. As a result, people with great interest
in American politics, even some who are experts in most aspects of politics,
often have only limited knowledge of the Court.

I have written this book to provide a better understanding of the
Supreme Court. The book is intended to serve as a short but comprehensive
guide, both for readers who already know much about the Court and for
those who have a more limited sense of it. I discuss how the Court
functions, the work that it does, and the effects of its rulings on the lives
of people in the United States. And I probe explanations of the decisions
that the Court and its justices make, of actions by other people and groups
that participate in cases, and of the Court's impact on government and
society.

The book gives attention to the Court's history, but it focuses primarily
on the current era. With that focus, this edition discusses recent
developments in and around the Court. President Obama made the two
most recent appointments to the Court in 2009 and 2010, but it is

President George W. Bush's appointments of John Roberts and Samuel Alito that have had a more powerful impact on the Court's direction. I examine that impact in broad terms. I also consider the Court's major decisions in the past few years and the conflicts that have arisen in its relationships with the other branches of government. Underlying some of these developments is the growth in partisan polarization that has touched all aspects of government and politics in the United States.

The first chapter introduces the Supreme Court. In that chapter I discuss the Court's role in general terms, examine the Court's place in the judicial system, analyze the Court as an institution, and present a brief summary of its history.

Each of the other chapters deals with an important aspect of the Court. Chapter 2 focuses on the justices: their selection, their backgrounds and careers, and the circumstances under which they leave the Court. Chapter 3 presents a discussion of how cases reach the Court and how the Court selects the small portion of those cases that it will hear.

In Chapter 4 I examine decision making in the cases that the Court accepts for full consideration. After outlining the Court's decision-making procedures, I turn to the chapter's primary concern: the factors that influence the Court's choices among alternative decisions and policies. Chapter 5 deals with the kinds of issues on which the Court concentrates, the policies it supports, and the extent of its activism in the making of public policy. I give special attention to changes in the Court's role as a policymaker and the sources of those changes. The final chapter examines the ways in which other government policymakers respond to the Court's decisions, as well as the Court's impact on American society as a whole. The chapter concludes with an assessment of the Court's significance in American life.

This new edition of the book reflects the very considerable help that many people gave me with earlier editions. In writing this edition I benefited from the information provided by the Office of the Solicitor General and the Public Information Office of the Supreme Court. The book was strengthened by suggestions for revision from Brett Curry, Georgia Southern University; Adrienne Fulco, Trinity College; Sheldon Goldman, University of Massachusetts; Robert Langran, Villanova University; Jonathan Parent, SUNY–Albany; Charles Smith, University of California, Irvine; and Conrad Weiler, Temple University.

As always, the professionals at CQ Press did much to make my life easier and, more important, to make the book better. I appreciate the excellent assistance of Nancy Loh and Laureen Gleason in the editing process. Charisse Kiino and Brenda Carter maintain a high standard for everything that is done at CQ Press, and their good work over the years has been of enormous help to me.

I benefit a great deal from the professional community of scholars who study the courts and American politics. Like its predecessors, this edition incorporates a good deal of recent research that provides new information and insights about the Supreme Court. I have learned much from my interactions with other scholars in this community. I have also learned from my colleagues in the political science department at Ohio State, a department and university that have offered valuable support for my work. And the students whom I teach have advanced my thinking with their questions and ideas about the Court. In this and other ways, they make teaching a great pleasure.

Chapter 1

The Court

O n March 23, 2010, President Barack Obama signed the Patient Protection and Affordable Care Act. The new law made fundamental changes in the nation's health care system. Congress had enacted the law after a fierce yearlong battle, and the president's signing ceremony seemed to be the culmination of that battle.

It was not. On March 23, the state of Virginia filed a lawsuit challenging the health care law, and that lawsuit was followed by several others arguing that the law was unconstitutional. These cases worked their way through the federal district courts and courts of appeals, and within eighteen months, three courts of appeals had issued rulings in these cases. In November 2011, the Supreme Court accepted a set of petitions for hearings from parties in the health care cases. After hearing three days of arguments on the cases in March 2012, the Court issued its rulings in June. Its decision upholding the health care law in most respects certainly did not end the political battle over the law. Indeed, the Court's decision became one focal point in that battle and in the broader partisan and ideological conflicts in American politics. But more than two years after Congress enacted the health care law, the Court settled the constitutional issue of whether Congress had the power to take that action.

The health care cases were hardly typical of the cases that the Supreme Court hears, cases that are mostly undramatic. But they were not unique. The Court has addressed major national issues again and again, and in doing so it has shaped the course of politics and policy. In the past fifty years the Court has reached significant rulings on policy issues such as abortion, capital punishment, gun rights, and the financing of political campaigns. One decision ensured that President Richard Nixon would leave office in 1974, and another ensured that George W. Bush would become president in 2001.[1]

1

Because of the role that the Supreme Court plays in American life, it is impossible to understand American government and society without understanding the Court. This book is an effort to provide that understanding. Who serves on the Court, and how do they get there? What determines which cases and issues the Court decides? In resolving the cases before it, how does the Court choose between alternative decisions? In what policy areas is it active, and what kinds of policies does it make? Finally, what happens to the Court's decisions after they are handed down, and what impact do they actually have?

Each of these questions is the subject of a chapter in the book. As I focus on each question, I try to show not only what happens in and around the Court but also why things work the way they do. This first chapter is an introduction to the Court, providing background for the chapters that follow.

A Perspective on the Court

The Supreme Court's position in government is more ambiguous than the positions of the other branches, so a good place to begin is with the Court's attributes as an institution and its work as a policymaker.

The Court in Law and Politics

The Supreme Court is, first of all, a court—the highest court in the federal judicial system. Like other courts it has jurisdiction to hear and decide certain kinds of cases. Like other courts it can decide legal issues only in cases that are brought to it. And as a court, it makes decisions within a legal framework. Congress writes new law, but the Court interprets existing law. In this respect the Court operates within a constraint from which legislators are free.

In another respect, however, the Supreme Court's identity as a court reduces the constraints on it. The widespread belief that courts should be insulated from the political process gives the Court a degree of actual insulation. The justices' lifetime appointments allow them some freedom from concerns about whether political leaders and voters approve of their decisions. Justices usually avoid open involvement in partisan activity, because such involvement is seen as inappropriate. And because direct contact between lobbyists and justices is generally considered unacceptable, interest group activity in the Court is basically restricted to the formal channels of legal argument.

The Court's insulation from politics should not be exaggerated, however. People sometimes speak of courts as if they are, or at least ought to be, "nonpolitical." In a literal sense, this is impossible: as a part of government, courts are political institutions by definition. What people really mean when they refer to courts as nonpolitical is that courts are separate from the political process and their decisions are affected only by legal considerations. This too is impossible for courts in general and certainly for the Supreme Court.

The Court is political chiefly because it makes important decisions on major issues. People care about those decisions and want to influence them. As a result, political battles regularly arise over appointments to the Court. Interest groups bring cases and present arguments to the Court in an effort to help shape its policies. Members of Congress pay attention to the Court's decisions and hold powers over the Court, and for that reason the justices may take Congress into account when they decide cases. Finally, the justices' political values affect the votes they cast and the opinions they write in the Court's decisions.

Thus, the Supreme Court should be viewed as both a legal institution and a political institution. The political process and the legal system each influence what the Court does. This ambiguous position adds to the complexity of the Court. It also makes the Court an interesting case study in political behavior.

The Court as a Policymaker

This book examines the Supreme Court broadly, but it emphasizes the Court's role in making public policy—the authoritative rules by which people in government institutions seek to influence government itself and to shape society as a whole. Legislation to provide funding for schools, the ruling of a trial court in an auto accident case, and a Supreme Court decision on rules of police procedure are all examples of public policy. The Court can be viewed as part of a policymaking system that includes lower courts and the other branches of government.

As I have noted, the Supreme Court makes public policy by interpreting provisions of law. Issues of public policy come to the Court in the form of legal questions. In this respect the Court's work as a policymaker differs fundamentally in form from that of Congress.

The Court does not face legal questions in the abstract. Rather, it addresses these questions in the process of settling specific controversies between parties (sometimes called litigants) that bring cases to it. In a sense, then, every decision by the Court has three aspects: it is a judgment about the specific dispute brought to it, an interpretation of the legal issues in that dispute, and a position on the policy questions that are raised by the legal issues.

These three aspects of the Court's rulings are illustrated by a 2011 decision, *Microsoft Corporation v. i4i Limited Partnership*. i4i held a patent for a method to edit computer documents, and in 2007 it sued Microsoft under federal law for infringement of the patent. If a defendant in a patent infringement case shows that the patent was invalid—that it should not have been issued—then the defendant wins the case. Microsoft claimed that i4i's patent was invalid, but a district court jury rejected that claim and ruled that Microsoft was guilty of patent infringement. Microsoft appealed, arguing that the district judge's instruction to the jury gave defendants too heavy a burden when they sought to prove that the patent was invalid. But the Court of Appeals for the Federal Circuit and then the Supreme Court upheld the district judge's standard and ruled against Microsoft.

In the first aspect of its decision, the Supreme Court affirmed the court of appeals decision against Microsoft. As a result, i4i won its case, including an award of $240 million and an injunction against Microsoft practices that infringed on its patent. If the Supreme Court had reversed the court of appeals decision and remanded the case for reconsideration under a different standard, Microsoft would have gained another chance to win the case.

The Court's decision was also a judgment about the meaning of the federal statute in question, the Patent Act of 1952. One section of that statute says that a patent is presumed to be valid and that a party arguing against its validity has the burden of proof. The Supreme Court interpreted that language to mean that an invalidity defense must be proved by clear and convincing evidence. In doing so, it established a rule that lower courts were obliged to follow in any future case.

Finally, the Supreme Court's decision shaped federal policy on the standards for the validity of patents. There has been a long-standing debate about how high a standard must be met to grant patents and to uphold them when they are challenged in court. Advocates of both rigorous and lenient standards argue that adoption of their positions would foster economic growth. By giving defendants a heavy burden when they challenge a patent, the Court favored the advocates of lenient standards on one specific but important issue.

The Supreme Court's role in patent policy is not unusual. Through its individual decisions and lines of decisions, the Court contributes to the content of government policy on a variety of issues. The Court's assumption of this role reflects several circumstances. For one thing, as the French observer Alexis de Tocqueville noted early in the nation's history, "Scarcely any political question arises in the United States that is not resolved, sooner or later, into a judicial question."[2] In part, this is because the United States has a written constitution that can be used to challenge the legality of government actions. Because so many policy questions come to the courts and ultimately to the Supreme Court, the Court has the opportunity to shape a wide range of policies. And the justices often accept and even welcome that opportunity, ruling on major issues and shaping public policy on those issues.

At the same time, the Court's role in policymaking is limited by several conditions, two of which are especially important. First, the Court can do only so much with the relatively few decisions it makes in a year. The Court currently issues decisions with full opinions in an average of about eighty cases each year. In deciding such a small number of cases, the Court addresses only a select group of policy issues. Inevitably, there are whole fields of policy that it barely touches. Even in the areas in which the Court does act, it deals with only a limited number of the issues that exist at a given time.

Second, the actions of other policymakers narrow the impact of the Court's decisions. The Court is seldom the final government institution to deal with the policy issues it addresses. Its decisions are implemented by lower-court judges and administrators, who often have considerable discretion over how they put a ruling into effect. The impact of a decision about police searches for evidence depends largely on how police officers react to it. Congress and the president influence how the Court's decisions are carried out, and they can overcome its interpretations of federal statutes simply by amending those statutes. As a result, there may be a great deal of difference between what the Court rules on an issue and the public policy that ultimately results from government actions on that issue.

For these reasons, those who see the Supreme Court as the dominant force in the U.S. government almost surely are wrong. But the Court does contribute a good deal to the making of public policy.

The Court in the Judicial System

The Supreme Court is part of a court system, and its place in that system structures its role by determining what cases it can hear and the routes those cases take.

State and Federal Court Systems

The United States has a federal court system and a separate court system for each state. Federal courts can hear only those cases that Congress has put under their jurisdiction. Nearly all of this jurisdiction falls into three categories.

First are the criminal and civil cases that arise under federal laws, including the Constitution. All prosecutions for federal crimes are brought to federal court. Some types of civil cases based on federal law, such as those involving antitrust and bankruptcy, must go to federal court.

Other types can go to either federal or state court, but they are typically brought to federal court.

Second are cases to which the U.S. government is a party. When the federal government brings a lawsuit, it nearly always does so in federal court. When someone sues the federal government, the case must go to federal court.

Third are civil cases involving citizens of different states in which the amount in question is more than $75,000. If this condition is met, either party may bring the case to federal court. If a citizen of New Jersey sues a citizen of Texas for $100,000 as compensation for injuries from an auto accident, the plaintiff (the New Jersey resident) might bring the case to federal court, or the defendant (the Texan) might have the case "removed" from state court to federal court. If neither does so, the case will be heard in state court—generally in the state where the accident occurred or the defendant lives.

Only a small proportion of all court cases fit in any of those categories. The most common kinds of cases—criminal prosecutions, personal injury suits, divorces, actions to collect debts—typically are heard in state court. The trial courts of a single populous state such as Illinois or Florida hear far more cases than the federal trial courts. However, federal cases are more likely than state cases to raise major issues of public policy.

State court systems vary considerably in their structure, but some general patterns exist (see Figure 1-1). Each state system has courts that are primarily trial courts, which hear cases initially as they enter the court system, and courts that are primarily appellate courts, which review lower-court decisions that are appealed to them. Most states have two sets of trial courts, one to handle major cases and the other to deal with minor cases. Major criminal cases usually concern what the law defines as felonies. Major civil cases are those involving large sums of money. Most often, appeals from decisions of minor trial courts are heard by major trial courts.

Appellate courts are structured in two ways. Eleven states, generally those with small populations, have a single appellate court—usually called the state supreme court. All appeals from major trial courts go to this supreme court. The other thirty-nine states have a set of intermediate appellate courts below the supreme court. These intermediate courts initially hear most appeals from major trial courts. In those states supreme courts have discretionary jurisdiction over most challenges to the decisions of intermediate courts. Discretionary jurisdiction means simply that a court can choose which cases to hear; cases that a court is required to hear fall under its mandatory jurisdiction.

The structure of federal courts is shown in Figure 1-2. At the base of the federal court system are the federal district courts. The United States

FIGURE 1-1
Most Common State Court Structures

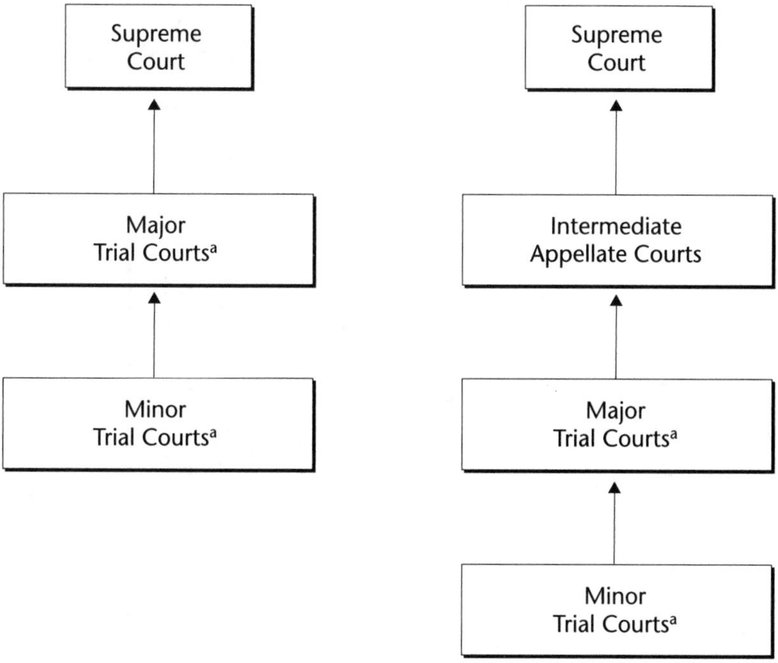

Note: Arrows indicate most common routes of appeals.

a. In many states, major trial courts or minor trial courts (or both) are composed of two or more different sets of courts. For instance, New York has several types of minor trial courts.

has ninety-four district courts. Each state has between one and four district courts, and there is a district court in the District of Columbia and in some of the territories, such as Guam. District courts hear all federal cases at the trial level, with the exception of a few types of cases that are heard in specialized courts.

Above the district courts are the twelve courts of appeals, each of which hears appeals in one of the federal judicial circuits. The District of Columbia constitutes one circuit; each of the other eleven circuits covers three or more states. The Second Circuit, for example, includes Connecticut, New York, and Vermont. Appeals from the district courts in one circuit generally go to the court of appeals for that circuit, along with appeals from the Tax Court and from some administrative agencies. Patent cases and some claims against the federal government go from the district courts to the specialized Court of Appeals for the Federal Circuit, as do

FIGURE 1-2
Basic Structure of the Federal Court System

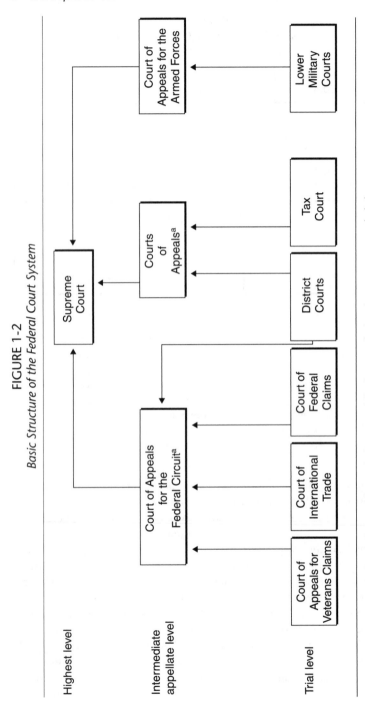

Note: Arrows indicate most common routes of appeals. Some specialized courts of minor importance are excluded.

a. These courts also hear appeals from administrative agencies.

TABLE 1-1
Summary of Supreme Court Jurisdiction

Types of jurisdiction	Categories of cases
Original	Disputes between states[a]
	Some types of cases brought by a state
	Disputes between a state and the federal government
	Cases involving foreign diplomatic personnel
Appellate[b]	All decisions of federal courts of appeals and specialized federal appellate courts
	All decisions of the highest state court with jurisdiction over a case, concerning issues of federal law
	Decisions of special three-judge federal district courts (mandatory)

a. It is unclear whether these cases are mandatory, and the Court treats them as discretionary.
b. Some minor categories are not listed.

appeals from three specialized trial courts. The Court of Appeals for the Armed Forces hears cases from lower courts in the military system.

The Supreme Court's Jurisdiction

The Supreme Court stands at the top of the federal judicial system. Its jurisdiction, summarized in Table 1-1, is of two types. First is the Court's original jurisdiction: the Constitution gives the Court jurisdiction over a few categories of cases as a trial court, so these cases may be brought directly to the Court without going through lower courts. The Court's original jurisdiction includes some cases to which a state is a party and cases involving foreign diplomatic personnel.

Most cases within the Court's original jurisdiction can be heard alternatively by a district court. Lawsuits between two states can be heard only by the Supreme Court, and these lawsuits account for most of the decisions based on the Court's original jurisdiction. These cases usually involve disputes over state borders or, increasingly, water rights. The Court frequently refuses to hear cases under its original jurisdiction, even some lawsuits by one state against another. In part for this reason, full decisions in these cases are not plentiful—fewer than 200 in the Court's history.[3] When the Court does accept a case under its original jurisdiction, it ordinarily appoints a "special master" to gather facts and propose a decision, which the Court tends to ratify. Most of the original cases that the Court hears are more technical than interesting, but they sometimes have high stakes. Certainly the justices take them seriously. In *Montana v. Wyoming and North Dakota* (2011), for instance, Antonin Scalia dissented from the Court's ruling about the rights of the three states to water from the Yellowstone River.

The second type of jurisdiction, appellate jurisdiction, accounts for the overwhelming majority of cases that the Court hears. Under its appellate jurisdiction the Court hears cases brought by parties that are dissatisfied with the lower-court decisions in their cases. Within the federal court system such cases can come from the federal courts of appeals and from the two specialized appellate courts. Cases may also come directly from special three-judge district courts; most of these cases involve voting and election issues.

State cases can come to the Supreme Court after decisions by the state supreme courts if they involve claims arising under federal law, including the Constitution. If a state supreme court chooses not to hear a case, the losing party can then go to the Supreme Court. Table 1-2 shows that a substantial majority of the cases that come to the Court, and an even larger majority of the cases that it hears, originated in federal court rather than in state court.

The rule under which state cases come to the Supreme Court may be confusing, because cases arising under federal law ordinarily start in federal court. But cases brought to state courts on the basis of state law sometimes contain issues of federal law as well. This situation is common in criminal cases. A person accused of burglary under state law will be tried in a state court. During the state court proceedings, the defendant may argue that the police violated rights protected by the U.S. Constitution during a search. The case eventually can be brought to the Supreme Court on that

TABLE 1-2

Sources of Supreme Court Cases in Recent Periods (in percentages)

	Federal courts			
	Courts of appeals	District courts	Specialized courts	State courts
Cases brought to the Court[a]	78	0	1	21
Cases heard by the Court[b]	83	1	5	11

Source: Data on cases heard by the Court are from the U.S. Supreme Court Database, archived at http://scdb.wustl.edu/.

Note: Original jurisdiction cases are not included. Nonfederal courts of the District of Columbia and of U.S. territories are treated as state courts. For cases heard by the Court, each oral argument is counted once unless it involves consolidated cases from two different categories of courts.

a. Cases in which the Court ruled on petitions for hearings, October 3, 2011 (1,793 cases).
b. Cases in which the Court heard oral argument, 2009 and 2010 terms (149 cases).

issue. If it is, the Court will have the power to rule only on the federal issue, not on the issues of state law involved in the case. Thus, the Court cannot rule on whether the defendant actually committed the burglary.

Nearly all cases brought to the Court are under its discretionary jurisdiction, so it can choose whether or not to hear them. With occasional exceptions discretionary cases come to the Court in the form of petitions for a writ of certiorari, a writ through which the Court calls up a case for decision from a lower court. The Court must hear certain cases, called appeals. In a series of steps culminating in 1988, Congress converted the Court's jurisdiction from mostly mandatory to almost entirely discretionary. Today, appeals can be brought in only the few small classes of cases that come directly from three-judge district courts.

The Supreme Court hears only a fraction of 1 percent of the cases brought to federal and state courts. As this figure suggests, courts other than the Supreme Court have ample opportunities to make policy on their own. Moreover, their decisions help determine the ultimate impact of the Court's policies. Important though it is, the Supreme Court certainly is not the only court that matters.

An Overview of the Court

Some attributes of the Supreme Court itself should be examined to provide a picture of what the Court is like. This section considers several aspects of the Court, with emphasis on the justices and the people who help them do their work.

The Court's Building

The Supreme Court did not move into its own building until 1935. In its first decade the Court met first in New York and then in Philadelphia. The Court moved to Washington, DC, with the rest of the federal government at the beginning of the nineteenth century. For the next 130 years, it sat in the Capitol, a "tenant" of Congress.

The Court's accommodations in the Capitol were not entirely adequate. Among other things the lack of office space meant that justices did most of their work at home. After an intensive lobbying effort by Chief Justice William Howard Taft, Congress appropriated money for the Supreme Court building in 1929. The five-story structure occupies a full square block across the street from the Capitol. Because the primary material in the impressive building is marble, it has been called a "marble palace." The aging of the Court's building and the need to house a staff that had grown considerably led to a major renovation project that was completed in 2011 after eight years.

The bronze doors at the main entrance to the Supreme Court building, above the marble steps on the west side of the building. Because of security concerns, the Court closed that entrance in 2010, though visitors can still exit through these doors.

The building houses all the Court's facilities. Formal sessions are held in the courtroom on the first floor. Behind the courtroom is the conference room, where the justices meet to decide cases. Also near the courtroom are the chambers that contain offices for the associate justices and their staffs. The chief justice's chambers are attached to the conference room.

In 2010 the Court closed its main public entrance at the top of the stairs in the front of the building, citing security concerns. The symbolism of that closure led to considerable criticism, including an unusual statement by Stephen Breyer opposing the closure, which Ruth Bader Ginsburg joined.[4]

Personnel: The Justices

Under the Constitution, Supreme Court justices must be nominated by the president and confirmed by the Senate. By long-established Senate practice, a simple majority is required for confirmation. The Constitution says that justices will hold office "during good behavior"—that is, for life unless they relinquish their posts voluntarily or are removed through impeachment proceedings. Beyond these basic rules, questions such as the number of justices, their qualifications, and their duties have been settled by federal statutes and by tradition.

The Constitution says nothing about the number of justices. The Judiciary Act of 1789 provided for six justices. Subsequent statutes changed the number successively to five, six, seven, nine, ten, seven, and nine. The changes were made in part to accommodate the justices' duties in the lower federal courts, in part to serve partisan and policy goals of the president and Congress. The most recent change to nine members was made in 1869, and any further changes in size seem quite unlikely.

In 2012 each associate justice received a salary of $213,900, and the chief justice received $223,500. Substantial as these salaries are, they are considerably lower than the incomes of leading lawyers in large private law firms. Justices are limited to about $26,000 in outside income from activities such as teaching, but there are no limits on income from books. Clarence Thomas and Sonia Sotomayor received advance payments of more than $1 million for their memoirs. Some of the current justices, including Stephen Breyer and John Roberts, were wealthy when they came to the Court. That certainly was not true of Thomas and Sotomayor, whose book advances improved their financial status considerably.[5]

The primary duty of the justices is to participate in the collective decisions of the Court: determining which cases to hear, deciding cases, and writing and contributing to opinions. Ordinarily, the Court's decisions are made by all nine members, but exceptions occur. At times the Court has only eight members because a justice has left the Court and a replacement has not been appointed. A justice's illness may leave the Court temporarily shorthanded, or a justice may decide not to participate in a case because of a perceived conflict of interest. Under federal law, judges should withdraw from cases—"recuse" themselves—when a decision would affect their self-interest substantially or their impartiality "might reasonably be questioned."[6] The Court leaves this decision entirely to the individual justice.

Justices seldom explain the reasons for their recusals, but those reasons often can be discerned. The most common reason is a financial interest in a case, usually a result of a justice's stock holdings. Both Chief Justice Roberts and Justice Breyer have sold some of their stock holdings to enable them to participate in cases from which they would otherwise have had to recuse.[7] Other recusals result when a justice was involved in a case in a prior position, such as a lower-court judgeship. Elena Kagan recused from about one-third of the cases during her first term on the Court because her office had worked on those cases when she was U.S. Solicitor General.

Controversies about justices' recusal decisions have arisen in recent years, spurred primarily by public statements by justices about matters related to pending cases and by interactions between justices and people who have an interest in the outcome of a case. Meanwhile, interest groups and others have sought recusals in particular cases to gain an advantage for positions they favor. A conservative group called attention to John Paul Stevens's ownership of Florida beachfront property, which might be affected by the Court's decision in a 2010 case involving property rights and environmental regulation. Stevens recused himself, and the Court had a 4–4 vote on a key issue in the case. The Court probably would have reached a liberal decision on that issue if Stevens had participated.[8] After Congress enacted the major health care law that President Obama proposed, conservative groups and members of Congress sought the recusal of Justice Kagan from any case involving a challenge to the law, arguing that she had dealt with the issue as solicitor general. For their part, liberal groups sought the recusal of Justice Clarence Thomas, arguing that his wife, Virginia Lamp Thomas, had been heavily involved in opposition to the law. These efforts intensified once the Court accepted a set of cases involving challenges to the law, but both justices participated in the cases.

As the Florida environmental case illustrates, the Court may have a tie vote when only eight justices participate in a decision. Because of Justice Kagan's recusals, there were two such decisions in the Court's 2010 term.[9] A tie vote affirms the lower-court decision. If the tie applies to the whole decision, the votes of individual justices are not announced and no opinions are written. Similarly, the lower-court decision in a case is affirmed if the Court cannot reach a quorum of six members. This situation has occurred a few times in recent years, most often because litigants named most of the justices as defendants in their lawsuits.[10]

In addition to their participation in collective decisions, the justices make some decisions individually as circuit justices. The United States has always been divided into federal judicial circuits. Originally, most appeals within a circuit were heard by ad hoc courts composed of a federal trial judge and two members of the Supreme Court who were assigned to that area as circuit justices. The circuit duties were arduous, especially when long-distance travel was difficult. Some justices even suffered ill health from "circuit riding." [11] Actions by Congress and by the justices themselves gradually reduced the extent of their circuit riding, and this duty ended altogether when Congress created the courts of appeals in 1891.

The justices today retain some duties as circuit justices, with each justice assigned to one or more circuits. As circuit justices they deal with applications for special action, such as a request to stay a lower-court decision (prevent it from taking effect) until the Court decides whether to hear the case. Such an application generally must go first to the circuit justice. That justice may rule on the application as an individual or refer the case to the whole Court. If the circuit justice rejects an application, it can then be made to a second justice. That justice ordinarily refers it to the whole Court.

Probably the most common subject of stay requests is the death penalty. The Court is confronted with numerous requests to stay executions or vacate (remove) stays of execution, many of which come near the scheduled execution time. The Court grants only a small proportion of requests for stays of execution. Other subjects of stay requests range widely. In an unusual case, the Court in 2010 issued a stay to prevent the broadcast of a federal trial to several other federal courthouses, in a case that had attracted wide interest. The Court's stay came by a 5–4 vote, and both the majority and the dissenters issued lengthy opinions justifying their positions.[12]

For the most part, the nine justices are equal in formal power. The exception is the chief justice, who is the formal leader of the Court. The chief justice presides over the Court's public sessions and conferences and assigns the Court's opinion whenever the chief voted with the majority. The chief also supervises administration of the Court with the assistance of committees.

By tradition, the junior justice sits on the Court's cafeteria committee. Apparently, that committee faces serious challenges: a 2010 review in the *Washington Post* gave the cafeteria a grade of F and concluded that "this food should be unconstitutional."[13] In her first year on the Court, Elena Kagan used her service on the cafeteria committee to get a frozen yogurt machine installed in the cafeteria. Chief Justice Roberts later said that "no one can remember" such a significant achievement for the justice on the committee.[14]

The chief justice is the formal leader of the federal judicial system as well.[15] This role is symbolized by the official title, "Chief Justice of the United States." In this role the chief chairs the federal Judicial Conference and conveys to Congress the views of the conference on legislative issues. The chief justice appoints judges to administrative committees and some specialized courts. The chief also delivers the annual "Year-End Report on the Federal Judiciary."

The chief justice traditionally swears in the president on Inauguration Day. When John Roberts performed this duty for President Barack Obama in 2009, it was the first time that a chief justice had sworn in a president who had voted in the Senate against the chief's confirmation to the Supreme Court.[16] After Roberts and Obama stumbled over the words of the oath specified by the Constitution, Roberts came to the White House the next day to administer the oath once again and thus eliminate any doubt that the constitutional requirement had been met.

The burdens of the justices' jobs are a matter of disagreement. The justices often refer to the enormous amount of material they must read in the cases that come to the Court. In contrast, some observers see the justices' workload as relatively light. They point to the relatively small number of cases that the Court now hears, the excellent support that the justices get from their law clerks, and the time that the justices are able to spend in activities outside the Court. One law professor, exaggerating for emphasis, said that in many ways "it's the cushiest job in the world."[17] The justices themselves surely would disagree with that characterization.

Personnel: Law Clerks and Other Support Staff

A staff of about 450 people, serving in several units, supports the justices. Most of the staff members carry out custodial and police functions under the supervision of the marshal of the Court. The clerk of the Court carries out the clerical processing of all the cases that come to the Court. The reporter of decisions supervises preparation of the official record of the Court's decisions, the *United States Reports*. The librarian is in charge of the libraries in the Supreme Court building. The court's public information office responds to inquiries and distributes information about the Court.

Of all the members of the support staff, the law clerks have the most direct effect on the Court's decisions.[18] Associate justices may employ four clerks each, the chief justice five (though the chief generally hires only four). Clerks usually work with a justice for only one year. The typical clerk is a recent, high-ranked graduate of a prestigious law school. The clerks who served in the 2007–2011 terms came from more than thirty law schools, but nearly half had gone to Harvard or Yale.[19] The great majority had clerked in a federal court of appeals before coming to the Supreme Court, and some had spent a short time in legal practice after their service in a court of appeals. Justices, especially those who are most conservative, tend to draw clerks from court of appeals judges who share the justices' ideological positions.[20]

Clerks typically spend much of their time on the petitions for hearings by the Court, reading the petitions and the lower-court records and summarizing them for the justices. Clerks also work on cases that have been accepted for decision. This work includes analysis of case materials and issues, discussions of issues with their justices, and drafting opinions. Typically, clerks write the first drafts of the justices' opinions. Justice Samuel Alito reported that his clerks "always do a draft for me."[21]

The extent of law clerks' influence over the Court's decisions is a matter of considerable interest and wide disagreement.[22] Observers who depict the clerks as quite powerful probably underestimate the justices' ability to maintain control over their decisions. Still, the jobs that justices give to their clerks ensure significant influence. Writing drafts of opinions, for instance, allows clerks to shape the content of those opinions, whether or not they seek to do so. The same is true of the other work that clerks do.

After leaving the Court, most law clerks initially go into the private practice of law. With "signing bonuses" that now run as high as $280,000, these clerks often earn far more than the justices in their first year after Court service.[23] Many former clerks go on to distinguished careers. Indeed, several have become justices themselves. Among the current justices, John Roberts, Stephen Breyer, and Elena Kagan were once law clerks in the Court.

The Court and the Outside World

The Supreme Court as an institution and the justices as individuals have complicated relationships with the world outside the Court, relationships that have been changing. Until recently, relatively little information about the Court and its justices has been available to the public. For instance, justices seldom gave public interviews, and the Court's oral arguments and other formal proceedings were accessible only to the small number of people who attended them in person. This paucity of information may have been part of an effort to win favorable public attitudes toward the Court by fostering the impression that the Court stands apart from ordinary politics.[24] If there was such a strategy, it appeared to achieve some success. The Court's public approval ratings rise and fall over time, but they are usually more positive than those of the president and Congress. In a 2011 survey, for instance, confidence in the Court was far higher than confidence in Congress and in the federal government as a whole.[25] This high level of approval may provide the Court with some protection from criticism and attacks by other policymakers.

The Court and the justices were never completely isolated from the world outside the Court, and they have become more open to that world.[26] The Court now provides a good deal of information about its work through its website. Transcripts of oral arguments are available on the same day as the arguments. Audio recordings are released later the same week, and occasionally on the same day, though most justices still oppose televised arguments despite some pressure from Congress to change their stance.

Justices have long been active within the legal community, appearing at law schools and speaking before groups of lawyers and judges. This continues to be true today, and justices travel a good deal to make these appearances. One common activity is teaching at summer law school programs outside the United States. In 2010, for instance, Justice Alito taught in France, Justice Breyer in Great Britain, Justice Kennedy in Austria, and Justice Scalia in Italy.[27]

As a group, the justices have become more willing to speak to audiences outside the legal system. Interviews with the news media are now fairly common, and in 2009 eight of the justices gave lengthy interviews for broadcast on C-SPAN. Altogether, the justices made nearly 400 appearances on C-SPAN between 1998 and 2007.[28] Several justices appear at public events for nonlawyers, as Justice Breyer and Justice Scalia have done in conjunction with their books about the Court. Describing the shift over the past few decades, one commentator wrote in 2009 that "the justices are everywhere. If they are not on book tours, they are opining on the authorship of Shakespeare's plays, or mingling with their peers in Europe, or on C-Span addressing high school students, or at least delivering named lectures at law schools."[29]

In their appearances before legal and public groups, the justices sometimes express their views about issues of legal and public policy. For instance, Justice Kennedy has spoken about what he sees as the excessive length of prison sentences in the United States.[30] Occasionally, those expressions arouse criticism, primarily because of charges that a justice has prejudged an issue that will come before the Court. Indeed, in 2003 Justice Scalia recused himself from a case at the request of one of the parties because he had criticized the lower court's decision in a speech.[31] None of the current justices seems to have the direct relationships with presidents and members of Congress that were common in earlier eras, but some interact with political interest groups. In 2007, for instance, four justices appeared at the twenty-fifth anniversary celebration of the Federalist Society, a conservative legal group.[32] These interactions too have aroused criticism, primarily from liberals who argue that some conservative justices (especially Justice Thomas) are too closely linked with conservative activists and groups.[33]

Even among the justices who are most active outside the Court, few are truly famous. Typically, justices attract widespread public attention when they are nominated and confirmed but then fade into relative obscurity. Given four names to choose from, only 28 percent of the public could identify John Roberts as chief justice in 2010, after he had served five years in that position.[34] Justices usually go unrecognized even at the Supreme Court building, though Clarence Thomas has reported that he is an exception.[35]

Within a subset of the public, however, the justices are truly celebrities.[36] Certainly that is true of the legal community, but the justices' celebrity increasingly extends beyond that community. The news media pay attention to their activities, even when they get into an auto accident (Antonin Scalia) or escape from a plane with a smoking engine by sliding down an emergency chute (Ruth Bader Ginsburg).[37] They are often targets of satire and cartoons, several have been the subjects of biographies, and Sonia Sotomayor even had a comic book devoted to her. A San Antonio school district has named most of its high schools after justices, so fans can cheer for the Stevens Falcons or the O'Connor Panthers.[38]

Justices differ in how they respond to their celebrity. Some justices, such as Antonin Scalia and Sonia Sotomayor, seem to enjoy the attention they receive. Among other things, their status allows them to participate in activities that are usually unavailable to ordinary people. Sotomayor and John Paul Stevens threw out the first ball at games of their favorite baseball teams (the Cubs for Stevens, the Yankees for Sotomayor). Opera fans Scalia and Ruth Bader Ginsburg have played nonspeaking roles in opera productions, and Stephen Breyer played the Ghost in *Hamlet.* When they were still married, Jennifer Lopez and Marc Anthony hosted Sotomayor for dinner.[39] And Sotomayor appeared on Sesame Street in 2012, adjudicating a dispute between Goldilocks and Baby Bear.

In contrast, David Souter would have preferred complete anonymity. He did his best to achieve it, keeping his distance from the news media and making few appearances at events outside the Court. Even justices who enjoy their celebrity generally prefer to go unrecognized in public, and that preference may help account for most justices' opposition to the televising of oral arguments.

Justice Sonia Sotomayor, a Yankees fan, on her way to throw out the first pitch at a game in Yankee Stadium in 2009. Some of the justices enjoy their celebrity and the opportunities it provides.

The Court's Schedule

The Court keeps to a constant annual schedule. It holds one term each year, lasting from the first Monday in October until the beginning of the succeeding term a year later.[40] The term is designated by the year in which it begins: the 2012 term began in October 2012. (However, the clerk's office treats a term as ending when the Court finishes its work in June.) Ordinarily, the Court does its collective work from late September to late June. This work begins when the justices meet to act on the petitions for hearings that have accumulated during the summer and ends when the Court has issued decisions in all the cases it heard during the term.

Most of the term is divided into sittings of about two weeks, when the Court holds sessions to hear oral arguments in cases and to announce decisions in cases that were argued earlier in the term, and recesses of two weeks or longer. In May and June the Court hears no arguments but holds one or more sessions each week to announce decisions. It issues few decisions early in the term because of the time required after oral arguments to write opinions and reach final positions. Typically, about one-third of the decisions are announced in June, as the justices scramble to finish their work by the end of the term. According to Justice Scalia, "Toward the end of the term when there are a lot of opinions outstanding that haven't come in yet," former Chief Justice Rehnquist was "wont to say, 'Ladies and gentlemen, time to stop thinking and start writing.'"[41]

When the Court has reached and announced decisions in all the cases it heard during the term, the summer recess begins. Cases that the Court accepted for hearing but that were not argued during the term are carried over to the next term. In summer the justices generally spend time away from Washington but continue their work on the petitions for hearings that arrive at the Court. During that time the Court and individual circuit justices respond to applications for special action. When the justices meet at the end of summer to dispose of the accumulated petitions, the annual cycle begins again.

The schedule of weekly activities, like the annual schedule, is fairly regular. During sittings, the Court generally holds sessions on Monday through Wednesday for two weeks and on Monday of the next week. The sessions begin at ten o'clock in the morning. Oral arguments usually are held during each session except on the last Monday of the sitting. They may be preceded by several types of business. On Mondays the Court announces the filing of its order list, which is a report of the Court's decisions on petitions for hearing and other actions taken at its conference the preceding Friday. On Tuesdays and Wednesdays, as well as the last Monday of the sitting, justices announce their opinions in any cases the Court has resolved. In May and June, however, opinions may be announced on any day of the week.

The oral arguments consume most of the time during sessions. The usual practice is to allot one hour, equally divided between the two sides, for arguments in a case. On most argument days the Court hears two cases.

During sittings, the Court holds two conferences each week. The Wednesday afternoon conference is devoted to discussion of the cases that were argued on Monday. In a longer conference on Friday the justices discuss the cases argued on Tuesday and Wednesday, as well as petitions for certiorari and other matters the Court must decide. In May and June, after oral arguments have ended for the year, the Court has weekly conferences on Thursdays.

The Court also holds a conference on the last Friday of each recess to deal with the continuing flow of business. The remainder of the justices' time during recess periods is devoted to their individual work: study of petitions for hearing and cases scheduled for argument, writing of opinions, and reaction to other justices' opinions. This work continues during the sittings.

The Court's History

This book is concerned primarily with the Supreme Court at present and in the recent past, but I frequently refer to the Court's history to provide perspective on the current Court. For this reason, an overview of that history will provide background for later chapters. Even a brief overview makes clear the links between the Court's own history and that of the nation as a whole. The Court has played a role in American political development, and it has been shaped by the development of other political institutions.

The Court from 1790 to 1865

The framers of the Constitution explicitly created the Supreme Court, but the Constitution says much less about the Court than about Congress and the president. In the Judiciary Act of 1789, which set up the federal court system, the Court's jurisdiction under the Constitution was used as the basis for granting the Court broad powers. Still, what the Court would do with its powers was uncertain, in part because their scope was ambiguous.

The Court started slowly, deciding only about fifty cases and making few significant decisions between 1790 and 1799.[42] Several people rejected offers to serve on the Court, and two justices—including Chief Justice John Jay—resigned to take more attractive positions in state government. The Court's fortunes improved considerably under John Marshall, chief justice from 1801 to 1835. Marshall, appointed by President John Adams, dominated the Court to a degree that no other justice has matched. He used his dominance to strengthen the Court's position and advance the policies he favored.

The Court's most important assertion of power under Marshall was probably its decision in *Marbury v. Madison* (1803), in which the Court struck down a federal statute for the first time. In his opinion for the Court, Marshall argued that when a federal law is inconsistent with the Constitution, the Court must declare the law unconstitutional and refuse to enforce it. A few years later, the Court also claimed the same right of judicial review over state acts.

The Court's aggressiveness brought denunciations and threats, including an effort by President Thomas Jefferson to have Congress remove at least one justice through impeachment. But Marshall's skill in minimizing confrontations helped protect the Court from a successful attack. The other branches of government and the general public gradually accepted the powers that he claimed for the Court and the Court's role in policy-making.

This acceptance was tested by the Court's decision in *Scott v. Sandford* (1857), generally known as the *Dred Scott* case. Prior to that decision, the Court had overturned only one federal statute, the minor law involved in *Marbury v. Madison*. In *Dred Scott*, however, Marshall's successor, Roger Taney (1836–1864), wrote the Court's opinion holding that Congress had exceeded its constitutional powers when it prohibited slavery in some territories. That decision was intended to resolve the legal controversy over slavery. Instead, the level of controversy increased, and the Court was vilified in the North. The Court's prestige suffered greatly, but its basic powers survived without serious challenge.[43]

During this period, the Court was concerned with more than its own position; it was addressing major issues of public policy. The primary area of its concern was federalism, the legal relationship between the national government and the states. Under Marshall, the Court gave strong support to national powers. Marshall wanted to restrict state policies where they interfered with activities of the national government, especially its power to regulate commerce. Under Taney, the Court was not as favorable to the national government, but Taney and his colleagues reversed the Marshall Court's general expansion of federal power only to a limited degree. As a result, the constitutional power of the federal government remained strong; the Court had permanently altered the lines between the national government and the state governments.

The Court from 1865 to 1937

After the Civil War, the Court began to focus its attention on government regulation of the economy. By the late nineteenth century, all levels of government were adopting new laws to regulate business activities. Among them were the federal antitrust laws, state regulations of railroad practices, and federal and state laws regulating employment conditions. Inevitably, much of this legislation was challenged in the courts on constitutional grounds.

The Supreme Court upheld a great many government policies regulating business in this period, but it gradually became less friendly toward those policies. That position was reflected in the development of constitutional doctrines limiting government power to control business activities. Those doctrines were used with increasing frequency to attack regulatory legislation, and in the 1920s the Supreme Court struck down more than 130 regulatory laws as unconstitutional.[44]

In the 1930s the Supreme Court's attacks on economic regulation brought it into serious conflict with the other branches. President Franklin Roosevelt's New Deal program to combat the Great Depression included sweeping statutes to control the economy, measures that enjoyed widespread support. In a series of decisions in 1935 and 1936, the Court struck down several of these statutes, including laws broadly regulating industry and agriculture, generally by 6–3 and 5–4 margins.[45]

Roosevelt responded in 1937 by proposing legislation under which an extra justice could be added to the Court for every sitting justice over the age of seventy who had served at least ten years, up to a maximum of six extra justices. If the legislation were enacted, Roosevelt could appoint six new justices, thereby "packing" the Court with justices favorable to his programs. While this plan was being debated in Congress, however, the Court weakened the impetus behind it. In several decisions in 1937, the Court reversed direction and upheld New Deal legislation and similar state laws by narrow margins.[46] Many observers, although not all, have concluded that this shift was a deliberate effort by one or two moderate justices to mend the Court's contentious relationship with the other branches.[47] In any event, the Court-packing plan died.

The Court from 1937 to 1969

During the congressional debate in 1937, one of the justices who had frequently voted to strike down New Deal laws retired. Several other justices left the Court in the next few years, giving Roosevelt the ideological control of the Court that he had sought through the Court-packing legislation. The new Court created by his appointments fully accepted New Deal regulation of the economy, giving very broad interpretations to the constitutional powers to tax and to regulate interstate commerce. And in the decades that followed, the Court continued to uphold major economic policies of the federal government.

Because of the Court's consistent position on issues of economic regulation, this field gradually became less central to its role. Instead, the Court increasingly focused on civil liberties. By the mid-1960s, the Court was giving the most attention to interpretation of legal protections for freedom of expression and freedom of religion, for the procedural rights of criminal defendants and others, and for equal treatment of disadvantaged groups.

During this period, the Court's overall support for civil liberties issues in conflict with other values varied considerably. That support peaked in the 1960s, the latter part of the period when Earl Warren was chief justice (1953–1969). The Court's policies during that period are often identified with Warren, but other liberal justices played roles of equal or greater importance: Roosevelt appointees Hugo Black and William Douglas, as well as Eisenhower appointee William Brennan.

The most prominent decision of the Warren era was *Brown v. Board of Education* (1954), in which the Court ordered desegregation of school systems that assigned students to separate schools by race. The Court supported the rights of African Americans in several other areas as well. During the 1960s the Court expanded the rights of criminal defendants in state cases. It issued landmark decisions on the right to counsel (*Gideon v. Wainwright*, 1963), police search and seizure practices (*Mapp v. Ohio*, 1961), and the questioning of suspects (*Miranda v. Arizona*, 1966). The Court supported freedom of expression by expanding First Amendment rights, especially on obscenity and libel. In a line of cases beginning with *Baker v. Carr* (1962), the Court required that legislative districts be equal in population.

The Court from 1969 to the Present

When Earl Warren retired in 1969, he was succeeded as chief justice by Warren Burger, President Nixon's first Court appointee. In 1970 and 1971 Nixon made three more appointments. The Court's membership changed much more slowly after that. But each new member until 1993 was appointed by a conservative Republican president—one by Gerald Ford, three by Ronald Reagan, and two by George H. W. Bush. In 1986 Reagan named Nixon appointee William Rehnquist, the Court's most conservative justice, to succeed Warren Burger as chief justice. Each president serving since then—Bill Clinton, George W. Bush, and Barack Obama—has made two appointments. In 2005 Bush appointed John Roberts as chief justice to succeed Rehnquist.

The Republican appointments from 1969 through 1991 gradually made the Court more conservative. Even though four of the six appointments since then have come from Democratic presidents, the net effect of personnel changes in this period has been to move the Court a bit more to the right.

This ideological change is reflected in the Court's civil liberties policies, to a greater degree on some issues than on others. Perhaps the most decisive shift has come on issues of criminal procedure. The Court has not directly overturned any of the Warren Court's landmark decisions expanding defendants' rights, but it cut back on the reach of decisions such as *Mapp* and *Miranda*. The Rehnquist and Roberts Courts generally have given narrow interpretations to federal statutes prohibiting discrimination.

However, the Burger Court acted decisively to expand protections against sex discrimination under the Constitution. The Court also issued rulings in 2006 and 2008 that provided legal protections for suspected terrorists who were detained at the Guantánamo Bay Naval Station.[48]

Especially under Chief Justice Roberts, the Court has expanded civil liberties that conservatives tend to favor. A series of decisions from 1976 through 2011 limited government power to regulate the financing of political campaigns.[49] In 2008 the Court held for the first time that the Second Amendment protected the right to individual gun ownership from federal abridgment, and two years later the Court ruled that this right applied to state governments as well.[50]

The Court has also shifted direction in economic policy. In general, its interpretations of federal laws on environmental protection and labor-management relations have become distinctly more conservative. Beginning in 1995 it narrowed congressional power to regulate the private sector and state governments in some respects.[51] This narrowing encouraged opponents of the federal health care law that was enacted in 2010 to challenge the law on constitutional grounds.

The absence of a more decisive shift in the Court's policies after 1969 has disappointed some conservative observers of the Court. Still, those policies have moved considerably to the right, underlining the impact of the Court's membership on its work. Because of that impact the selection of justices is a crucial process, a process that I will examine in the next chapter.

NOTES

1. Those decisions were *United States v. Nixon* (1974) and *Bush v. Gore* (2000).
2. Alexis de Tocqueville, *Democracy in America*, 2 vols., trans. Henry Reeve, rev. Francis Bowen (New York: Knopf, 1945), 1: 280.
3. This figure is updated from Henry J. Abraham, *The Judicial Process*, 7th ed. (New York: Oxford University Press, 1998), 188.
4. *Statement Concerning the Supreme Court's Front Entrance*, 176 L. Ed. 2d i (2010).
5. The justices' annual financial disclosure reports list the (very) approximate values of their investments at the end of each calendar year. They also list the justices' outside income, including book royalties. The reports for the justices since 2002 are posted at http://moneyline.cq.com/pml/home.do.
6. 28 U.S.C. § 455.
7. Brent Kendall, "Chief Justice Roberts Sells Pfizer Shares," *Wall Street Journal*, September 28, 2010, http://online.wsj.com/article/SB10001424 05274870388240457552013227381308.html; Greg Stohr, "Breyer Sold Wal-Mart Shares in Advance of Supreme Court Case," *Bloomberg News*, May 27, 2011, http://www.bloomberg.com/news/2011-05-27/breyer-sold-wal-mart-shares-in-advance-of-supreme-court-case.html.

8. Tony Mauro, "Stevens' Recusal Makes Difference in Florida Property Ruling," *The BLT: The Blog of Legal Times,* June 17, 2010, http://legaltimes. typad.com/blt/2010/06/stop-the-beach-the-difference-a-recusal-can-make-.html. The case was *Stop the Beach Renourishment, Inc. v. Florida Department of Environmental Protection* (2010).

9. The cases were *Flores-Villar v. United States* (2011) and *Costco Wholesale Corp. v. Omega, S.A.* (2010).

10. Two examples are *Jones v. Supreme Court* (2011) and *Smith v. Thomas* (2011).

11. David N. Atkinson, *Leaving the Bench: Supreme Court Justices at the End* (Lawrence: University Press of Kansas, 1999), chap. 2.

12. *Hollingsworth v. Perry* (2010).

13. Becky Krystal, "Supreme Court Cafeteria," *Washington Post,* July 14, 2010, E2.

14. Tony Mauro and Marcia Coyle, "Aside from Wal-Mart, Few Huge Cases at High Court," *National Law Journal,* December 26, 2011, 7.

15. See Russell R. Wheeler, "Chief Justice Rehnquist as Third Branch Leader," *Judicature* 89 (November–December 2005): 116–120.

16. Lawrence Hurley, "Will Obama Have an Awkward Inaugural Moment?" *Daily Journal,* November 20, 2008.

17. Devin Dwyer, "'Cushy' Job, or 'Isolated' Hell? Life as a Supreme Court Justice," *ABC News,* April 23, 2010, http://abcnews.go.com/print?id= 10449434.

18. On law clerks and justices, see Todd C. Peppers and Artemus Ward, eds., *In Chambers: Stories of Supreme Court Law Clerks and Their Justices* (Charlottesville: University of Virginia Press, 2012).

19. This figure was calculated from information sheets provided by the Supreme Court.

20. See Lawrence Baum and Corey Ditslear, "Supreme Court Clerkships and 'Feeder' Judges," *Justice System Journal* 31 (2010): 26–48.

21. Brian Lamb, Susan Swain, and Mark Farkas, eds., *The Supreme Court: A C-Span Book Featuring the Justices in Their Own Words* (New York: PublicAffairs, 2010), 155.

22. Todd C. Peppers and Christopher Zorn, "Law Clerk Influence on Supreme Court Decision Making: An Empirical Assessment," *DePaul Law Review* 58 (2008): 410–427.

23. David Lat, "Supreme Court Clerk Bonuses Are Heading Higher," *Above the Law Blog,* August 30, 2011, http://abovethelaw.com/2011/08/supreme-court-clerk-bonuses-are-heading-higher/.

24. Barbara A. Perry, *The Priestly Tribe: The Supreme Court's Image in the American Mind* (Westport, CT: Praeger, 1999).

25. The survey was by the Associated Press and the National Constitution Center, August 18–22, 2011. The results were reported by the Roper Center for Public Opinion Research, http://webapps.ropercenter.uconn.edu.

26. Richard Davis, *Justices and Journalists: The U.S. Supreme Court and the Media* (New York: Cambridge University Press, 2011), 170–186.

27. Information on public appearances is taken from the justices' financial disclosure reports, discussed in Note 5.

28. Davis, *Justices and Journalists,* 173.

29. Linda Greenhouse, "Justice Unbound," *New York Times,* May 3, 2009, WK1.

30. Carol J. Williams, "Justice Kennedy Laments the State of Prisons in California, U.S.," *Los Angeles Times*, February 4, 2010.

31. Charles Lane, "High Court to Consider Pledge in Schools," *Washington Post*, October 15, 2003, A1, A9. The case was *Elk Grove v. Newdow* (2004).

32. Robert Barnes, "Federalists Relish Well-Placed Friends," *Washington Post*, November 16, 2007, A3.

33. See Jeffrey Toobin, "Partners: Will Clarence and Virginia Thomas Succeed in Killing Obama's Health-Care Plan?" *The New Yorker*, August 29, 2011, 39–51.

34. Pew Research Center, "8%—Chief Justice Thurgood Marshall?", http://pewresearch.org/databank/dailynumber/?NumberID=1056.

35. Lamb, Swain, and Farkas, *The Supreme Court*, 101–102.

36. See Craig S. Lerner and Nelson Lund, "Judicial Duty and the Supreme Court's Cult of Celebrity," *George Washington Law Review* 78 (September 2010), 1267–1268; and Davis, *Justices and Journalists*, 21–33.

37. "Antonin Scalia's Traffic Jam," *Washington Post*, March 30, 2011, C2; "Ginsburg Slides Down Plane Chute at Dulles," *USA Today*, September 15, 2011, 3A.

38. The schools and mascots are listed at http://www.nisd.net/schools/info/High.

39. Lisa Robinson, "Jenny Back on the Block," *Vanity Fair*, September 2011, 302.

40. The Court's schedule is described in Eugene Gressman, Kenneth S. Geller, Stephen M. Shapiro, Timothy S. Bishop, and Edward A. Hartnett, *Supreme Court Practice*, 9th ed. (Arlington, VA: BNA Books, 2007), 11–16.

41. Joan Biskupic, "It's Crunch Time for Some of High Court's Biggest Decisions," *USA Today*, June 6, 2005, 7A.

42. See William R. Casto, *The Supreme Court in the Early Republic: The Chief Justiceships of John Jay and Oliver Ellsworth* (Columbia: University of South Carolina Press, 1995). For another perspective, see Scott Douglas Gerber, ed., *Seriatim: The Supreme Court before John Marshall* (New York: New York University Press, 1998).

43. Robert G. McCloskey, *The American Supreme Court*, 6th ed., rev. Sanford Levinson (Chicago: University of Chicago Press, 2010), 64–66.

44. This figure was calculated from data in Congressional Research Service, *The Constitution of the United States of America: Analysis and Interpretation* (Washington, DC: Government Printing Office, 1987), 1885–2113.

45. The cases included *Carter v. Carter Coal Co.* (1936); *United States v. Butler* (1936); and *Schechter Poultry Corp. v. United States* (1935).

46. The cases included *National Labor Relations Board v. Jones & Laughlin Steel Corp.* (1937); *Steward Machine Co. v. Davis* (1937); and *West Coast Hotel Co. v. Parrish* (1937).

47. William G. Ross, *The Chief Justiceship of Charles Evans Hughes, 1930–1941* (Columbia: University of South Carolina Press, 2007), ix–xi and chap. 4.

48. The decisions were *Hamdan v. Rumsfeld* (2006) and *Boumediene v. Bush* (2008).

49. The most important decisions were *Buckley v. Valeo* (1976) and *Citizens United v. Federal Election Commission* (2010).

50. *District of Columbia v. Heller* (2008); *McDonald v. City of Chicago* (2010).

51. See *United States v. Morrison* (2000) and *Gonzales v. Raich* (2005).

Chapter 2

The Justices

A year before the 2012 presidential election, Michelle Obama reminded an audience of the impact that Supreme Court decisions have on people's lives. "That is what's at stake in this election," she said.[1] She did not need to spell out the connection between presidential elections and the Court's work. Observers of the Court recognize that the Court's membership has a fundamental effect on its decisions and that its membership is determined primarily by presidents.

As of mid-2012, presidents have made 153 nominations to the Supreme Court, and 112 justices have served on it. Four candidates were nominated and confirmed twice, and eight declined appointments or died before beginning service on the Court. Twenty-nine did not secure Senate confirmation; a few of these nominees dropped out before the Senate could consider them.[2]

Table 2-1 lists the thirty-three nominations to the Court since 1953 and the twenty-six justices chosen since that time. This chapter focuses on that period and primarily on the past few decades. In the chapter's three sections I discuss the selection of justices, the characteristics of the people who are selected, and how and why they leave the Court.

The Selection of Justices

The formal process for selection of Supreme Court justices is simple. When a vacancy occurs, the president makes a nomination. The nomination must then be confirmed by the Senate, with a simple majority of participating senators required for confirmation. When the chief justice's position is vacant, the president has two options: to nominate a

TABLE 2-1

Nominations to the Supreme Court Since 1953

Name	Nominating president	Justice replaced	Years served
Earl Warren (CJ)	Eisenhower	Vinson	1953–1969
John Harlan	Eisenhower	Jackson	1955–1971
William Brennan	Eisenhower	Minton	1956–1990
Charles Whittaker	Eisenhower	Reed	1957–1962
Potter Stewart	Eisenhower	Burton	1958–1981
Byron White	Kennedy	Whittaker	1962–1993
Arthur Goldberg	Kennedy	Frankfurter	1962–1965
Abe Fortas	Johnson	Goldberg	1965–1969
Thurgood Marshall	Johnson	Clark	1967–1991
Abe Fortas (CJ)	Johnson	(Warren)	Withdrew, 1968
Homer Thornberry	Johnson	(Fortas)	Moot, 1968
Warren Burger (CJ)	Nixon	Warren	1969–1986
Clement Haynsworth	Nixon	(Fortas)	Defeated, 1969
G. Harrold Carswell	Nixon	(Fortas)	Defeated, 1970
Harry Blackmun	Nixon	Fortas	1970–1994
Lewis Powell	Nixon	Black	1971–1987
William Rehnquist	Nixon	Harlan	1971–2005
John Paul Stevens	Ford	Douglas	1975–2010
Sandra Day O'Connor	Reagan	Stewart	1981–2006
William Rehnquist (CJ)	Reagan	Burger	1986–2005
Antonin Scalia	Reagan	Rehnquist	1986–
Robert Bork	Reagan	(Powell)	Defeated, 1987
Douglas Ginsburg	Reagan	(Powell)	Withdrew, 1987
Anthony Kennedy	Reagan	Powell	1988–
David Souter	G. H. W. Bush	Brennan	1990–2009
Clarence Thomas	G. H. W. Bush	Marshall	1991–
Ruth Bader Ginsburg	Clinton	White	1993–
Stephen Breyer	Clinton	Blackmun	1994–
John Roberts (CJ)	G. W. Bush	Rehnquist	2005–
Harriet Miers	G. W. Bush	(O'Connor)	Withdrew, 2005
Samuel Alito	G. W. Bush	O'Connor	2006–
Sonia Sotomayor	Obama	Souter	2009–
Elena Kagan	Obama	Stevens	2010–

Note: CJ = chief justice. Fortas and Rehnquist were associate justices when nominated as chief justice. Roberts was originally nominated to replace O'Connor, then was nominated for chief justice after Rehnquist's death.

Defeated = Senate voted against confirmation.

Withdrew = Nomination or planned nomination was withdrawn. The Fortas nomination was withdrawn after a vote to end a filibuster failed. Douglas Ginsburg withdrew before he was formally nominated.

Moot = When Fortas withdrew as nominee for chief justice, the Thornberry nomination to take Fortas's position as associate justice became moot.

sitting justice to that position and also nominate a new associate justice, or to nominate a person as chief justice from outside the Court. Presidents usually take the latter course, as President Bush did when he selected John Roberts to succeed William Rehnquist in 2005. But President Ronald Reagan elevated Rehnquist from associate justice to chief justice after Warren Burger retired in 1986.

The actual process of selection is more complicated than the simple formal process suggests. The decisions of presidents and senators are shaped by individuals and groups with a strong interest in these decisions, and the process of nomination and confirmation can be complex. I will discuss the roles of unofficial participants in the process and then consider how the president and the Senate reach their decisions.

Unofficial Participants

Because Supreme Court appointments are so important, many people seek to influence the president and the Senate. When a vacancy occurs, presidents and other administration officials may hear from a wide array of individuals and groups. The same is true of senators who are deciding whether to support a nominee's confirmation. The most important of these individuals and groups fall into three categories: the legal community, other interest groups, and people who seek nominations for themselves.

The Legal Community. Lawyers have a particular interest in the Court's membership, and their views about potential justices may carry special weight. As the largest and most prominent organization of lawyers, the American Bar Association (ABA) occupies an important position. An ABA committee investigates presidential nominees who await confirmation and evaluates them as "well-qualified," "qualified," or "not qualified."

Because they believe that the ABA committee is biased against conservative nominees, some Republican senators give little weight to its judgment. Still, the committee's level of enthusiasm for a nominee can affect the confirmation process. (It has never rated a Supreme Court nominee as "not qualified.") A unanimous rating of "well-qualified," which most nominees receive, assists a nominee in winning Senate approval. By the same token, when four committee members rated Robert Bork as "not qualified" in 1987 and two gave that rating to Clarence Thomas in 1991, the nominees' prospects for confirmation were weakened. Those negative ratings of two conservative Republicans, one of them (Bork) a prestigious legal scholar, fostered the perception of bias in the ABA committee's decisions.

Other legal groups and individual lawyers also participate in the selection process. Law professors and other prominent attorneys often announce their evaluations of nominees the Senate is considering. For Republican presidents, the conservative Federalist Society of lawyers serves as one source of advice. Seven of Samuel Alito's current and past colleagues on the federal court of appeals for the Third Circuit testified on his behalf in the Judiciary Committee. And each lawyer who had served from 1985 to 2009 as solicitor general, head of the office that represents the federal government in the Supreme Court, joined a letter supporting Elena Kagan, who held that position when President Obama nominated her to the Court in 2010.

Supreme Court justices sometimes participate in the selection process, most often by recommending a potential nominee. Chief Justice Warren Burger went further. Appointed by Richard Nixon in 1969, he was active in suggesting names to fill other vacancies during the Nixon administration. He played an important role in G. Harrold Carswell's nomination and a crucial role in the nomination of his longtime friend Harry Blackmun. Some years later, Burger lobbied the Reagan administration on behalf of Sandra Day O'Connor.[3]

Other Interest Groups. Many interest groups have a stake in Supreme Court decisions, so groups often seek to influence the selection of justices. The level of group activity has grown substantially in the past half-century, and it now pervades both the nomination and the confirmation stages of the selection process.

Interest groups would like to influence the president's nomination decision. The groups that actually exert influence at this stage are typically those that are politically important to the president. Democratic presidents usually give some weight to the views of labor and civil rights groups. Republican presidents usually pay attention to groups that take conservative positions on social issues such as abortion.

The influence of these core groups was underlined in 2005, after President Bush nominated White House counsel Harriet Miers to succeed Sandra Day O'Connor. Many conservatives were unsure whether Miers held views similar to their own, and conservative groups and individuals mounted a strong campaign against her. After their campaign secured Miers's withdrawal, President Bush chose Samuel Alito, a judge who was popular with conservative groups.

Once a nomination has been announced, groups often work for or against Senate confirmation. Significant interest group activity was limited and sporadic until the late 1960s.[4] Its growth since then reflects growth in the number of interest groups and the intensity of group activity, greater awareness that nominations to the Court are important, and group leaders' increased understanding of how to influence the confirmation process. Ideological groups have also found that opposition to controversial nominees is a good way to generate interest in their causes and monetary contributions from their supporters.

Groups that opposed specific nominees achieved noteworthy successes between 1968 and 1970. Conservative groups helped to defeat Abe Fortas, nominated for elevation to chief justice by President Lyndon Johnson in 1968, and labor and civil rights groups helped to secure the defeats of Nixon nominees Clement Haynsworth and G. Harrold Carswell. President Reagan's nomination of Robert Bork in 1987 gave rise to an unprecedented level of group activity, and the strong mobilization by liberal groups was one key to Bork's defeat in the Senate.[5]

Since the Bork nomination, interest groups have played active roles in response to every Supreme Court nomination. Group activity increases with the perception that a nominee would shift the ideological balance in the Court substantially and that a nominee might be vulnerable to defeat. Both conditions existed with President George H. W. Bush's nomination of Clarence Thomas in 1991, and that nomination produced a heated battle between competing groups. But even when these conditions are lacking, there are always some groups that mount campaigns against nominees. That was true of Elena Kagan, whose nomination aroused opposition from groups such as Americans United for Life and the National Rifle Association. As one commentator described it, opposition to Kagan "is an appeal to their bases, to keep them energized."[6]

Candidates for the Court. Some Supreme Court nominees had never thought of themselves as potential justices. President George W. Bush has reported that Harriet Miers "was surprised—more like shocked" when Bush asked about her interest in a nomination.[7] Some prospective nominees withdraw from consideration, some turn down nominations, and others accept them reluctantly. But for many lawyers, the Supreme Court is a long-standing dream. A decade before his appointment to the Court, Clarence Thomas told a reporter, "I want to be on the Supreme Court."[8] Samuel Alito had that goal in mind much earlier. The 1972 Princeton University yearbook recorded Alito's hope to "warm a seat on the Supreme Court" (though Alito has said that the statement was a joke and that "it was a dream that I never thought I would come close to realizing").[9] Not surprisingly, most people who are offered nominations accept them readily.

Some lawyers conduct concerted private campaigns for Supreme Court nominations. William Howard Taft became chief justice in 1921 after years of efforts. As an ex-president he had a great deal of influence, and one commentator described Taft as "virtually appointing himself" chief justice.[10] While serving on a federal court of appeals, Warren Burger undertook considerable labor to make himself a candidate for the

Supreme Court. When his effort succeeded, President Nixon's attorney general—overlooking Taft's example—said that "Burger's the first guy to run for the job of Chief Justice—and get it."[11] Burger and Taft are unusual cases, both in the extent of their efforts and in their success. More often, prospective nominees engage in quieter campaigns to enhance their chances through means such as writing opinions that garner attention. Because there are only a limited number of nominations to the Court, however, most of these campaigns fail.

Nominees participate actively in the confirmation process. They visit with senators, provide voluminous written materials to the Senate Judiciary Committee, and testify before the Committee at its hearings on confirmation. The visits have become a major activity. Sonia Sotomayor met with 89 senators before her confirmation hearings and three others afterward.[12]

Because nominees' testimony receives so much attention, it has become a key to confirmation. In 1987 Robert Bork's testimony weakened his prospects for confirmation because it left the impression that he was strongly conservative and because it exposed his rough edges. Clarence Thomas's testimony four years later increased opposition to him because what he said about his views on certain issues raised doubts about his candor. Seeking to avoid such negative results, nominees work hard to prepare for the hearings.

The questions that senators ask nominees range widely, but one important aim is to ascertain a nominee's views about the issues that the Supreme Court addresses.[13] Senators who seek to defeat a nominee try to get the nominee to take unpopular positions. But well-prepared nominees can usually overcome those efforts. They can turn back questions about matters such as abortion or the death penalty on the ground—largely legitimate—that they do not want to "prejudge" issues that might come before the Court. Nominees can limit criticism for being unresponsive by addressing questions about issues on which they know their answers will be popular or uncontroversial. As one senator said during the hearing on Samuel Alito, a hearing is "a subtle minuet, with the nominee answering as many questions as he thinks are necessary in order to be confirmed."[14]

Nominees differ in their approaches. John Roberts in 2005 impressed senators with his expertise and personality, and he adroitly avoided the traps that some Democratic committee members sought to lay for him. Alito was not quite as effective in putting forth a positive image, but he too avoided traps. One commentator said, "John Roberts charmed his way through the proceedings. Sam Alito has chosen to simply bore his way through."[15] Sonia Sotomayor faced questions from Republican senators about decisions and out-of-court statements she had made that they saw as potentially damaging to her. She was cautious in her testimony but sought to address the concerns

Supreme Court nominee Elena Kagan with Senators Patrick Leahy and Jeff Sessions before the beginning of her confirmation hearing in 2010. A nominee's testimony at the hearing is usually the most important event in the confirmation process.

that Republicans raised. Her testimony did not satisfy her critics, but she did not say anything that aroused broader opposition.

Senators often express frustration that nominees are not more forth-coming, and some have complained that nominees such as Roberts and Alito portray themselves as more moderate in their views than their sub-sequent records as justices show them to be.[16] These complaints have some validity, although perceptions that nominees have become less can-did over time do not seem to be accurate.[17] But it is not surprising that some nominees tailor their testimony to avoid saying anything that makes their confirmation more controversial.

One of the strongest criticisms of the confirmation hearings was writ-ten by law professor Elena Kagan in 1995. Kagan criticized nominees for their evasions and senators for failing to press nominees harder, and she said that the hearings had become "a vapid and hollow charade."[18] But at her own confirmation hearings fifteen years later, she said that she had been wrong when she wrote the article, and she was as cautious as other recent nominees. And like some of those nominees, she portrayed herself as someone whose personal views would not affect her decisions as a jus-tice: "I think it's law all the way down."[19] Whatever she may have thought about the confirmation process, Kagan had little reason to abandon an approach that had proved successful for other nominees.

The President's Decision

For the president, a Supreme Court vacancy provides a valuable opportunity to influence the Court's direction, and presidents seek to make the most of these opportunities. But the individuals and groups for whom nominations are important can subject the president to heavy and conflicting pressures, and the pressures have grown stronger in recent years.[20]

Presidents differ in their involvement in the selection process. Bill Clinton, George W. Bush, and Barack Obama played a more active role in the process than did their predecessors Ronald Reagan and George H. W. Bush. Obama, a former constitutional law professor with a strong interest in the Court, has been especially active. Obama interviewed several prospective nominees before selecting Sonia Sotomayor and Elena Kagan, and he met with Senate leaders from both parties prior to the Kagan nomination.

Still, all presidents delegate most of the search process to other officials in the executive branch. In recent administrations the process has been centered in the Office of the White House Counsel.[21] Obama's search for a nominee in 2009 involved intense activity within his administration. Staff in the White House counsel's office and Vice President Biden's office, among others, worked to identify and gather information on prospective nominees, and they enlisted people within and outside the administration to do extensive research on the candidates. Staff members and Biden himself interviewed candidates.

Administrations in the current era typically do a good deal of preparatory work even before a vacancy in the Court actually arises. In the George W. Bush administration, White House officials interviewed prospective nominees in 2001, four years before there was a vacancy to fill.[22] Once a vacancy occurs, occasionally a president fixes on a single candidate for nomination. When Chief Justice Rehnquist died, President Bush quickly chose John Roberts for that position; he had already nominated Roberts to succeed Justice O'Connor. More often, administrations create a short list and then work to identify the best candidate from that list. President Obama chose Elena Kagan from a group of finalists that included three judges on the federal courts of appeals.[23] This process allows presidents and other officials to work systematically through the advantages and disadvantages of choosing different names from the list. But uncertainties about potential nominees and shifting conditions often introduce an element of chaos to the process. That was certainly true of President Clinton's nominations. And there was a degree of chaos even in the George W. Bush nominations, despite the administration's careful preparations.

Administrations differ in the mix of criteria that presidents and their advisers use in choosing nominees. The possible criteria fall into several categories: the "objective" qualifications of potential nominees, their policy preferences, rewards to political and personal associates, and building political support. Cutting across these criteria and helping to determine their use is the reality that the Senate decides whether to confirm a nominee.

"Objective" Qualifications. Presidents have strong incentives to select Supreme Court nominees who have demonstrated high levels of legal competence and adherence to ethical standards. Most presidents have respect for the Court. Further, highly competent justices are in the best position to influence their colleagues. Finally, serious questions about a candidate's competence or ethical behavior work against Senate confirmation.

In general, presidents' choices reflect an interest in competence. This does not mean that all nominees are highly skilled in the law, but only in a few cases has a nominee's capacity to serve on the Court been seriously questioned. One of those was Nixon's nominee G. Harrold Carswell, who was denied confirmation. Perceptions that Harriet Miers had only limited knowledge of constitutional law were one source of the opposition that ultimately led her to withdraw as a nominee.

The ethical behavior of several nominees has been questioned. Opponents of Abe Fortas (when nominated to be chief justice), Clement Haynsworth, Stephen Breyer, and Samuel Alito pointed to what they saw as financial conflicts of interest. Fortas was also criticized for continuing to consult with President Johnson while serving as an associate justice. The charges against Fortas and Haynsworth helped bring about their defeats in the Senate. After Douglas Ginsburg was announced as a Reagan nominee, disclosures were made about a possible financial conflict of interest when he was in the Justice Department and about his past use of marijuana. The latter disclosure was especially damaging, and Ginsburg withdrew his name from consideration. An allegation that Clarence Thomas had sexually harassed an assistant while he was a federal administrator resulted in a special set of Senate hearings on the charge and put his confirmation in jeopardy.

To minimize the possibility of such embarrassments, administrations today give close scrutiny to the competence and ethics of potential nominees. Although these criteria eliminate some people from consideration, enough candidates survive to give presidents a wide range of choices for a nomination.

Policy Preferences. By policy preferences I mean an individual's attitudes toward policy issues. These criteria have always been a consideration in the selection of Supreme Court justices. In the current era every president gives considerable weight to the policy preferences of prospective nominees because of the Court's prominence as a policymaker and because interest groups associated with both parties care so much about the Court's direction.

But presidents continue to differ in how much they focus on nominees' policy views. Richard Nixon and Ronald Reagan, who wanted to change the Court's direction, gave this consideration some emphasis. Speaking of potential nominees, Nixon told his chief of staff that he did not care "if the guy can read or write, just so he votes right."[24] Policy considerations were even more important to George W. Bush, in part because he and other conservatives were unhappy that a string of appointments by his Republican predecessors had changed the Court less than they had hoped. In contrast, Bill Clinton was less concerned with the policy views of his prospective nominees.

This criterion can create a dilemma for presidents. Interest groups and political activists associated with the two parties tend to favor nominees with strong ideological views—liberal Democrats or conservative Republicans. Most presidents themselves have similar preferences. But a nominee who is perceived as relatively extreme may be vulnerable to defeat in the Senate because interest groups on the other side are more likely to mobilize against such a nominee and more senators will perceive the nominee as ideologically unacceptable.

Thus, presidents often perceive that they must choose between two imperfect options. One is to select a nominee with strong ideological views and risk difficulty with confirmation. The other is to choose a more moderate nominee, potentially annoying interest groups that are important to their party and reducing the president's impact on the Court's direction. Presidents have responded to this dilemma in different ways, depending in part on their willingness to get into conflicts over the selection of nominees. President Obama chose Sonia Sotomayor and Elena Kagan over other candidates who seemed more liberal, in part to minimize problems in the confirmation process.

Presidents who want to put like-minded people on the Supreme Court need to ascertain that their nominees really *are* like-minded. This is one reason why every nominee since 1986 except for Kagan and Harriet Miers has come from a federal court of appeals. If a judge has a long record of judicial votes and opinions on issues of federal law, as Sotomayor and Samuel Alito did, presidents and their advisers can be fairly confident about the kinds of positions the judge would take on many issues as a justice. In the George W. Bush administration, one prospective nominee with a strong conservative reputation was nonetheless eliminated from consideration because of a single opinion in which he had taken a liberal position.[25]

Some nominees do not have these long records. Miers and Kagan had never served as judges. Sandra Day O'Connor had served only on state courts, and nearly all of David Souter's judicial service was at the state level. Most kinds of issues that come to the Supreme Court are uncommon in state courts. Clarence Thomas had served only one year on a federal court of appeals and John Roberts, only two. For candidates such as these, other sources of information can be consulted, such as their record in nonjudicial positions and people who know them well. In Harriet Miers's case, George W. Bush had a good sense of her views from their long association, including her work in the White House. Sometimes presidents or their representatives ask prospective nominees directly about their views. According to one report, presidential advisers questioned John Roberts closely in order to ascertain the strength of his conservatism.[26]

Presidents concerned with confirmation of their nominees prefer a situation in which they have a clear sense of their nominees' views but there is little public evidence of those views for opponents to attack. As George W. Bush said about Harriet Miers, who had not served as a judge, "There's not a lot of opinions for people to look at."[27] But the lack of hard evidence that Miers was strongly conservative on judicial issues bothered members of the president's own party. In the case of David Souter, President George H. W. Bush had what he thought was good evidence of the nominee's conservatism from people who knew him, but Senate Democrats had little evidence of their own with which to raise questions about Souter. Souter was confirmed with little difficulty, but his record as a justice indicates that he was not nearly as conservative as Bush thought. That record has served as a cautionary tale for conservatives, and fear of another Souter helps explain the strong opposition to Miers.

Exceptions such as Souter get considerable attention, but most justices turn out to be ideologically compatible with the presidents who appoint them. Those who deviate from the appointing president generally fall into two categories. First, some of them were chosen by presidents who were not especially interested in choosing compatible justices or who were not careful about doing so. Gerald Ford selected John Paul Stevens without regard for his nominee's policy preferences, so the gap between Ford's conservatism and Stevens's liberalism is not surprising. According to a story that is widely circulated but of uncertain accuracy, Dwight Eisenhower cited his appointees Earl Warren and William Brennan as the two mistakes he had made as president.[28] But as California governor, Warren had shown signs of the liberalism he later manifested as chief justice, and Brennan's own liberalism was apparent from his record as a state judge.

Second, some justices shift their ideological positions after reaching the Court. Richard Nixon's one "failure" was Harry Blackmun, who had a distinctly conservative record in his early years on the Court but gradually adopted more liberal positions. Anthony Kennedy also may have shifted in a liberal direction after reaching the Court, albeit to a lesser degree. A conservative publication later referred to Kennedy as "surely Reagan's biggest disappointment."[29]

Political and Personal Reward. When George W. Bush nominated Harriet Miers to the Supreme Court in 2005, he had known Miers for a dozen years. In Texas she was general counsel for Bush's transition team after he was elected governor, and she was also his personal lawyer. She joined his presidential administration in 2001, serving in the White House as staff secretary, deputy chief of staff, and counsel to the president.

In choosing Miers, Bush took what had been a common approach for most of the Supreme Court's history. As of the late 1960s, about 60 percent of the nominees to the Court had known the nominating president personally.[30] With the exception of Dwight Eisenhower, all the presidents from Franklin Roosevelt through Lyndon Johnson selected primarily personal acquaintances.

Rewarding political associates seemed to be the main criterion for Harry Truman in selecting justices. One of those associates was Sherman Minton, a friend and former Senate colleague of Truman's, who was serving as a federal judge in Indiana when he learned that one of the justices had died. He quickly boarded a train to Washington, went to the White House, and asked Truman to nominate him for the vacancy. Truman immediately agreed, and Minton became a justice.[31]

Some appointments to the Court were direct rewards for political help. Eisenhower selected Earl Warren to serve as chief justice largely because of Warren's crucial support of Eisenhower at the 1952 Republican convention. As governor of California and leader of that state's delegation, Warren had provided the needed votes on a preliminary issue, and Eisenhower's success on that issue helped secure his nomination.

Of the more recent nominees, Miers certainly falls in the category of close associates of appointing presidents. Elena Kagan may fit in that category as well. President Obama met her when both taught at the University of Chicago Law School, kept in contact with her after that, and selected her as solicitor general after he was elected president. In announcing Kagan's nomination, Obama called her "my friend."[32] But Miers and Kagan stand alone among the people whom presidents have selected since 1968. Indeed, few nominees in that period have had any contact with the president before being considered for the Court. Obama first met Sonia Sotomayor a few days before choosing her as his nominee in 2009.[33]

Perhaps the main reason for the decline in the selection of personal acquaintances is that such nominees are vulnerable to charges of "cronyism." That charge was made in 1968 when President Johnson nominated

Justice Abe Fortas for elevation to chief justice and nominated Judge Homer Thornberry to succeed Fortas as associate justice; both Fortas and Thornberry were close to Johnson. The charge played a small role in building opposition to Fortas and Thornberry in the Senate. Ultimately, Fortas's confirmation was blocked by a filibuster, and Thornberry's nomination thus became moot. Miers's nomination was also attacked as a case of cronyism, and that charge was one factor in the pressures that led to her withdrawal.

One element of political reward has remained strong, however: about 90 percent of all nominees to the Court—and all those chosen since 1975—have been members of the president's party. One reason is that lawyers who share the president's policy views are more likely to come from the same party, but there is also a widespread feeling that such an attractive prize should go to one of the party faithful.

Building Political Support. Nominations can be made to reward people who helped the president in the past, but they can also be used to seek political benefits in the future. Most often, presidents select justices with certain attributes in order to appeal to leaders and voters who share those attributes.

Geography and religion were important criteria for selecting justices in some past eras, but their role in nominations has nearly disappeared. The decline of interest in maintaining geographical diversity is symbolized by the fact that four of the current justices grew up in New York City. Similarly, the decline of religion as a consideration is symbolized by the fact that the current Court includes no Protestants, even though they constitute a clear majority in the country.

In contrast, representation by race, gender, and ethnicity has become quite important. President George H. W. Bush's nomination of Clarence Thomas to succeed Thurgood Marshall reflected the pressure he felt to maintain black representation on the Court. And according to one scholar, "gender was the primary and decisive factor" in President Reagan's nomination of Sandra Day O'Connor at a time when there was a widespread feeling that a woman should be appointed.[34] The nominations of Harriet Miers, Sonia Sotomayor, and Elena Kagan reflected an interest in putting women on the Court. Miers and Sotomayor were selected from sets of finalists who were all female. Barack Obama's choice of Sotomayor over the other finalists was heavily influenced by the desire to select the first Hispanic justice, largely to please an important group in the electorate.

Summary. Presidents use several criteria to choose Supreme Court nominees. The importance of these considerations changes over time and varies from one nomination to another.

The Court's importance has powerful effects on the criteria for selection of justices. First, it leads presidents and their representatives to weigh all the criteria more carefully than they generally do in nominating judges to lower courts. Second, it leads to an emphasis on competence and policy preferences rather than the "political" considerations of reward and support building. If Supreme Court justices are better jurists than the judges on lower federal courts, and if their policy preferences are more accurate reflections of their nominators' views, it is chiefly because presidents have a strong incentive to achieve those results.

Senate Confirmation

A president's nomination to the Court goes to the Senate for confirmation. The nomination is referred to the Judiciary Committee, which gathers extensive information on the nominee, holds hearings at which the nominee and other witnesses testify, and then votes its recommendation for Senate action. After this vote the nomination is referred to the floor, where it is debated and a confirmation vote taken.

A simple majority is needed for confirmation, although a large minority of senators (under the current rules, forty-one) could block confirmation through a filibuster that uses extended debate to prevent a confirmation vote. That was the fate of Abe Fortas's nomination for chief justice in 1968. In 2006 some Democrats called for a filibuster against confirmation of Samuel Alito, but the Senate voted 75–25 to end debate and proceed to a vote.

The Senate's Role and Record. When the president nominates someone to any position, the presumption typically is in favor of confirmation. That presumption applies to the Supreme Court. But the Senate gives Supreme Court nominations close scrutiny, and confirmation is far from automatic.

Indeed, defeats of nominees are hardly rare. Through mid-2012 the Senate has refused to confirm twenty-six nominations to the Supreme Court, through either an adverse vote or nonaction. These twenty-six cases constitute about one-sixth of the nominations that the Senate has considered. This proportion of defeats is the highest of any position to which the president makes appointments. For example, presidents have made far more nominations of cabinet members, but only nine have been defeated.

Presidents have been more successful with Supreme Court nominations in the twentieth century and the early twenty-first century than in the nineteenth. Since 1900 only five of the sixty-three nominations considered by the Senate have failed: Herbert Hoover's nomination of John Parker in 1930, Johnson's elevation of Abe Fortas to chief justice in 1968,

Nixon's nominations of Clement Haynsworth in 1969 and G. Harrold Carswell in 1970 (both for the same vacancy), and Reagan's nomination of Robert Bork in 1987. Only five successful nominees were confirmed by less than a two-thirds margin in the Senate.

This record of success is a bit misleading, because the Senate has continued to scrutinize nominations carefully. Of the thirty-two nominees the Senate considered from 1949 through mid-2012, four were defeated and many others faced serious opposition. The Senate votes in this period are shown in Table 2-2. As suggested by these votes, nominees have faced especially close scrutiny since 1967, and it is noteworthy that the last four successful nominees all received more than twenty negative votes. Closer scrutiny is also reflected in the length of time that confirmation requires: the median time from nomination to confirmation vote was twenty-eight days between 1949 and 1980 and eighty-four days since then.[35]

Nominees and Situations. Nominees vary a great deal in the degree of difficulty they face in the Senate, from those who face no opposition to those who fail to win the needed majority. This variation reflects the attributes of nominees and of the situations in which the Senate considers them.[36]

The attributes of nominees that affect confirmation the most are their perceived ideological positions and qualifications. Nominees who are thought to be highly liberal or highly conservative have greater difficulty than those who seem to be moderate. And nominees who seem less qualified than they should be also arouse opposition. The two attributes can become intertwined, in that senators who are ideologically distant from a nominee often use doubts about a nominee's legal skills or ethical standards as a seemingly objective justification for opposing the nominee. But senators who are not distant from a nominee may oppose confirmation because they conclude that the nominee's qualifications are deficient.

Several aspects of the situation at the time of nomination also affect the Senate's action. One is the president's political strength in the Senate. According to one count, presidents whose party holds a Senate majority have had 90 percent of their nominees confirmed, as against 61 percent for presidents who faced an opposition majority.[37] One reason for this difference is that senators of the majority party chair the Judiciary Committee and schedule votes on the floor. Another reason is that a Senate controlled by the opposition has more senators who are politically opposed to the president and who are ideologically distant from a nominee. For both reasons, President Obama began with a significant advantage when he made his nominations in 2009 and 2010.

Other factors affect the president's strength. Presidents with high public approval ratings have an advantage because strong public support

TABLE 2-2
Senate Votes on Supreme Court Nominations Since 1949

Nominee	Year	Vote
Tom Clark	1949	73–8
Sherman Minton	1949	48–16
Earl Warren	1954	NRV
John Harlan	1955	71–11
William Brennan	1956	NRV
Charles Whittaker	1957	NRV
Potter Stewart	1959	70–17
Byron White	1962	NRV
Arthur Goldberg	1962	NRV
Abe Fortas	1965	NRV
Thurgood Marshall	1967	69–11
Abe Fortas[a]	1968	Withdrawn
Homer Thornberry	(1968)	No action
Warren Burger	1969	74–3
Clement Haynsworth	1969	45–55
G. Harrold Carswell	1970	45–51
Harry Blackmun	1970	94–0
Lewis Powell	1971	89–1
William Rehnquist	1971	68–26
John Paul Stevens	1975	98–0
Sandra Day O'Connor	1981	99–0
William Rehnquist[b]	1986	65–33
Antonin Scalia	1986	98–0
Robert Bork	1987	42–58
Douglas Ginsburg	(1987)	No action
Anthony Kennedy	1988	97–0
David Souter	1990	90–9
Clarence Thomas	1991	52–48
Ruth Bader Ginsburg	1993	96–3
Stephen Breyer	1994	87–9
John Roberts	2005	78–22
Harriet Miers	(2005)	No action
Samuel Alito	2006	58–42
Sonia Sotomayor	2009	68–31
Elena Kagan	2010	63–37

Source: Joan Biskupic and Elder Witt, *Guide to the U.S. Supreme Court*, 3d ed. (Washington, DC: Congressional Quarterly, 1997), 1099; table updated by the author.

Note: NRV = no recorded vote.

a. Elevation to chief justice; nomination withdrawn after the Senate vote of 45–43 failed to end a filibuster against the nomination (two-thirds majority was required).
b. Elevation to chief justice.

deters opposition to their nominees. And nominations made late in a president's term are more vulnerable for several reasons: the president's popularity tends to decline over time, second-term presidents are "lame ducks" who will leave office shortly, and partisanship often increases. Only 54 percent of the nominees selected in the last year of a presidential term won confirmation.[38] No justice has left the Court in the last year of a term since 1968, primarily because justices recognize the controversy that often arises when nominations are made in that year.

A second aspect of the situation is the mobilization of support and opposition to the nominee. It makes a difference whether some senators decide to play an active role in mustering votes against a nominee and whether the administration mounts a strong effort to secure confirmation.[39] Outside government, a strong interest group campaign against a nomination can overcome the assumption that the nominee will be confirmed and thereby get senators to consider voting against confirmation. Such campaigns can also reduce public support for a nominee, and public opinion affects senators' votes for or against nominees.[40]

Finally, the perceived impact of a nomination helps to determine whether senators believe that efforts to defeat the nominee are worthwhile. In part, the intense scrutiny given to recent nominations reflects the increased prominence of the Supreme Court as a policymaker on controversial issues. Senators attach particular importance to a nomination if the nominee might change the Court's policies substantially, either because the nominee is much more liberal or conservative than the justice leaving the Court or because of a close ideological balance on the Court.

Among nominees in the past three decades, David Souter and Clarence Thomas illustrate the importance of personal attributes. The two were chosen by President George H. W. Bush a year apart, with the Democrats holding majorities in the Senate. Each would replace a strongly liberal justice, so both seemed likely to change the Court's ideological tenor considerably. Souter won confirmation with only moderate difficulty, but Thomas's margin was only four votes. The difference can be explained primarily by two widespread perceptions: that Souter was a moderate conservative and Thomas a strong conservative and that Souter was well-qualified but Thomas's qualifications might be questioned.

Another pair of nominees illustrates the importance of the situation. President Reagan selected Antonin Scalia in 1986 and Robert Bork in 1987. Both were viewed as highly conservative, and both were considered well-qualified for service on the Court. Scalia was confirmed unanimously, and Bork was defeated. One difference was that the Senate had a Republican majority in 1986 but a Democratic majority the next year. Another was that Scalia would replace another strong conservative but Bork would replace a moderate conservative on a Court that was closely divided between liberals and conservatives. Finally, in 1986, liberal senators and interest groups focused their efforts on defeating William Rehnquist's nomination for chief justice and largely ignored Scalia. In 1987, in contrast, liberals in and out of the Senate gave intense attention to Bork.

These generalizations can be illustrated further by looking at two sets of nominations. The first set includes the four defeats of nominees in the past half-century. The second includes the six nominees considered by the Senate since 1993, all of whom won confirmation.

The Defeats. From 1930 to 1967 a long series of Supreme Court nominees won confirmation. Then, in the period from 1968 to 1970 three nominees lost in the Senate. The first was Abe Fortas, a sitting justice whom President Johnson nominated to be chief justice in 1968. The Senate had a Democratic majority, but many of the Democrats were conservative, and Fortas's strong liberalism on the liberal Warren Court aroused conservative opposition. Further, some Republicans wanted to prevent Fortas's confirmation in order to reserve the vacancy for a new president—expected to be Republican—in 1969. These opponents pointed to two activities that raised doubts about Fortas's ethical fitness: his continued consultation with the president about policy matters while serving on the Court and an arrangement by which he gave nine lectures at American University, in Washington, DC, for a fee of $15,000 raised from businesses. The Judiciary Committee approved the nomination by a divided vote, but it ran into a filibuster on the Senate floor. A vote to end the filibuster fell fourteen votes short of the two-thirds majority then required; the opposition came almost entirely from Republicans and southern Democrats. President Johnson then withdrew the nomination at Fortas's request.

In 1969 Fortas resigned from the Court. President Nixon selected Clement Haynsworth, chief judge of a federal court of appeals, to replace him. Haynsworth was opposed by labor groups and the National Association for the Advancement of Colored People, both of which disliked his judicial record. Liberal senators, unhappy about that record themselves, sought revenge for Fortas's defeat as well. Haynsworth was also charged with unethical conduct: he had sat on two cases involving subsidiaries of companies in which he owned stock, and in another case he had bought the stock of a corporation in the interval between his court's decision in its favor and the announcement of that decision. These charges led to additional opposition from Senate moderates. Haynsworth ultimately was defeated by a 45–55 vote, with a large minority of Republicans voting against confirmation.

President Nixon then nominated another court of appeals judge, G. Harrold Carswell. After the fight over Haynsworth, most senators were inclined to support the next nominee. One senator predicted that any new Nixon nominee "will have no trouble getting confirmed unless he has committed murder—recently."[41] But Carswell drew opposition from civil rights groups for what they perceived as his hostility to their interests, and their cause gained strength from a series of revelations about the nominee that suggested active opposition to racial equality. Carswell was also criticized for an alleged lack of judicial competence. After escorting Carswell to talk with senators, one of Nixon's staffers reported to the president that "they think Carswell's a boob, a dummy. And what counter is there to that? He is."[42] The nomination was defeated by a 45–51 vote, with a lineup similar to the vote on Haynsworth.

Robert Bork's 1987 defeat differed from the three that preceded it in that no serious charges were made about Bork's competence or his ethical standards. But liberals were concerned about his strong conservatism on civil liberties issues and his potential to shift the Court's ideological balance. Senator Ted Kennedy and liberal interest groups worked hard to secure votes against Bork. Concern about Bork's views was intensified by his testimony before the Senate Judiciary Committee, in which he discussed in detail his positions on issues such as the right to privacy.

This growing concern, combined with the unprecedented level of interest group activity against Bork, made his defeat possible. Also important was President Reagan's political weakness: not only did the Democrats control the Senate, but Reagan's popularity inside and outside Congress had declined. Even so, a more effective campaign for Bork by the administration might have secured his confirmation. In any event, confirmation was denied by a 42–58 vote. All but eight senators voted along party lines; the overwhelming and unexpected opposition of southern Democrats made the difference in the outcome.

These four defeats, different though they were, have some things in common. In each instance, many senators were inclined to oppose the nominee on ideological grounds. All but Fortas faced a Senate controlled by the opposite party, and Fortas was confronted by a conservative majority. And each nominee was weakened by a "smoking gun" that provided a basis for opposition: the ethical questions about Fortas and Haynsworth, the allegations of racism and incompetence against Carswell, and the charge that Bork was outside the mainstream in his views on judicial issues. The combination of these problems led to enough negative votes to prevent confirmation in each instance.

The Recent Confirmations. Between 1993 and 2010 the Senate voted on six nominations. All six nominees won confirmation, but their paths to victory differed considerably.

When President Clinton nominated Ruth Bader Ginsburg in 1993 and Stephen Breyer in 1994, there remained a good deal of resentment among Republicans over the defeat of Robert Bork. As the fates of Haynsworth and Carswell indicate, such resentment can lead to retaliation. However, the Democrats held a majority in the Senate. Just as important, Clinton made an effort to avoid confirmation battles by nominating relatively moderate liberals. Ginsburg had helped lead the litigation campaign on behalf of equal rights for women, but her record as a court of appeals judge was fairly centrist. And neither nominee would change the Court's ideological balance very much.

Ginsburg won confirmation with no serious obstacles and only three negative votes. Breyer had a slightly more difficult time. Some Republican senators argued that he had shown a lack of prudence in investing in an insurance syndicate and that the investment had created conflicts of interest in some cases. Ultimately, nine Republicans cast votes against him, but his nomination was never in real jeopardy.

George W. Bush's nominations of John Roberts and Samuel Alito in 2005 came at a time of increased polarization between the parties and concern about the Supreme Court's future direction. As a result, it was likely that Senate Democrats would oppose a nominee who seemed to be a strong conservative. Yet interest groups allied with the Republican Party were adamant that the president choose strong conservatives, and the president's own inclination seemed to be the same. Bush had the advantage of a moderately large Republican majority in the Senate, increasing the chances of a favorable outcome for any nominee. Under the circumstances, he chose two nominees whose records suggested that they were quite conservative. (Bush also saw Harriet Miers as strongly conservative.)

Nothing like a smoking gun emerged for Roberts. Indeed, his testimony in the Judiciary Committee left most observers with a highly positive image of him. Ultimately, he was confirmed by a 78–22 vote, with all the negative votes coming from Democrats.

Like Roberts, Alito had demonstrated a high level of legal skills. But he was more vulnerable than Roberts because he had a more extensive record of strongly conservative positions. Some opponents thought they had a smoking gun in two statements he had made in 1985. In those statements Alito said that he was proud of his contributions to the Reagan administration's arguments that the "Constitution does not protect the right to an abortion" and implied that his goal was "the eventual overruling of *Roe v. Wade*."[43] Alito was also criticized for participating as a judge in one case involving a mutual fund firm that held a substantial investment of his, despite a pledge to recuse himself from such cases when he was nominated to the court of appeals. Perhaps most important, Alito would replace moderate conservative Sandra Day O'Connor. Thus, unlike Roberts, who succeeded William Rehnquist, Alito could move the Court substantially to the right.

Most senators seemed to regard Alito's participation in the case that was related to his investment as inadvertent and inconsequential. In contrast, Alito's efforts to reassure senators that he was not an extreme conservative and that he would not necessarily vote to overturn *Roe* had limited success with Democrats. But it was clear early in the process that nearly all Republican senators would vote for him. As the minority party in the Senate, the Democrats could block Alito only with a successful filibuster, and many Democratic senators saw a filibuster as inappropriate or at least bad political strategy. After the vote to end debate, Alito won confirmation by a 58–42 margin. One Republican and all but four Democrats voted against him.

Sonia Sotomayor entered the confirmation process with the great advantage of a large Democratic majority in the Senate and the additional advantage that her replacement of David Souter was unlikely to change the Court's overall ideological balance very much. Still, some Senate Republicans joined conservative interest groups in expressing strong opposition to Sotomayor. She had said in one talk, "I would hope that a wise Latina woman with the richness of her experiences would more often than not reach a better conclusion than a white male who hasn't lived that life."[44] Opponents argued that this passage and other statements and actions indicated a lack of impartiality on her part. They also charged that some of her positions in court of appeals decisions were unduly liberal and departed from good interpretations of the law.

None of these criticisms constituted the kind of smoking gun that might have attracted Democratic opposition to the nomination. Indeed, no Democratic senator voted against Sotomayor. But the great majority of Republicans—31 of 40—cast negative votes. Although those Republicans cited specific concerns about Sotomayor, their votes were primarily a product of ideological considerations: conservative senators and interest groups that were important to those senators saw the nominee as unduly liberal.

Elena Kagan benefited from the same Democratic majority as Sotomayor. And like Sotomayor, she would not change the ideological balance of the Court. Indeed, some liberals complained that she was probably more conservative than John Paul Stevens, the justice she would succeed.

Yet Kagan still faced widespread opposition from Senate Republicans and conservative interest groups. Opponents cited her lack of judicial experience and her limited experience as a practicing lawyer. Even in the absence of a prior judicial record, they found evidence of what they saw as strongly liberal views. Republicans were especially critical of her actions as dean at Harvard Law School limiting the access of military recruiters to law students because of the military's prohibition of service by openly gay and lesbian people. Ultimately, Kagan won even less Republican support than Sotomayor, with 36 of the 41 Republicans voting against her. The difference may have reflected the reluctance of a few Republicans to vote against the first Hispanic nominee to the Court.

The Current Picture. The Senate's use of its power over confirmation of Supreme Court nominees has varied a good deal over time. For most of the twentieth century, senators were generally willing to defer to presidents in their votes on nominees. But since 1968 the Senate has taken a more assertive role in scrutinizing nominees. One reason for this change is the growth in efforts by interest groups to defeat nominees whose views run counter to group positions. Another spur has been the growing awareness that a single Court appointment can affect national policy in important ways. In both respects one issue—abortion—has been especially important.

Still, until the last decade many nominees faced little opposition. By 2005, however, the growing polarization of the parties had changed the picture.[45] All four nominees between 2005 and 2010 probably would have been uncontroversial as late as the early 1990s. Each seemed well-qualified, and three of the four (all but Samuel Alito) seemed likely to leave the Court's ideological balance unchanged. But each attracted strong criticism from the opposition party, and only John Roberts—the first of the four—won as many as ten votes from the opposition.

None of the four nominees was ever in serious danger of defeat, but that was only because the president's party had a Senate majority in each instance. So long as partisan polarization remains strong, a president who lacks that majority may well have difficulty in winning confirmation for nominees. Under that condition, a president might select a nominee with especially strong qualifications and a record of ideological moderation in order to maximize the chances for success. In the current period, even more than in some past periods, which people reach the Supreme Court depends on Senate elections as well as presidential elections.

Who Is Selected

In some respects the people who have become Supreme Court justices are a diverse group. But because of the workings of the selection process, certain kinds of people are far more likely to reach the Court than others.

Career Paths

The kinds of people who become justices can be understood largely in terms of the paths that people take to get to the Court. These paths have changed over time. In order to highlight that change, in this section I examine the set of thirty-seven justices appointed since 1937. Recent justices are of particular interest, and the box on pages 52–53 summarizes the careers of the justices who sat on the Court in 2012.[46]

The Legal Profession. The Constitution specifies no requirements for Supreme Court justices, so they need not be attorneys. In practice, however, this restriction has been absolute. Nearly everyone involved in the selection process assumes that only a person with legal training can serve effectively on the Court. If a president nominated a nonlawyer to the Court, this assumption—and the large number of lawyers in the Senate—almost surely would prevent confirmation.

Thus, holding a law degree constitutes the first and least flexible requirement for recruitment to the Court. Most of the justices who served during the first century of the Court's history followed what was then the standard practice, apprenticing under a practicing attorney. In several instances the practicing attorney was a leading member of the bar. James Byrnes (chosen in 1941) was the last justice to study law through apprenticeship; all his successors have taken what is now the nearly universal route of law school training. A high proportion of justices have graduated from prestigious schools.

High Positions. If legal education is a necessary first step in the paths to the Court, almost equally important as a last step is attaining a high position in government or the legal profession. Obscure private practitioners or state trial judges might be superbly qualified for the Court, but their qualifications would be questioned because of their lowly positions. A high position in government or the legal profession also makes a person more visible to the president and to the officials who identify potential nominees.

At the time they were selected, the justices appointed since 1937 held positions of four types. They were judges, executive branch officials, elected officials, or well-respected leaders in the legal profession.

Nineteen of the justices appointed in this period were appellate judges at the time of selection. Seventeen sat on the federal courts of appeals. The other two (William Brennan and Sandra Day O'Connor) served on state courts. Six of the seventeen federal judges came from the District of

Columbia circuit, which is especially visible to the president and other federal officials.

Eleven justices served in the federal executive branch, eight of them in the Justice Department. The other three justices served as chair of the Securities and Exchange Commission (William Douglas), secretary of the Treasury (Fred Vinson), and secretary of labor (Arthur Goldberg).

Of the other seven justices appointed since 1937, four held high elective office. Three were senators (Hugo Black, James Byrnes, and Harold Burton), and the fourth was the governor of California (Earl Warren). The other three held positions outside government. Each had attained extraordinary success and respect—as a legal scholar (Felix Frankfurter), a Washington lawyer (Abe Fortas), and a leader of the legal profession (Lewis Powell). Frankfurter and Fortas had also been informal presidential advisers.

The Steps Between. The people who have become Supreme Court justices took several routes from their legal education to the high positions that made them credible candidates for the Court. Frankfurter, Fortas, and Powell illustrate one simple route: entry into legal practice or academia, followed by a gradual rise to high standing in the legal profession. Some justices took a similar route through public office. Earl Warren held a series of appointive and elective offices, leading to his California governorship. Clarence Thomas and Samuel Alito each served in several nonelected government positions and then as a judge on a federal court of appeals.

Since 1975 the most common route to the Court has been through private practice or law teaching, often combined with some time in government, before appointment to a federal court of appeals. Antonin Scalia, Ruth Bader Ginsburg, and Stephen Breyer were law professors. Anthony Kennedy and John Roberts were in private practice. In a variant of that path, Sonia Sotomayor left private practice to become a federal district judge and was later elevated to a court of appeals. During their prejudicial careers, all six had held government positions or participated informally in the governmental process.

Justice O'Connor took a unique path to the Court. She spent time in private practice and government legal positions, with some career interruptions for family reasons, before becoming an Arizona state senator and majority leader of the senate. O'Connor left the legislature for a trial judgeship. Her promotion to the state court of appeals through a gubernatorial appointment put her in a position to be considered for the Supreme Court.

Careers of the Supreme Court ...

John G. Roberts Jr. (born 1955)

Law degree, Harvard University, 1979
Law clerk, U.S. Court of Appeals, 1979–1980
Supreme Court law clerk, 1980–1981
U.S. Justice Department, 1981–1982
White House Counsel's Office, 1982–1986
U.S. Solicitor General's Office, 1989–1993
Private law practice, 1986–1989, 1993–2003
Judge, U.S. Court of Appeals, 2003–2005
Appointed chief justice, 2005

Antonin Scalia (born 1936)

Law degree, Harvard University, 1960
Private law practice, 1960–1967
Law school teaching, 1967–1971
Legal positions in federal government, 1971–1977
Law school teaching, 1977–1982
Judge, U.S. Court of Appeals, 1982–1986
Appointed to Supreme Court, 1986

Anthony M. Kennedy (born 1936)

Law degree, Harvard University, 1961
Private law practice, 1961–1975
Judge, U.S. Court of Appeals, 1975–1988
Appointed to Supreme Court, 1988

Clarence Thomas (born 1948)

Law degree, Yale University, 1974
Missouri attorney general's office, 1974–1977
Attorney for Monsanto Company, 1977–1979
Legislative assistant to a U.S. senator, 1979–1981
Assistant U.S. secretary of education, 1981–1982
Chair, U.S. Equal Employment Opportunity Commission, 1982–1990
Judge, U.S. Court of Appeals, 1990–1991
Appointed to Supreme Court, 1991

Ruth Bader Ginsburg (born 1933)

Law degree, Columbia University, 1959
Federal district court law clerk, 1959–1961
Law school research position, 1961–1963
Law school teaching, 1963–1980
Judge, U.S. Court of Appeals, 1980–1993
Appointed to Supreme Court, 1993

...Justices (2012)

Stephen G. Breyer (born 1938)

Law degree, Harvard University, 1964

Supreme Court law clerk, 1964–1965

U.S. Justice Department, 1965–1967

Law school teaching, 1967–1980

Staff, U.S. Senate Judiciary Committee, 1974–1975, 1979–1980

Judge, U.S. Court of Appeals, 1980–1994

Appointed to Supreme Court, 1994

Samuel A. Alito Jr. (born 1950)

Law degree, Yale University, 1975

Law clerk, U.S. Court of Appeals, 1976–1977

Assistant U.S. Attorney, 1977–1981

U.S. Solicitor General's Office, 1981–1985

U.S. Justice Department, 1985–1987

U.S. Attorney, 1987–1990

Judge, U.S. Court of Appeals, 1990–2006

Appointed to Supreme Court, 2006

Sonia Sotomayor (born 1954)

Law degree, Yale University, 1979

Assistant district attorney, 1979–1984

Private law practice, 1984–1992

Judge, U.S. District Court, 1992–1998

Judge, U.S. Court of Appeals, 1998–2009

Appointed to Supreme Court, 2009

Elena Kagan (born 1960)

Law degree, Harvard University, 1986

Law clerk, U.S. Court of Appeals, 1986–1987

Supreme Court law clerk, 1987–1988

Private law practice, 1989–1991

Law school teaching, 1991–1995

Positions in executive branch, 1995–1999

Law school teaching and administration, 1999–2009

U.S. Solicitor General, 2009–2010

Appointed to Supreme Court, 2010

Sources: Biographical Directory of Federal Judges, Federal Judicial Center, http://www.fjc
.gov/history/home.nsf/page/judges.html.

Note: With the exception of Justice Breyer's Senate staff service, only the primary
position held by a future justice during each career stage is listed.

TABLE 2-3
Selected Career Experiences of Justices Appointed Since 1937 (in percentages)

	Experience during career		
Years appointed	Elective office	Head of federal agency	Judgeship
1937–1968	43	29	48
1969–2012	7	0	81
	Position at appointment		
1937–1968	19	29	29
1969–2012	0	0	81

Source: Biographical Directory of Federal Judges, Federal Judicial Center, http://www.fjc.gov/history/home.nsf/page/judges.html.

Note: Federal agencies include cabinet departments and independent agencies. Heads of offices within departments (e.g., the Office of the Solicitor General in the Justice Department) are not counted.

Changes in Paths. Even within the period since 1937, there has been a striking change in justices' pre-Court careers. Put simply, those careers have come to involve less politics and more law. As shown in Table 2-3, there is a substantial difference in those respects between the justices who were appointed between 1937 and 1968 and the justices chosen since then.

The twenty-one justices appointed to the Court between 1937 and 1968 were reasonably typical of those selected in earlier periods. About half had judicial experience, nearly as many had held elective office, and more than a quarter had headed a federal administrative agency.

The sixteen justices who have arrived at the Court since 1969 are a different kind of group. All but three have come directly from lower courts. Only one, Sandra Day O'Connor, had ever held elective office. None had headed a federal agency, and several had spent little or no time in government before winning judgeships. For these justices, the median proportion of their careers spent in what might be called the legal system— private practice, law school teaching, and the judiciary—was 85 percent. For the justices appointed between 1937 and 1968, the median was 67 percent.[47] The extent of this change was underlined in the period between 2006 and 2010, when all nine sitting justices had come to the Court from a federal court of appeals.

One reason for this change, perhaps the primary one, is that a prior judicial record helps presidents and their advisers to predict the positions that prospective nominees might take as justices. In an era in which most presidents care a great deal about the Court's direction, any help in making these predictions is valued. There may also be a growing feeling that service on a lower court helps to prepare a judge for the Supreme Court. Harriet Miers and Elena Kagan were criticized for the absence of that service.

Whether or not lower-court experience is needed as preparation for the Supreme Court, the change in paths to the Court since 1968 may affect the justices' perspectives and their thinking about legal issues. Some commentators argue that justices today do not understand government and politics as much as their counterparts in earlier periods and that this lack of understanding reduces their ability to recognize the likely consequences of some decisions.[48] There may be some truth in this argument, and the shift in the backgrounds of justices from politics to law may have other effects on the Court's decisions. But today, as in the past, people who had no contact at all with the political world would have little chance to reach the Court. None of the current justices fits that description.

Other Attributes of the Justices

Career experience is only one important characteristic of the people who become justices. But other attributes can be understood partly in terms of the career paths that take people to the Court.

Age. Since 1937 most Supreme Court justices have been in their fifties at the time of their appointments and the rest in their forties or early sixties. William Douglas was the youngest appointee, at age forty; at the other end of the spectrum, Lewis Powell was sixty-four.

The ages of Court appointees reflect a balance between two considerations. On the one hand, lawyers need time to develop the record of achievement that makes them credible candidates for the Court. On the other hand, presidents would like their appointees to serve for many years in order to achieve the maximum impact on the Court. Thus a candidate such as Clarence Thomas, forty-three when George H. W. Bush appointed him, can be especially attractive. Elena Kagan was fifty when Barack Obama nominated her to the Court in 2010. Almost surely, her relative youth compared with the other leading candidates worked in her favor.

Class, Race, and Sex. The Supreme Court's membership has diverged from the general population in regard to social class: most justices grew up in families that were relatively well off. One study found that one-third of the justices were from the upper class and one-quarter were from the upper middle class. Less than one-quarter were from the lower middle class or below.[49]

The justices selected since the 1930s have been less of a high-status group than were their predecessors, and the current Court reflects that change. Of the justices who sat on the Court in 2012, Clarence Thomas's family was impoverished, and Sonia Sotomayor's family can be characterized as lower middle class. The families of the other seven justices on the 2012 Court were divided about evenly between the middle class and upper middle class.

The historic predominance of higher-status backgrounds can be explained by the career paths that most justices take. First and most important, a justice must obtain a legal education. To do so is easiest for individuals of high status, because of the cost of law school and the college education that precedes it. Early in the Court's history, when most justices had apprenticed with an attorney, such advantaged people had the best opportunity to apprentice with leading lawyers.

Second, individuals of high status have a variety of advantages in their careers. Those who can afford to attend elite law schools, for instance, have the easiest time obtaining Supreme Court clerkships and positions in successful law firms. The partial deviation from this pattern since the 1930s reflects the increased availability of college and legal education as well as other social changes. Despite their limited financial resources, Sonia Sotomayor and Clarence Thomas were able to go to private colleges and then to Yale Law School.

Until 1967 all the justices were white men. This pattern is not difficult to understand. Because of various restrictions, women and members of racial minority groups long had extreme difficulty pursuing a legal education. As a result, few members of these groups passed the first barrier to selection. In addition, prejudice limited their ability to advance in the legal profession and in politics. Thus, very few individuals who were not white men could achieve the high positions that people generally must obtain to be considered for nomination to the Court.

Since 1967 four women (Sandra Day O'Connor, Ruth Bader Ginsburg, Sonia Sotomayor, and Elena Kagan), two African Americans (Thurgood Marshall and Clarence Thomas), and a Hispanic American (Sotomayor) have won appointments to the Court. These appointments reflect changes in society that made it less difficult for people other than white men to achieve high positions. They also reflect the growing willingness of presidents to consider women and members of racial minority groups as prospective nominees. Still, because of the various advantages they enjoy, white men are likely to enjoy disproportionate representation on the Court for some time.

If the Court has been composed primarily of white men with higher-status backgrounds, how has this affected its policies? One possible effect involves the legal claims of racial minority groups and of women. It seems likely that those claims would have been taken seriously at an earlier time if members of these groups had sat on the Court, because these justices would have influenced their colleagues' perceptions of discrimination.

The effect of female representation on the Court was symbolized by a 2009 case involving a middle-school girl who had been subjected to a highly intrusive search for drugs by school personnel. After some justices treated the search as a trivial matter during oral argument, Ginsburg spoke to a reporter about what she saw as her colleagues' insensitivity to the feelings of a thirteen-year-old girl. What she said to her colleagues directly is not known, but ultimately all but one of them agreed that the search had been unconstitutional.[50] Both Ginsburg and Sandra Day O'Connor have expressed their view that the presence of female justices affects the Court's collective judgments in some cases.[51]

Political and social attitudes differ somewhat between people of higher and lower socioeconomic status, so justices' social class origins might affect the Court's decisions. But the sympathies of people who have "climbed" upward from a low socioeconomic level may differ little from those of people who started out with social and economic advantages. Notably, the justices with humble backgrounds have included conservatives such

Justice Ruth Bader Ginsburg, retired Justice Sandra Day O'Connor, Justice Sonia Sotomayor, and Justice Elena Kagan at a panel discussion in 2012. The presence of women on the Court since O'Connor's appointment in 1981 has affected the Court's decisions on some issues.

as Warren Burger and Clarence Thomas as well as liberals such as Earl Warren and Sonia Sotomayor.

In terms of class origins, race, and sex, the current Court is the most diverse in history. On the other hand, the Court has become much less diverse in terms of the justices' educational backgrounds. All nine justices in 2012 graduated from private undergraduate schools, including five who went to Ivy League schools and two who studied at Stanford. And all nine justices went to law school at Harvard or Yale, though Ruth Bader Ginsburg transferred from Harvard to Columbia for her final year. In educational terms, then, today's Court is very much an elite group. This fact reflects the respect and career advantages gained by graduates of prestigious schools and perhaps the special aura attached to the Yale and Harvard law schools. Some commentators have expressed concern about what they see as the insularity of a Court that comes from such a narrow range of schools.[52] That concern may be merited, but the nine current justices are hardly homogeneous in their thinking about legal and policy issues.

Partisan Political Activity. One attribute shared by most current justices, like their predecessors, is a degree of involvement in partisan politics. Antonin Scalia, John Roberts, and Samuel Alito each held multiple positions in Republican administrations. Anthony Kennedy drafted a state ballot proposition for California governor Ronald Reagan. Clarence Thomas worked with John Danforth when Danforth was the Missouri attorney general and a U.S. senator, and Thomas later served in the Reagan and George H. W. Bush administrations. Stephen Breyer interrupted his law school teaching twice to work with Democrats on the Senate Judiciary Committee.

This pattern reflects the criteria for selecting judges. Even when nominations to the Court are not used as political rewards, presidents look more favorably on people who have contributed to their party's success. Partisan activity also brings people to the attention of presidents, their staff members, and others who influence nomination decisions. Perhaps more important, it enables people to win the high government positions that make them credible candidates for the Court.

The Role of Chance. No one becomes a Supreme Court justice through an inevitable process. Rather, advancement from membership in the bar to a seat on the Court results from luck as much as anything else. This luck comes in two stages. First, good fortune is often necessary to achieve the high positions in government or law that make individuals possible candidates for the Court. Second, even after they achieve such positions, whether candidates are seriously considered for the Court and actually win an appointment depends largely on several circumstances.

For one thing, a potential justice gains enormously by belonging to a particular political party at the appropriate time. Every appointment to the Court between 1969 and 1992 was made by a Republican president. As a result, a whole generation of potential justices who were liberal Democrats had no chance to win appointments. Further, someone whose friend or associate achieves a powerful position becomes a far stronger candidate for a seat on the Court. Elena Kagan achieved a great deal, culminating in her appointment as dean at Harvard Law School. But if she had not known Barack Obama, it is highly unlikely that she would have become solicitor general and then won a Supreme Court appointment.

More broadly, everyone appointed to the Court has benefited from a favorable series of circumstances. John Paul Stevens has reported that his pro bono volunteer services for a client led to favorable publicity that later helped him win a judicial appointment.[53] If William Rehnquist had retired during George W. Bush's first term rather than remaining on the Court, it is unlikely that John Roberts would have succeeded him as chief justice, because Roberts did not become a lower-court judge until 2003.[54]

This does not mean that the effects of presidential appointments to the Court are random. No matter which individuals they choose, Democratic presidents generally nominate people with liberal views, and Republicans tend to select conservatives. Presidents and their aides increasingly make systematic efforts to identify the nominees who serve their goals best. But it does mean that specific individuals achieve membership on the Court in large part through good fortune. "You have to be lucky," said Sandra Day O'Connor about her appointment, a statement that reflects realism as well as modesty.[55]

Leaving the Court

In the Supreme Court's first century, Congress sometimes increased the Court's size to allow new appointments of justices. Such legislation has become almost unthinkable. Today, new members come to the Court only when a sitting justice leaves.

Justices can leave the Court in three ways: through death, a voluntary decision, or external pressure.[56] In contrast with the nineteenth century, justices today seldom stay on the Court until they die. Before William Rehnquist's death in 2005, the last justice to die in office had been Robert Jackson in 1954. Thus, departures from the Court result primarily from voluntary choices and external pressure. Table 2-4 summarizes the reasons for departure since 1965.

TABLE 2-4
Reasons for Leaving the Court Since 1965

Year	Justice	Age	Primary reasons for leaving	Length of time from leaving until death
1965	Goldberg	56	Appointment as ambassador to the United Nations	24 years
1967	Clark	67	Son's appointment as attorney general	10 years
1969	Fortas	58	Pressures based on possible ethical violations	13 years
1969[a]	Warren	78[b]	Age	5 years
1971	Black	85	Age and ill health	1 month
1971	Harlan	72	Age and ill health	3 months
1975	Douglas	77	Age and ill health	4 years
1981	Stewart	66	Age	4 years
1986	Burger	78	Uncertain: age, demands of service on a federal commission may have been factors	9 years
1987	Powell	79	Age and health concerns	11 years
1990	Brennan	84	Age and ill health	7 years
1991	Marshall	83[b]	Age and ill health	2 years
1993	White	76[b]	Desire to allow another person to serve, possibly age	9 years
1994	Blackmun	85	Age	5 years
2005	Rehnquist	80	Death	Same time
2006[a]	O'Connor	75	Spouse's ill health	NA
2009	Souter	69	Desire to return to New Hampshire	NA
2010	Stevens	90[b]	Age	NA

Sources: Biographical sources, newspaper stories.

Note: NA = not applicable.

a. Warren originally announced the intent to leave the Court in 1968, O'Connor in 2005.

b. When they announced their intent to leave the Court, Warren was 77, Marshall 82, White 75, and Stevens 89.

Voluntary Departures

After its somewhat rocky start, the Supreme Court became a prestigious body with considerable influence on American life. As a result, justices typically are reluctant to leave the Court.

This reluctance is reflected in the rarity of instances in which justices leave to take other positions or opportunities. In the past century only a handful of justices have done so. The most recent was Arthur Goldberg, who resigned in 1965 to become U.S. ambassador to the United Nations.

Still, justices must decide whether and when to retire from the Court. Financial considerations once played an important part in those choices: several justices stayed on the Court, sometimes with serious infirmities, to keep receiving their salaries. Congress established a judicial pension in 1869, and it is now quite generous. Justices who have served as federal judges for at least ten years and who are at least sixty-five years old can retire and continue to receive the salary earned at the time of retirement if their age and years of service add up to eighty or more. Justices can also receive any salary increases granted to sitting justices if they are disabled or if they perform a certain amount of service for the federal courts— generally equal to one-quarter of full-time work.

Thereby freed from financial concerns, older justices weigh the satisfactions of remaining on the Court against the somewhat different satisfactions of retirement and against concern about their capacity to handle their work. David Souter left the Court at the age of sixty-nine, when he was in good health. By all accounts, he did so because he found it attractive to return to his native New Hampshire, which he much preferred to Washington, DC.[57] But the satisfactions of Court service are so great that most justices stay well past the usual retirement age, and most are reluctant to leave. Early in his time on the Court, John Paul Stevens asked a law clerk to calculate the average age of retirement for justices, "so I would have a feel for when I should leave." But he stayed on the Court long after that point, retiring at the age of ninety. When he did retire, he said that "if I have overstayed my welcome, it is because this is such a unique and wonderful job."[58]

Writing in 2000, one scholar argued that since World War II, seven justices had stayed on the Court "years or months" too long, after a decline in their mental capacities.[59] William Rehnquist remained on the Court in 2005 even after he was unable to fully participate in the Court's work because of cancer. But most justices do leave the Court when they can no longer ignore their infirmities. It is noteworthy that Rehnquist was the only justice in the past half-century to die in office. John Paul Stevens asked his colleague David Souter to let him know when he was no longer doing his job effectively. In early 2010, after Souter had retired, Stevens was troubled when he found himself stumbling over words for the first time while presenting his opinion in a case. That experience helped to move him toward retirement, which he announced three months later. Still, shortly after his retirement he said that he "may have jumped the gun a little bit" in leaving the Court.[60]

Other factors affect decisions on whether to leave the Court. Some justices time their retirements so that a president whose views are compatible with theirs will choose their successor. It appears that the election of President Obama made retirement more attractive to David Souter, a relatively liberal Republican. Souter reportedly said that he "probably" would have retired if John McCain had won the 2008 election.[61] Family considerations sometimes come into play as well.

One current justice gave very early notice of his retirement. In 1992, a year after he joined the Court, Clarence Thomas told two of his clerks that he would remain on the Court until 2034. He explained, "The liberals made my life miserable for 43 years, and I'm going to make their lives miserable for 43 years."[62]

Retired Justice John Paul Stevens at the Court in 2011, holding the book he wrote in the year after his retirement. Like Sandra Day O'Connor and David Souter, Stevens remained quite active after retiring from the Court.

Some justices remain active after their retirement. David Souter has served frequently in the federal court of appeals in Boston, near his New Hampshire home. Within eighteen months of his 2010 retirement, he had participated in more than 100 decisions.[63] John Paul Stevens was among the justices who made the fewest outside appearances while he sat on the Court, but since retirement he has given many speeches and interviews. Some of his interviews have promoted his memoir, focusing on the most recent five chief justices, which he wrote in the year after his retirement.

He has expressed his views about an array of public issues in the book and his public appearances, and he has criticized some Court decisions that were handed down before and after his retirement.[64]

Sandra Day O'Connor has combined the two pursuits, sitting with all eleven regional courts of appeals and speaking on behalf of causes such as civic education and replacement of state judicial elections with appointment systems. Some critics have argued that her combination of hearing cases and public advocacy was inappropriate, while others have defended her. In any event, her example—like that of Stevens and Souter—underlines the fact that many justices leave the Court while they still have the capacity to play active roles.

External Pressure

Although justices make their own decisions whether to resign or retire, Congress and the president can try to influence those decisions. The legislation creating attractive pension rights has had considerable effect. People in the other branches can also try to persuade specific justices to leave the Court. Presidents have good reason to do so—to create vacancies they can fill. John Kennedy reportedly persuaded Felix Frankfurter to retire after ill health had decreased his effectiveness, but Thurgood Marshall bitterly resisted efforts by the Carter administration to persuade him to retire.

Presidents can also try to lure justices away from the Court by offering them other positions. Lyndon Johnson offered Arthur Goldberg the position of ambassador to the United Nations and then exerted intense personal pressure on him until he accepted that position. Byron White, however, rejected the idea of becoming FBI director when the Reagan administration sounded him out about it.

In contrast with those kinds of pressures, impeachment is beyond the justices' control. Under the Constitution, justices, like other federal officials, can be removed through impeachment proceedings for "treason, bribery, or other high crimes and misdemeanors."[65] President Thomas Jefferson actually sought to gain control of the largely Federalist (and anti-Jefferson) judiciary through the use of impeachment, and Congress did impeach and convict a federal district judge in 1803. Justice Samuel Chase made himself vulnerable to impeachment by participating in President John Adams's campaign for reelection in 1800 and by making some injudicious and partisan remarks to a Maryland grand jury in 1803. Chase was impeached, but the Senate acquitted him in 1805. His acquittal effectively ended Jefferson's plans to seek the impeachment of other justices.

No justice has been impeached since then, but the possible impeachment of two justices has been the subject of serious discussion. Several efforts were made to remove William Douglas (most seriously in 1969 and 1970), motivated by opposition to his strong liberalism. The reasons stated publicly by opponents were his financial connections with a foundation and his outside writings.[66] A special House committee failed to approve a resolution to impeach Douglas, however, and the resolution died in 1970.

Had Abe Fortas not resigned from the Court in 1969, he actually might have been removed by Congress.[67] Fortas had been criticized for his financial dealings at the time of his unsuccessful nomination as chief justice in 1968. A year later it was disclosed that he had a lifetime contract as a consultant to a foundation and had received money from the foundation at a time when the person who directed it was being prosecuted by the federal government. Under considerable pressure, Fortas resigned. The resignation came too quickly to determine how successful an impeachment effort would have been, but almost certainly it would have been serious.

The campaigns against Douglas and Fortas came primarily from the Nixon administration, which sought to replace the two liberals with more conservative justices. John Dean, a lawyer on Nixon's staff, later reported that Fortas's resignation led to "a small celebration in the attorney general's office," which "was capped with a call from the president, congratulating" Justice Department officials "on a job well done."[68] In contrast, according to Dean, the unsuccessful campaign against Douglas "created an intractable resolve by Douglas never to resign while Nixon was president."[69]

The Fortas episode seems unlikely to be repeated, in part because it reminded justices of the need to avoid questionable financial conduct. The occasional removal of federal judges through impeachment proceedings makes it clear that impeachment is a real option. But it is used only in cases with strong evidence of serious misdeeds, often involving allegations of corrupt behavior.

Thus, the timing of a justice's leaving the Court reflects primarily the justice's own inclinations, health, and longevity. Those who want to influence the Court's membership may have their say when a vacancy occurs, but they have little control over the creation of vacancies.

Conclusion

The recruitment of Supreme Court justices is a complex process. People do not rise to the Court in an orderly fashion. Rather, whether they become credible candidates for the Court and whether they actually win appointments depend on a wide range of circumstances. Indeed, something close to pure luck plays a powerful role in determining who becomes a justice.

The recruitment process has evolved over the Court's history. To take one example, the balance of power between president and Senate in selecting justices has shifted back and forth. Further, justices today are drawn from a broader subset of society than they were during most of the Court's history, and their backgrounds are more "legal" and less "political" than they once were.

The Court's power and prestige have fundamental effects on its membership. For one thing, presidents take nominations to the Court very seriously, and they have a wide range of prospective nominees to choose from. For another, justices are usually reluctant to give up their positions.

Also consequential is the perception of a strong link between the Court's membership and its decisions. Because of this perception, presidents accord heavy weight to the policy preferences of candidates when they choose a nominee. For the same reason, the Senate gives Court nominees greater scrutiny than it does nominees to any other position. Interest groups regularly seek to influence the president and the Senate, and they sometimes engage in massive campaigns over nominees.

This perception is well-founded. In later chapters I will discuss how the identities of the justices shape the Court's positions on legal and policy issues.

NOTES

1. "Remarks by First Lady Michelle Obama at 2012 Reception in Providence, Rhode Island," September 30, 2011, http:/www.whitehouse.gov/.
2. The four who were nominated and confirmed twice include three individuals elevated from associate justice to chief justice (Edward White, Harlan Stone, and William Rehnquist) and one (Charles Evans Hughes) who resigned from the Court and was later appointed chief justice. Douglas Ginsburg is counted as a nominee even though he withdrew from consideration in 1987, before he was officially nominated. Harriet Miers was nominated in 2005 but withdrew before the Senate could consider her nomination.
3. Joan Biskupic, *Sandra Day O'Connor* (New York: HarperCollins, 2005), 72–73. Burger's role in the Nixon nominations is discussed in John W. Dean, *The Rehnquist Choice* (New York: Free Press, 2001), 19, 52, 179–185.
4. This discussion is based in part on John Anthony Maltese, *The Selling of Supreme Court Nominees* (Baltimore, MD: Johns Hopkins University Press, 1995); and Gregory A. Caldeira and John R. Wright, "Lobbying for Justice: The Rise of Organized Conflict in the Politics of Federal Judgeships," in *Contemplating Courts*, ed. Lee Epstein (Washington, DC: CQ Press, 1995), 44–71.
5. Michael Pertschuk and Wendy Schaetzel, *The People Rising: The Campaign against the Bork Nomination* (New York: Thunder's Mouth Press, 1989); Patrick B. McGuigan and Dawn M. Weyrich, *Ninth Justice: The Fight for Bork* (Washington, DC: Free Congress Research and Education Foundation, 1990); Mark Gitenstein, *Matters of Principle: An Insider's Account of America's Rejection of Robert Bork's Nomination to the Supreme Court* (New York: Simon & Schuster, 1992).
6. Mark Arsenault, "Groups Seek Forum by Fighting Kagan," *Boston Globe*, June 10, 2010, A1.
7. George W. Bush, *Decision Points* (New York: Crown Publishers, 2010), 100.

8. Andrew Peyton Thomas, *Clarence Thomas: A Biography* (San Francisco, Calif.: Encounter Books, 2001), 179.

9. Brian Lamb, Susan Swain, and Mark Farkas, eds., *The Supreme Court: A C-Span Book Featuring the Justices in Their Own Words* (New York: PublicAffairs, 2010), 160.

10. Henry J. Abraham, *Justices, Presidents, and Senators: A History of U.S. Supreme Court Appointments from Washington to Bush II*, 5th ed. (Lanham, MD: Rowman & Littlefield, 2008), 146.

11. Dean, *The Rehnquist Choice*, 14.

12. Lamb, Swain, and Farkas, eds., *The Supreme Court*, 183.

13. See Lori A. Ringhand and Paul M. Collins Jr., "May It Please the Senate: An Empirical Analysis of the Senate Judiciary Committee Hearings of Supreme Court Nominees, 1939–2009," *American University Law Review* 60 (February 2011): 589–641.

14. Richard Brust, "No More Kabuki Confirmations," *ABA Journal* 95 (October 2009): 39.

15. Dahlia Lithwick, "Revenge of the Nerd," *Slate Magazine*, January 10, 2006.

16. Carrie Budoff, "Specter to Probe Supreme Court Decisions," *Politico*, July 25, 2007.

17. Dion Farganis and Justin Wedeking, "'No Hints, No Forecasts, No Previews': An Empirical Analysis of Supreme Court Nominee Candor from Harlan to Kagan," *Law & Society Review* 45 (2011): 525–559.

18. Elena Kagan, "Confirmation Messes, Old and New," *University of Chicago Law Review* 62 (Spring 1995): 941.

19. "Sticking to the Law," *Washington Post*, June 30, 2010, A6.

20. The discussion of nomination decisions that follows draws much from Christine L. Nemacheck, *Strategic Selection: Presidential Nomination of Supreme Court Justices from Herbert Hoover through George W. Bush* (Charlottesville: University of Virginia Press, 2007); and from David Alistair Yalof, *Pursuit of Justices: Presidential Politics and the Selection of Supreme Court Justices* (Chicago: University of Chicago Press, 1999).

21. Nemacheck, *Strategic Selection*, chap. 5; Sheldon Goldman, Elliot Slotnick, and Sara Schiavoni, "Obama's Judiciary at Midterm," *Judicature* 94 (May–June 2011): 275.

22. Lamb, Swain, and Farkas, eds., *The Supreme Court*, 160.

23. Nemacheck, *Strategic Selection*, chap. 3; Goldman, Slotnick, and Schiavoni, "Obama's Judiciary at Midterm," 277.

24. Dean, *The Rehnquist Choice*, 96. See Kevin J. McMahon, *Nixon's Court: His Challenge to Judicial Liberalism and Its Political Consequences* (Chicago: University of Chicago Press, 2011).

25. Jan Crawford Greenburg, *Supreme Conflict: The Inside Story of the Struggle for Control of the United States Supreme Court* (New York: Penguin Press, 2007), 199.

26. Steve Holland, "Bush Defends Pick for Supreme Court," *Toronto Star*, October 5, 2005, A11.

27. Fred Barnes, "Souter-Phobia," *Weekly Standard*, August 1, 2005, 11–12.

28. Alyssa Sepinwall, "The Making of a Presidential Myth" (letter), *Wall Street Journal*, September 4, 1990, A11; Tony Mauro, "Leak of Souter Keeps McGuigan in Plan," *Legal Times*, September 10, 1990, 11.

29. "Justice Anthony Kennedy: Surely Reagan's Biggest Disappointment," *Human Events*, May 31–June 7, 1996, 3.

30. Robert Scigliano, *The Supreme Court and the Presidency* (New York: Free Press, 1971), 95.

31. John Paul Stevens, *Five Chiefs: A Supreme Court Memoir* (New York: Little, Brown, 2011), 60–61.
32. White House Office of the Press Secretary, "Remarks by the President and Solicitor General Elena Kagan at the Nomination of Solicitor General Elena Kagan to the Supreme Court," May 10, 2010, http://www.white house.gov.
33. Peter Baker and Jeff Zeleny, "Obama Nominates Hispanic Judge for Supreme Court," *New York Times,* May 27, 2009, A17.
34. Barbara A. Perry, *A "Representative" Supreme Court? The Impact of Race, Religion, and Gender on Appointments* (New York: Greenwood Press, 1991), 122.
35. These figures were calculated from data in R. Sam Garrett and Denis Steven Rutkus, *Speed of Presidential and Senate Actions on Supreme Court Nominations, 1900–2010* (Washington, DC: Congressional Research Service, 2010), 37–42, with the figures for the Kagan confirmation added.
36. See Lee Epstein, René Lindstädt, Jeffrey A. Segal, and Chad Westerland, "The Changing Dynamics of Senate Voting on Supreme Court Nominees," *Journal of Politics* 68 (May 2006): 296–307.
37. These percentages are based on figures in Jeffrey Segal, "Senate Confirmation of Supreme Court Justices: Partisan and Institutional Politics," *Journal of Politics* 49 (November 1987): 1008 (updated by the author).
38. Based on ibid., updated by the author. Nominations made during a president's fourth year but after the president's reelection are not included.
39. See Maltese, *Selling of Supreme Court Nominees.*
40. Jonathan P. Kastellec, Jeffrey R. Lax, and Justin H. Phillips, "Public Opinion and Senate Confirmation of Supreme Court Nominees," *Journal of Politics* 72 (July 2010): 767–784.
41. "Here Comes the Judge," *Newsweek,* February 2, 1970, 19. Quoted in John Massaro, *Supremely Political: The Role of Ideology and Presidential Management in Unsuccessful Supreme Court Nominations* (Albany: State University of New York Press, 1990), 105.
42. Richard Reeves, *President Nixon: Alone in the White House* (New York: Simon & Schuster, 2001), 161.
43. Ronald Brownstein, "Alito's Remarks on Roe May Not Be Fighting Words," *Los Angeles Times,* December 12, 2005, A11.
44. Sonia Sotomayor, "A Latina Judge's Voice," *Berkeley La Raza Law Journal* 13 (2002): 92.
45. See Geoffrey R. Stone, "Understanding Supreme Court Confirmations," in *Supreme Court Review 2010,* eds. Dennis J. Hutchinson, David A. Strauss, and Geoffrey R. Stone (Chicago: University of Chicago Press, 2011), 440–455.
46. This discussion of justices' backgrounds is based in part on John R. Schmidhauser, *Judges and Justices: The Federal Appellate Judiciary* (Boston, MA: Little, Brown, 1979), 41–100.
47. These proportions are based on biographies in the *Biographical Directory of Federal Judges,* compiled by the Federal Judicial Center, http://www.fjc.gov/history/home.nsf/page/judges.html.
48. Terri L. Peretti, "Where Have All the Politicians Gone? Recruiting for the Modern Supreme Court," *Judicature* 91 (November–December 2007): 121–122.
49. Lee Epstein, Jeffrey A. Segal, Harold J. Spaeth, and Thomas G. Walker, *The Supreme Court Compendium,* 4th ed. (Washington, DC: CQ Press, 2007), 271–279. This source was also used in the next paragraph to classify most of the justices sitting in 2012.

50. *Safford Unified School District #1 v. Redding* (2009); Joan Biskupic, "Ginsburg: The Court Needs Another Woman," *USA Today*, May 6, 2009, 1A.

51. Bradley Blackburn, "Justices Ruth Bader Ginsburg and Sandra Day O'Connor on Life and the Supreme Court," *ABC News*, October 26, 2010, http://abcnews.go.com/.

52. See John Schwartz, "Weighing the Effect of an Ivy-Colored Path to the Court," *New York Times*, June 9, 2009, A15; and Patrick J. Glen, "Harvard and Yale Ascendant: The Legal Education of the Justices from Holmes to Kagan," *UCLA Law Review Discourse* 58 (2010): 129–154.

53. Richard C. Reuben, "Justice Stevens: I Benefited from Pro Bono Work," *Los Angeles Daily Journal*, August 11, 1992, 11. See Kenneth A. Manaster, *Illinois Justice: The Scandal of 1969 and the Rise of John Paul Stevens* (Chicago: University of Chicago Press, 2001).

54. See Greenburg, *Supreme Conflict*, 242–243.

55. Laurence Bodine, "Sandra Day O'Connor," *American Bar Association Journal* 69 (October 1983): 1394.

56. This discussion of resignation and retirement draws on David N. Atkinson, *Leaving the Bench: Supreme Court Justices at the End* (Lawrence: University Press of Kansas, 1999); and Artemus Ward, *Deciding to Leave: The Politics of Retirement from the United States Supreme Court* (Albany: State University of New York Press, 2003).

57. Philip Rucker, "Quiet N.H. Home Is Where Souter's Heart Has Always Been," *Washington Post*, May 3, 2009, A1.

58. Interview with John Paul Stevens, "Inside E Street," AARP television program, July 5, 2011, http://www.aarp.org/health/longevity/info-07-2011/video-john-paul-stevens-conversation-on-longevity.html; and Adam Liptak, "Justices Bid Farewells on Last Day," *New York Times*, June 29, 2010, A18.

59. David J. Garrow, "Mental Decrepitude on the U.S. Supreme Court: The Historical Case for a 28th Amendment," *University of Chicago Law Review* 67 (Fall 2000): 1085. See also Susan Okie, "Illness and Secrecy on the Supreme Court," *New England Journal of Medicine* 351 (December 23, 2004): 2675–2678.

60. Interview with Stevens, "Inside E Street."

61. Jeanette Lee, "Justice Souter's Dream," The Atlantic Politics Channel, May 4, 2009, at http://politics.theatlantic.com/2009/05/justice_souters_dream.php. See Peter Baker and Jeff Zeleny, "Souter Said to Have Plans to Leave Court in June," *New York Times*, May 1, 2009, A1.

62. Neil A. Lewis, "2 Years After His Bruising Hearing, Justice Thomas Still Shows the Hurt," *New York Times*, November 27, 1993, 6.

63. Information on participation in cases by Justices Souter and O'Connor was drawn from the LexisNexis archive of court of appeals decisions.

64. Robert Barnes, "Retired Justice Stevens Is Still Cheerfully Issuing Opinions—of His Colleagues," *Washington Post*, October 3, 2011, A15; Stevens, *Five Chiefs*, 150, 184–186, 198–200, 219–221.

65. U.S. Constitution, art. 2, § 4.

66. John Ehrlichman, *Witness to Power: The Nixon Years* (New York: Simon & Schuster, 1982), 122.

67. Laura Kalman, *Abe Fortas: A Biography* (New Haven: Yale University Press, 1990), 359–376; Bruce Allen Murphy, *Fortas: The Rise and Ruin of a Supreme Court Justice* (New York: Morrow, 1988).

68. Dean, *The Rehnquist Choice*, 11.

69. Ibid., 26.

Chapter 3

The Cases

The Supreme Court reaches full decisions in a limited number of cases, currently fewer than eighty a year. Those cases are a very small proportion of all the court cases and potential cases that might eventually reach the Court. This chapter examines the process of agenda setting that produces those rare events. In the first stage of that process, people make a series of decisions that bring their cases to the Supreme Court. In the second stage, the Court selects from those cases the few—currently about 1 in 100—that it will fully consider and decide.

Several sets of people and institutions help to set the Court's agenda. In the first stage, litigants file cases and bring them through the legal system to the Court. Most of these litigants are represented by lawyers in at least part of this process, and some receive direct or indirect help from interest groups. Although the Court itself plays no direct part at this stage, people's predictions of how the Court might respond to a case affect their decisions about whether to bring it to the Court. In the second stage, the justices are the sole decision makers. But their choices may be influenced by the litigants, lawyers, and interest groups that participate in cases. For their part, the other branches of government structure both stages by setting the Court's jurisdiction and writing other rules that affect cases, and they participate directly in many cases.

The first two sections of this chapter examine the two stages of agenda setting in the Court. In the first section, I consider how and why cases are brought to the Court. In the second, I discuss how and why the justices choose certain cases to decide on the merits. In the final section, I take a different perspective on agenda setting by examining the size of the Court's agenda.

Reaching the Court:
Litigants, Attorneys, and Interest Groups

Litigants, their attorneys, and interest groups are all important in determining which cases get to the Supreme Court, and I will examine the role of each in turn. The federal government is the most frequent and most distinctive participant in Supreme Court cases, and its role merits separate consideration.

Litigants

Every case that comes to the Supreme Court has at least one formal party, or litigant, on each side. For a case to reach the Court, one or more of the parties must act to initiate the litigation and move it upward through the court system.

Litigants in the Supreme Court are a diverse lot. Among those who petition the Court to hear cases, the great majority are individuals. Most of these individuals are criminal defendants; the others occupy a variety of roles. Among respondents, the litigants who are on the other side from petitioners, the largest category consists of governments and government agencies. Individuals are also respondents in many cases. Businesses frequently appear as petitioners or respondents. Other kinds of organizations, such as nonprofit groups and labor unions, appear in some Court cases.

One key question about litigants is why they become involved in court cases and carry those cases to the Supreme Court. The motives of litigants can be thought of as taking two general forms. In two ideal types of Supreme Court litigation, one motive or the other is dominant. Some litigants have mixed motives, so they fit neither ideal type.

The first ideal type can be called ordinary litigation because it is so common. Most of the time, parties bring cases to court or appeal unfavorable decisions because they seek to advance a direct personal or organizational interest. For instance, plaintiffs file personal injury suits because they hope to receive money through a court verdict or an out-of-court settlement.

One example of ordinary litigation is *Henderson v. Shinseki* (2011).[1] David Henderson served in the military from 1950 to 1952, when he was discharged because of a psychological disability. In 2001 he applied to the Department of Veterans Affairs for money to pay the costs of care in his home. After the Department denied his application, he appealed to the federal Court of Appeals for Veterans Claims. His appeal came 15 days after the 120-day limit established by federal law. When the court raised that issue, Henderson asked to have the time limit waived on the ground that his disability had caused the delay. The court ruled that federal law did not allow such a waiver, and the Court of Appeals for the Federal Circuit upheld that ruling. Henderson went to the Supreme Court, which agreed to hear his case. He died before the oral argument, but his widow was allowed to substitute for him as a party. The Court ruled unanimously in her favor, holding that the time limit for appeals to the Veterans Court could be waived. Henderson had brought the case on his own, acting without a lawyer for several years, and his only goal was to get the benefits that he sought.

The second ideal type can be called political litigation. In political cases, litigants seek to influence public policy rather than advancing their personal self-interest. The most common purpose of political litigation is gaining a judicial decision that favors the litigant's policy goals. Litigants with that purpose often care more about the legal rules that the Court issues than about simply winning the case.

The challenges to the 2010 federal health care law that the Supreme Court addressed in 2012 were an instance of political litigation. In the set of six cases that were brought to the Court, the challengers included state governments and officials from twenty-seven states, the National Federation of Independent Business (NFIB), Liberty University, Thomas More Law Center, and several individuals. (In the three cases that the Court accepted, the challengers were the NFIB, two individual business owners associated with the NFIB, twenty-four states, and officials of two other states.)

Some of these challengers had a direct stake in their cases because they would be required to purchase health insurance for themselves or for their employees if the law went fully into effect. But the lawsuits were organized by public officials and private groups that opposed the health care law as public policy. They shared the primary goal of eliminating the law as a whole or major provisions of the law. For some, shaping the Court's interpretation of constitutional provisions such as the commerce clause may have been a secondary goal.

Many cases have large elements of both ordinary and political litigation. For instance, individuals or companies usually bring lawsuits with the aim of gaining something directly, but as their cases proceed through the court system they often become concerned with the larger policy issues that arise from the cases. In cases brought by government agencies, ordinary and political elements may be difficult to separate: prosecutors file criminal cases to advance the specific mission of their agencies, but that mission is linked to the broader policy goal of attacking crime.

The proportion of cases that can be classified as fully or partly political increases with each step upward in the judicial system, so political litigation is most common in the Supreme Court. This pattern is not accidental.

Ordinary litigation usually ends at a relatively early stage, because the parties find it more advantageous to settle their dispute or even to accept defeat than to fight on. In contrast, political litigants often want to get a case to the highest court, where a victory may establish a national policy they favor. In addition, political litigation sometimes attracts the support of interest groups that help to shoulder the costs and other burdens of carrying a case through the judicial system.

Even so, the great majority of cases brought to the Supreme Court are best classified as ordinary litigation. Most are criminal cases in which a convicted defendant wants to get out of prison, or to stay out. Other cases result from efforts by individuals to obtain monetary benefits from government agencies or monetary damages for personal injuries. Some cases come from business corporations whose economic stake in a dispute with other businesses or government justifies a petition to the Court.

Political litigation is more common in the cases that the Court agrees to hear because those cases are more likely to contain broad legal issues that interest the justices. Yet, as David Henderson's case illustrates, ordinary litigation is by no means absent from the cases that the Court hears. Even in the biggest cases, the chief motivation of the litigants is often their own direct interests. In *Wyeth v. Levine* (2009), which involved the liability of drug companies for injuries caused by their products, the high stakes in the case attracted thirty amicus briefs from interest groups and other interested parties. But the lawyer who argued on behalf of the injured woman reported that she "still viewed the case as about her" when it was in the Supreme Court.[2]

Organizations that are Supreme Court litigants often play active roles in their cases. Indeed, the lawyers that represent governments in the Court are usually employees of those governments. In contrast, most litigants who are individuals have limited involvement in their own cases. An extreme example is *Rasul v. Bush* (2004), which concerned the jurisdiction of federal courts to review the detention of suspected terrorists at the Guantánamo Bay Naval Station in Cuba. The cases were initiated by relatives of detainees on their behalf. Because the detainees were kept isolated from the outside world at that time, those still in detention did not know that their cases existed.[3]

Attorneys

In October 2011 the Supreme Court heard oral arguments in *Florence v. Board of Chosen Freeholders*, a case involving searches of new inmates in jails. Three lawyers argued in the case. Speaking for the federal government as amicus curiae ("friend of the court") was Nicole Saharsky of the Office of the Solicitor General in the Justice Department. The solicitor general's office represents the federal government in the Supreme Court, and its small group of lawyers quickly gains experience in the Court because the government is involved in so many cases. Saharsky presented her first argument to the Court in 2008, and her argument in *Florence* three and a half years later was her twelfth. But she was still far behind some of her colleagues in the solicitor general's office. One lawyer in the office, Edwin Kneedler, had argued more than 100 cases by 2011.

Carter Phillips argued for the local government that was defending its practices. Phillips represents a relatively new phenomenon. Traditionally, the federal government stood out for the experience of its lawyers in the Supreme Court. Other parties were generally represented by lawyers who worked on their cases in the lower courts, and most of those lawyers argued in the Court only once during their careers.

But gradually the picture changed. In the 1980s large law firms began to seek out work in Supreme Court litigation, recruiting attorneys with experience as law clerks in the Court or members of the solicitor general's staff. That trend has accelerated in recent years. For their part, businesses that have large stakes in cases increasingly seek experienced Supreme Court advocates to represent them. As a result, some lawyers in private firms have become regular participants in oral argument.

Carter Phillips is the leading example today. After clerking for Chief Justice Warren Burger and serving in the solicitor general's office, he moved into private practice in 1983 and became a regular participant in Supreme Court litigation. Altogether, he has now argued more than seventy-five cases in the Court, and he has worked on many other Court cases in roles such as writing petitions for certiorari.

Carter Phillips, who has presented oral arguments in more than seventy-five cases in the Supreme Court.

The third lawyer in the *Florence* case, representing the former inmate, was Thomas Goldstein. As a Supreme Court advocate, Goldstein is unique.[4] Early in his career, he set out to argue cases in the Supreme Court. He lacked a Supreme Court clerkship and experience in the solicitor general's office, and he worked out of his home rather than in a large law firm. But he had a strategy: he identified cases decided by the federal courts of appeals that the Supreme Court might be willing to hear, and he offered to represent the losing parties in those cases for free. The strategy worked, and he established himself as a Supreme Court advocate. Goldstein has now argued two dozen cases in the Court. Goldstein moved to a large firm in 2006. But in 2011 he returned to his old firm, now grown to four lawyers.

The *Florence* case illustrates the increasing prominence of experienced Supreme Court advocates. That change is documented more systematically in Table 3-1. Leaving aside lawyers for the federal government, the average level of experience for lawyers who present oral arguments has increased enormously, and regular participants—lawyers who argue more than ten cases over a five-term period—have gone from being nearly nonexistent to common.

Typically, these lawyers do not specialize in a particular subject matter. Former solicitor general Paul Clement argued the extraordinary number of seven cases in the Court's 2011 term, even if his participation in three of the four phases of the arguments on the federal health care law is counted only once. The seven cases ranged widely in subject matter. However, three of his cases had something important in common. In each, Clement represented the conservative position on an important issue—a partisan battle over the drawing of legislative districts in Texas and the federal government's challenge to Arizona's broad law regulating immigration along with the constitutional challenges to the health care law.[5]

Important as it is, the movement toward experienced advocates in the Court should not be exaggerated. Again omitting lawyers in the solicitor general's office, a majority of arguments in the 2010 term were presented by lawyers who appeared in the Court only once over the five-term period. In all likelihood, most of these lawyers will present only one oral argument before the Court in their careers.

Who are these one-time advocates? As in the past, most of them become involved in a case early in its history and continue to represent their client in the Supreme Court. In contrast, one 2011 case was argued by a Cleveland solo practitioner (with a mother who served as his part-time paralegal) whose client had been unable to find any other lawyer to petition the Court for certiorari in her case.[6]

Experience has obvious benefits. It helps lawyers to build expertise, and frequent participants in Supreme Court cases can develop credibility

TABLE 3-1
Numbers of Oral Arguments over a Five-Term Period by Lawyers Arguing Cases in the 1992 and 2010 Terms (Lawyers for Federal Government Excluded)

Number of arguments	1992 (%)	2010 (%)
1	81.4	60.0
2	6.6	10.0
3–5	8.2	9.3
6–10	3.8	7.9
11–15	0.0	7.9
16–25	0.0	5.0

Note: For lawyers who argued cases in 1992, the five-term period is 1988–1992; for lawyers who argued cases in 2010, the period is 2006–2010. Lawyers who argued multiple cases in 1992 or 2010 are counted each time they argued a case. Thus, the 5.0% in the lower-right cell of the table means that, leaving aside arguments by lawyers for the federal government, 5.0% of the oral arguments in the 2010 term were made by lawyers who had 16–20 arguments in the 2006–2010 terms.

with the justices. In contrast, some advocates who lack experience in the Court do a decidedly poor job. Unaware that his microphone was on, Justice Potter Stewart once asked in the middle of an inept argument, "Where did this guy come from?"[7] In a 2012 case a reporter concluded that a lawyer in the New Orleans district attorney's office had "found ways to botch virtually every point."[8]

But many first-time advocates in the Court are effective. Speaking about oral argument, Justice Antonin Scalia has said that "I'm often amazed at how good some of these people from nowhere are—court appointed counsel from Podunk."[9] Acting at an earlier stage in the process, one "jailhouse lawyer," who lacked any legal training, wrote a petition for certiorari for a fellow inmate and won a hearing for the inmate, beating the enormous odds against the Court's accepting a prisoner's case. A distinguished Supreme Court advocate said that "it was probably one of the best cert. petitions I have ever read," and he agreed to take on the case after it was accepted only if the jailhouse lawyer would help him. They won in a unanimous decision.[10]

Overall, however, lawyers with experience in the Court are better advocates than those without that experience.[11] Despite his praise for some first-time advocates, Justice Scalia concluded that the "specialists" in Supreme Court litigation "generally are better."[12] The growing role of specialists from law firms has contributed to a general improvement in the quality of advocacy in the Court, a development that Justice Samuel Alito and retired Justice John Paul Stevens have noted. Another source of improvement is the efforts of states to strengthen their advocacy in the Court.[13]

It is impossible to pinpoint the effect that good or bad advocacy has on Supreme Court decisions, but it surely makes a difference. There is some evidence, for instance, that the quality of oral argument affects outcomes.[14] But there are limits to this effect, because justices are not entirely dependent on the lawyers for their understanding of a case. Poor advocates sometimes win cases, and some parties have such weak cases that even the best lawyering could not alter the outcome.

In the legal system as a whole, a relationship exists between the wealth of an individual or institution and the quality of the legal services available to that party. To a degree, this is true of the Supreme Court. The experienced Supreme Court advocates in private practice are most readily available to large corporations and other prosperous organizations that can afford their regular fees.

But several mechanisms improve the position of people who lack wealth. First, the Court appoints an attorney to represent an indigent litigant whose cases it accepts, and some of those lawyers are highly skilled. Further, Supreme Court cases are both scarce and attractive to lawyers. For that reason, Supreme Court specialists sometimes offer their services at no cost to litigants whose cases have been accepted by the Court and even to litigants who have lost in a federal court of appeals. Meanwhile, several prestigious law schools have established clinics to handle Supreme Court cases for no charge, and they too seek out cases. These clinics, sometimes affiliated with law firms that have Supreme Court specialists, can provide high-quality legal services.[15] Still, as a group, those litigants that can afford to hire the most experienced advocates have an advantage over those that cannot.

Lawyers are eligible to participate in cases if they join the Supreme Court bar, for which the most important requirement is that they have been admitted to practice in a state for at least the last three years. Lawyers who cannot meet this requirement, however, usually are allowed to argue cases they have brought to the Court. Lawyers join the Supreme Court bar primarily for the prestige. More than 250,000 lawyers are members,[16] and the great majority will never participate in a Supreme Court case.

Interest Groups

The leaders of interest groups have to decide where their resources can do the most good. Many groups devote some resources to the Supreme Court, and some give high priority to the Court. One reason is that the Court is highly visible, so groups can publicize themselves to members

Bob Edgar, President of Common Cause, speaking at a 2012 rally against the Court's ruling on regulation of campaign spending in *Citizens United v. Federal Election Commission.* Members of interest groups sometimes speak and demonstrate at the Court in an effort to influence legal policy.

and others by giving attention to the Court. More important, the Court's decisions affect a wide array of interests in society. As a result, interest groups are regular participants in the Court.

Forms of Group Activity. In contrast with Congress, it is considered highly improper to lobby judges directly. Because of this norm, Supreme Court justices generally try to avoid contact with litigants and the groups that support them.

But interest groups have several other ways by which they can attempt to influence the Court. As described in Chapter 2, some groups participate in the nomination and confirmation of justices. Groups can also lobby the Court indirectly through marches and demonstrations or by seeking favorable coverage for positions they favor in the news media.

The primary route used to influence the Court is participation in the litigation process, participation that takes multiple forms.[17] First, groups can initiate litigation or help bring it to the Court. Organizations that exist primarily as interest groups generally lack standing, a legal stake in a case, to bring cases in their own names. But other organizations that may be considered interest groups, especially businesses and governments, are often parties in Supreme Court cases.

A group that is not a party can sponsor a case on an issue that concerns it, providing attorneys' services and bearing the costs from the start. Sponsorship is costly, and it can be difficult to carry out, so relatively few groups undertake full sponsorship of cases. But sometimes groups engage in limited sponsorship of cases that have already been initiated, helping to bear the financial costs and supplying legal services and advice. A substantial portion of the cases the Court actually hears involve full or limited sponsorship.

One example of sponsorship was *Brown v. Plata* (2011).[18] A small California public interest law firm, the Prison Law Office, takes cases involving efforts to improve prison conditions. Lawyers from the Office, working with lawyers from other firms, brought a class action case in 2001 to challenge the quality of medical treatment for inmates in California prisons. The Office carried the case forward through a series of steps that culminated in a 2009 order by a three-judge district court. That court mandated a reduction in the number of inmates to remedy deficiencies in medical care and deficiencies in mental health care that had been raised in a separate lawsuit. The state appealed to the Supreme Court, and the Court agreed to give the case full consideration. (Appeals that go directly from district courts to the Supreme Court are discussed later in the chapter.) A lawyer from the Prison Law Office argued on behalf of the prisoners in the two cases, and the Court upheld the district court's order by a 5–4 vote.

Whether or not it sponsors cases, a group can try to influence the Court's decisions to accept or reject cases and how the Court decides those cases that it accepts. If a group effectively controls a case, its attorneys submit a brief that asks the Court to grant or deny a writ of certiorari. If the case is accepted for decision on the merits, the group's attorneys submit new briefs and participate in oral argument.

When a group does not control the case, it still may submit arguments to the Court in amicus curiae briefs.[19] With the consent of the parties to a case or by permission of the Court, any person or organization may submit an amicus brief to supplement the arguments of the parties. (Legal representatives of governments do not need to obtain permission.) Most of the time, the parties give their consent for the submission of amicus briefs. When the Court's consent is needed, it seldom is denied. Amicus briefs can be submitted on whether a case should be heard or, after a case is accepted for hearing, directly on the merits.

Amicus briefs are by far the most common way in which groups other than parties participate in litigation before the Court. As might be expected, amicus briefs are especially common in cases that the Court has accepted for consideration on the merits. In the 2010 term amicus briefs were submitted in 95 percent of the cases decided after oral argument, 67 percent of the cases had at least five briefs, and 34 percent had at least ten briefs.[20] And because groups or individuals can join in submitting a brief, the number of participants is considerably larger than the number of briefs. Amicus briefs are much less common at the certiorari stage, but they are not rare. In the Court's 2005 term 270 amicus briefs were submitted on behalf of 144 paid petitions, about 10 percent of all the paid petitions.[21] (Paid petitions are those submitted by parties that are not indigent.) In *Wal-Mart Stores v. Dukes* (2011), a case involving the use of class action suits in employment discrimination cases, the Court received nine amicus briefs from businesses and interest groups asking it to hear the case. The Court did so, and its 5–4 decision limiting class actions produced the result that these amici sought.

Amicus briefs are popular for several reasons. First, although the costs of preparing them are substantial, they are considerably cheaper than sponsoring cases. Second, it is much simpler to submit an amicus brief than to engage in the complex task of sponsorship. Finally, many lawyers and other people believe that amicus briefs influence the Court's decisions. For this reason, groups whose interests are implicated by a case may feel that they need to have their say, and parties to cases often encourage or even orchestrate supportive briefs.

Group leaders can also use amicus briefs to attract support for the group. As one law professor pointed out, "They can recruit members and do direct fund raising, whether they win or lose. If they win, they say, 'We are only one justice away from losing,' and if they lose, they say, 'We are only one justice away from winning.' Both letters say, 'Send money.'"[22]

The Array of Groups in the Court. Interest group participation in Supreme Court litigation has increased dramatically in the past half-century. Groups are sponsoring more cases, and amicus briefs have proliferated. To take one indicator, in cases with oral arguments the Court received an average of 0.63 briefs per case in the 1956–1965 terms and 8.93 per case in the 2010 term.[23] One reason for this growth is that the number of active interest groups and the level of their activity have increased considerably. Another is that the apparent success of some groups in shaping the Supreme Court's policies has encouraged other groups to seek similar success.

Hundreds of interest groups now participate in Supreme Court cases in some way. Among them are nearly all the groups that are most active in Congress and the executive branch. The box on page 81 provides a sampling of this participation by listing some of the groups that submitted amicus briefs in the 2011 term.

The groups that participate in Supreme Court cases can be placed in four broad categories. The first is economic: individual businesses, trade associations, professional groups, labor unions, and farm groups. Much of the Court's work affects the interests of these groups, on issues that range from employment discrimination to regulation of product safety. The business community is especially well represented in the Court. Individual businesses frequently are parties to cases, and businesses and business groups regularly submit amicus briefs.

The economic group that stands out is the National Chamber Litigation Center, the litigation arm of the U.S. Chamber of Commerce.[24] The Center is very active as an amicus. In one recent three-year period it filed more amicus briefs at the certiorari stage than any other group, and in the Court's 2010 term it acted as amicus in about one-quarter of all the Court's decisions on the merits. The Chamber sometimes acts directly as a litigant. It did so in *Chamber of Commerce v. Whiting* (2011), in which it joined with other groups to challenge an Arizona immigration law under which employers could lose their business licenses. The Center also holds moot courts to prepare lawyers representing business interests for their arguments in the Court.

In the second category are groups that represent segments of the population defined by something other than economics. Most of these groups are based on personal attributes such as race, gender, age, and sexual orientation. The prototype for these groups is the NAACP Legal Defense and Educational Fund (sometimes called the NAACP Legal Defense Fund or simply the Fund). The Fund initially focused its efforts on voting rights and school desegregation. It later turned to other areas such as employment and criminal justice, giving special attention to the death penalty. The Fund's successes in the Supreme Court encouraged the creation of organizations that were concerned with discrimination on grounds other than race, groups that proliferated from the 1960s onward.

The groups in the third category represent broad ideological positions or more specific issue positions rather than the interests of a specific segment of society. Here, the prototype is the American Civil Liberties Union (ACLU).[25] Established in 1920 to protect civil liberties, the ACLU involves itself in virtually every area of civil liberties law. The ACLU also has created special projects to undertake concerted litigation campaigns in specific areas of concern, such as women's rights, capital punishment, and national security. Other groups that work to achieve liberal policy goals include Earthjustice, which litigates on environmental issues, and the Planned Parenthood Federation of America, for which abortion is a primary concern.

A Sampling of Groups
Submitting Amicus Curiae Briefs to
the Supreme Court in the 2011 Term

Economic Groups: Business and Occupational

AFL-CIO
American Bar Association
American Society of Composers
Google, Inc.
National Association of Chain Drug Stores
National Association of Criminal Defense Lawyers
National Association of Manufacturers

Noneconomic Interests

AARP
American Humanist Association
Asian American Justice Center
United States Conference of Catholic Bishops

Ideological and Issue Groups

American Center for Law and Justice
American Civil Liberties Union
Electronic Privacy Information Center
Innocence Network
Washington Legal Foundation

Governments and Governmental Groups

Cook County, Illinois
Former FCC Officials
League of California Cities
National School Boards Association
State of Michigan

Issue and ideological groups that favor conservative positions were slower to involve themselves in litigation, but many such groups are now active. Some focus primarily on economic issues. The Institute for Justice, for instance, litigates against government regulation of economic activity and government action to take private property. Others give primary attention to civil liberties issues. The most prominent activity of the Center for Individual Rights is a long-term campaign against affirmative action programs. Several litigating groups, such as the American Center for Law and Justice, represent conservative religious interests.

The final category consists of governments and groups of government officials. Governments regularly appear as interest groups in the Court. The federal government is a special case, discussed later in this section. State and local governments often come to the Court as litigants. In addition, they frequently file amicus briefs, as state governments did in about half of the Court's decisions in the 2010 term.

It has become standard practice for many or most states to join in a brief to emphasize their strong shared interest in a case. In *Snyder v. Phelps* (2011), a case involving hostile demonstrations at military funerals by a religious group, forty-eight states and the District of Columbia joined in an amicus brief to defend state laws limiting such demonstrations and allowing lawsuits against the demonstrators. In *Brown v. Entertainment Merchants Association* (2011), a case in which California's ban on the sale or rental of violent video games to juveniles was challenged, eleven states joined an amicus brief supporting California. But nine joined a brief on the other side, an outcome that came after lobbying by the video game industry.[26] That lobbying reflected a perception that the states' views have considerable effect on the justices.

Group Strategies and Tactics. Any interest group that engages in litigation must make strategic and tactical decisions. At the strategic level, groups that are not set up solely to litigate must decide how much of their energy and resources to devote to litigation rather than other forms of political action. Groups must also decide what kinds of issues to emphasize in their litigation work and how to coordinate their efforts with those of other groups that have similar interests. At the tactical level a group's lawyers consider whether initiating a specific case or supporting a litigant in an existing case would serve the group's goals. They sometimes have a choice among different locations in which to initiate cases or between federal and state courts. And like other lawyers, they have to choose which arguments to make in specific cases.

Many considerations affect these decisions, including the views of group members and the availability of resources. Perhaps the most fundamental consideration is a group's perceptions of the courts in general and the Supreme Court in particular. It is not surprising that conservative groups have become more active in Supreme Court litigation as the Court has grown more receptive to conservative arguments. Similarly, choices of specific cases and arguments reflect judgments about potential responses from the justices.

Some groups establish long-term litigation strategies in which they seek to shape legal policy over time. When groups are skilled and their goals align with the Supreme Court's disposition, they can win major victories. The NAACP Legal Defense Fund successfully attacked racial segregation in education in a series of cases that culminated in *Brown v. Board of Education* (1954). The ACLU's Women's Rights Project won most of the cases it brought to the Supreme Court in the 1970s, once the Court began to look skeptically at government practices that treated women and men differently. But litigation campaigns face serious obstacles. One is that a group cannot fully control cases in a field. Some gay rights groups thought it would be best to avoid challenging laws that prohibited same-sex marriage so long as the Supreme Court seemed unsympathetic to such a challenge, but two lawyers acted independently to challenge the California prohibition in 2009.[27] And success is not guaranteed even when a group's goals and the Court's collective views seem to be aligned, as some conservative groups have found in the past quarter-century.

The Significance of Interest Groups. Interest groups can influence whether the Supreme Court accepts a case and the Court's rulings in the cases it does accept. That influence is discussed later in this chapter and in Chapter 4. Here, I focus on their influence on whether cases get to the Court. In this respect, cases may be placed in three categories.

The largest category includes the cases that come to the Court without any participation by interest groups. The issues in these cases are too narrow to interest any group. They reach the Court because the parties and attorneys have strong incentives to seek a Supreme Court hearing and sufficient resources to finance the litigation. Indigent criminal defendants who face significant prison terms have the needed incentive, and they need not pay lawyers' fees or other expenses to get a case to the Court.

The second category consists of cases that would have reached the Court without any interest group involvement but in which groups are involved in some way. An interest group may assist one of the parties by providing attorneys' services or financing, or it may submit an amicus brief supporting a petition for hearing.

The third category includes cases that would not reach the Court without group sponsorship. There are many important legal questions in civil liberties that no individual litigant would take to the Supreme Court without help. For example, most of the individuals whom the ACLU assists could not have gone to court without the group's legal assistance.

Because group sponsorship of cases in the Court is relatively rare, only a small proportion of cases brought to the Court fall into this third category. But groups are most likely to sponsor cases that have the potential to be heard by the Court and to produce major legal rulings. Indeed, much of the Court's support for legal protections for civil liberties over the past century was made possible by interest group action.[28]

The Federal Government as Litigant

Of all the litigants in the Supreme Court, the federal government appears most frequently. It is a party in a large minority of the cases brought to the Court for consideration. Of the cases actually argued before the Court, the federal government participates as a party or an amicus in a substantial majority—about three-quarters in the 2009 and 2010 terms.[29] As a result of its frequent participation, the federal government is the most important interest group in the Court.

In turn, the group of about two dozen lawyers in the Office of the Solicitor General in the Justice Department has more impact on the Court than any other set of attorneys. Those lawyers represent the federal government in the Supreme Court. They decide whether to bring federal government cases to the Court; only a few federal agencies can take cases to the Court without the solicitor general's approval. They also do the bulk of the government's legal work in Supreme Court cases, including petitions for hearings, the writing of briefs, and oral arguments.

The solicitor general's office occupies a complicated position.[30] On the one hand, it represents the president and the executive branch, functioning as their law firm. In this role, the office helps to carry out the president's policies. But the office also has a unique relationship with the Supreme Court, one in which it serves as an adviser as well as an advocate. As Richard Pacelle put it, the solicitor general's office straddles the line "between law and politics."[31]

The office's unique relationship with the Court rests on the fact that it represents a unique litigant. For one thing, the executive branch and the Supreme Court are both part of the federal government. And because the executive branch is involved in so many potential and actual Supreme Court cases, the solicitor general has the opportunity to build a mutually advantageous relationship with the Court.

One way the solicitor general does so is by exercising self-restraint in requesting that the Court hear cases. The federal government asked the Court to hear fifteen cases in the 2010 term, a very small percentage of all the cases it had lost in the courts of appeals. In contrast, the government's opponents filed around 3,500 petitions. One solicitor general described himself as "Dr. No" because he frequently turned down federal agencies that wanted him to petition for certiorari in their cases.[32]

The solicitor general's office also seeks to maintain credibility by taking a more neutral stance than other litigants. For instance, the government occasionally "confesses error" in the Supreme Court, taking the side of the party that challenges a government victory in a court of appeals.[33] The office tries to show that it is above politics by generally adhering to the position that a prior administration has taken in a case even though the new administration has a different point of view. And with occasional exceptions, the office defends all federal laws against constitutional challenges, whether or not the president agrees with those laws.

For their part, the justices have given the solicitor general's office a unique role. The Court frequently "invites" (in reality, orders) the solicitor general to file amicus briefs in cases that do not affect the federal government directly, because the justices are interested in the government's views.[34] In the 2010 term the solicitor general's office filed amicus briefs in response to twenty-seven petitions for hearings, all of them at the Court's invitation. And the solicitor general often participates in oral argument as amicus by invitation or its own request, as it did in thirty-five cases—nearly half of all cases with oral argument—in the 2010 term. With the occasional exception of state governments, other litigants seldom receive that privilege.

The office's special relationship with the Court leads to a degree of independence from the president and the attorney general, who understand the value of maintaining that relationship. But the solicitor general usually is someone who shares the president's general point of view about legal policy. Further, the office operates in a climate created by the president and the attorney general.

These superiors occasionally intervene in specific cases. In a 2009 case President Obama overruled the Justice Department and asked the Supreme Court to hear a case in which the government sought to block the release of photos of mistreatment of prisoners held by the United States in Iraq and Afghanistan.[35] Because the stakes were so high, it seems likely that Obama also participated in the government's 2011 decision to ask the Court to hear one of the cases involving a challenge to the 2010 health care law.

As Pacelle has shown, the impact of a presidential administration on the solicitor general's choices varies with the situation.[36] There are certain positions that the office would take regardless of who the president is. When the federal government is a party to a case, the solicitor general nearly always supports the government's position as a litigant. When the solicitor general participates as amicus, the office necessarily supports government interests. Thus, when the office acts as an amicus in a state criminal case, it generally supports the prosecution even in a Democratic administration. In a case early in the Obama administration, for instance, the office argued as amicus that the Supreme Court should overrule a 1986 decision that limited police questioning of suspects under certain circumstances.[37]

In many other cases the solicitor general chooses a position without regard to the liberalism or conservatism of the administration. But there are some cases—primarily those involving contentious issues in civil rights and civil liberties—in which the ideological coloration of the administration affects the solicitor general's position.

Adding all this together, the solicitor general has considerable independence from the president, an independence that helps to make the office an effective advocate in the Court. However, that independence is most limited on issues that presidents and their administrations care the most about. And in some administrations the office has reflected the president's positions and priorities to more than the usual degree.

Deciding What to Hear: The Court's Role

In its 2010 term the Supreme Court considered nearly eight thousand petitions for hearings. The Court granted certiorari and full consideration to only ninety of those petitions.[38] Of the thousands of other petitions, the overwhelming majority were simply denied, allowing the lower-court decision to become final. Many of these cases had high stakes for the people who petitioned the Court, and some raised important legal and policy issues. Nonetheless, the Court chose not to hear them. In selecting a few dozen cases from the thousands brought to them, the justices determined which legal claims and policy questions they would address.

Options

In screening petitions for hearings, the Court makes choices that are more complicated than simply accepting and rejecting individual cases. To begin with, petitions are not always considered in isolation from one another. The justices may accept a case to clarify or expand on an earlier decision in the same policy area. They may accept multiple cases that raise the same issue to address that issue more fully than a single case would allow them to do. They may reject a case because they are looking for a more suitable case on the same issue.

When the Court does accept a case, the justices can choose which issues they will consider. In the set of cases that the Court heard in its 2010 term, there were nine in which the Court announced when it granted certiorari that it would consider only one (or in one instance, three) of the issues presented by the petitioner. In three cases the Court specified an additional issue that it wanted the parties to address. Occasionally, the Court decides a case on the basis of an issue that the parties never addressed, and such an action sometimes provokes a dissent from justices who see it as inappropriate. Justice Clarence Thomas issued such a dissent in *Turner v. Rogers* (2011), a case involving the procedural rights of a man who had been jailed for contempt of court. The most famous example of a decision based on a new issue was *Mapp v. Ohio* (1961), in which the Court reached a landmark decision on police searches and seizures after the parties had argued the case as one about constitutional limits on the regulation of obscenity.

In accepting a case the Court also determines what kind of consideration the case will receive. It may give the case full consideration, which means that the Court receives a new set of briefs on the merits from the parties and holds oral argument, then issues a decision on the merits with a full opinion explaining the decision. Alternatively, it may give the case summary consideration. This usually means that the case is decided without new briefs or oral argument; the Court relies on the materials that the parties have already submitted.

In most summary decisions, typically several dozen each term, the Supreme Court issues a GVR order—that is, granting certiorari, vacating the lower-court decision, and remanding the case to that court for reconsideration. The great majority of these orders are issued because some event after the lower-court decision, usually a recent Supreme Court decision, is relevant to the case.

In other summary decisions, the Court actually reaches a decision on the merits and issues an opinion of several paragraphs or even several pages. This opinion typically is labeled *per curiam*, meaning "by the Court," rather than being signed by a justice, but it has the same legal force as a signed opinion. Such decisions are usually reversals of lower-court decisions, and most come in criminal cases.

Finally, the Court sometimes issues summary decisions in the appeals from three-judge federal district courts that it is required to decide. *Bluman v. Federal Election Commission* (2012) involved a First Amendment challenge to a federal statutory provision that prohibited political campaign donations by people who are not U.S. citizens and who are not lawful permanent residents of the United States. The three-judge court upheld the provision. When the case was appealed to the Supreme Court, it received considerable attention because some people thought the Court would use it as a vehicle to continue its process of limiting federal power to regulate campaign finance. But the Court simply issued a four-word decision: "The judgment is affirmed."

Even after accepting a case, the Court occasionally avoids a decision by issuing what is called a DIG, or "Dismissed as Improvidently Granted," as it did three times in its 2010 term.[39] A DIG occurs when the parties' briefs on the merits or the oral arguments suggest to the justices that the case is inappropriate for a decision. Like GVRs, DIGs seem routine, but both sometimes draw heated dissents from justices who think they are inappropriate in a particular case. Justice Antonin Scalia has issued a series of dissents arguing that the Court overuses GVRs as a way to get lower courts to reconsider their decisions, and one GVR in 2010 was by a 5–4 vote. A DIG in 2010 also came on a 5–4 vote, and the dissenters wrote two opinions to explain their positions.[40]

Screening Procedures

The Court screens petitions for hearing through a series of procedures, which are made more complex by two distinctions. The first distinction is between the certiorari cases, over which the Court's jurisdiction is discretionary, and the cases labeled appeals, which the Court is required to decide. Few appeals reach the Court. As the *Bluman* case illustrates, the Court has the option of deciding appeals without holding oral argument or issuing full opinions. The second distinction, between paid cases and paupers' cases, requires more extensive discussion.

Paid Cases and Paupers' Cases. In recent years only about one-fifth of the requests for hearings that arrive at the Supreme Court have been paid cases, for which the petitioner pays the Court's filing fee of $300. The remaining cases are brought in forma pauperis by indigent people, for whom the fee is waived and requirements for the format of litigants' written materials are relaxed. The great majority of the paupers' cases (also called "unpaid") are brought by federal and state prisoners. (A person responding to a petition may also be given pauper status.)

Criminal defendants who have had counsel provided to them in the lower federal courts because of their low incomes are automatically entitled to bring paupers' cases in the Supreme Court. Other litigants must submit an affidavit supporting their motion for leave to file as paupers. The Court has never developed precise rules for when a litigant can claim pauper status. However, it has denied many litigants the right to proceed as paupers in particular cases on the grounds that they were not truly paupers or that their petitions were frivolous or malicious. The Court has also issued a general denial of pauper status in noncriminal cases to some litigants who have filed large numbers of paupers' petitions.

A very small proportion of paupers' petitions are accepted for full decisions on the merits—0.16 percent in the 2007–2010 terms, compared with 4.8 percent of the paid cases in the same period.[41] The low acceptance rate reflects the lack of inherent merit in many of these cases and the fact that many litigants have to draft petitions without a lawyer's assistance. It may also be that the justices and law clerks look less closely at paupers' petitions than at the paid petitions. There is some evidence that, all else being equal, the Court is less likely to accept a pauper's petition than a paid petition.[42] Because there are so many paupers' petitions, even the small proportion that are accepted add up to a significant number of cases—an average of ten a term in the 2007–2010 terms—and they constitute an important part of the Court's work on issues of criminal procedure.

Prescreening: The Discuss List. Under its "rule of four," the Court grants a writ of certiorari and hears a case on the merits if at least four justices vote at conference to grant the writ. But petitions for hearings are considered at conference only if they are put on the Court's "discuss list." The chief justice creates the discuss list, but other justices can and do add cases to it. Cases left off the discuss list are denied hearings automatically, and that is the fate of the great majority of petitions.

The discuss list procedure serves to limit the Court's workload. But this procedure also reflects a belief that most petitions do not require collective consideration because they are such poor candidates for acceptance. It is easy to reject petitions that raise only narrow issues or that make weak legal claims.

Action in Conference. In conference the chief justice or the justice who added a case to the discuss list opens consideration of the case. In order of seniority, from senior to junior, the justices then speak and usually announce their votes. If the discussion does not make the justices' positions clear, a formal vote is taken, also in order of seniority. Despite the prescreening of cases, a large majority of the petitions considered in conference are denied.

Most cases receive only brief discussion in conference. Some cases get more consideration, which sometimes extends beyond the initial discussion. In conference any justice can ask that a case be "distributed" once again for a later conference. This step might be taken to obtain additional information, such as the full record of the case in the lower courts. A justice also might ask for another distribution to circulate an opinion dissenting from the Court's tentative denial of a hearing and thereby try to change the Court's decision. Of the cases in which the Court held oral argument in its 2010 term, a slight majority were discussed at multiple conferences and several were distributed four or more times.

When it accepts a case, the Court also decides whether to allow oral argument or to decide the case summarily on the basis of the written materials. Four votes are required for oral argument. With GVRs and other summary decisions, typically certiorari is granted and the disposition of the case is decided at the same conference, so the two stages of decision in effect become one.

The Court does not issue opinions to explain its acceptance or rejection of cases. Nor are individual votes announced. But justices occasionally record their dissents from denials of petitions for hearings, usually accompanied by dissenting opinions. There were seven cases with such dissents in the 2010 term. Sometimes justices write opinions to explain their votes not to grant certiorari, as they did in three cases in that term. *Buck v. Thaler* (2011) and *Cash v. Maxwell* (2012), two criminal cases, each had one opinion dissenting from the denial of certiorari and another opinion justifying the denial.

The Clerks' Role. One of the law clerks' primary functions is to scrutinize requests for hearings. As of 2012 all the justices except Samuel Alito are part of the "cert. (for certiorari) pool." Petitions and other materials on each case are divided among the clerks for the justices in the pool. The clerk who has responsibility for a case writes a memorandum, one that typically includes a summary of the case and a recommendation that the petition be granted or denied.

Because there are so many petitions, and because pool memos are the most extensive source of information about them, recommendations in the memos surely have some impact on the justices' certiorari votes. Indeed, one study provides evidence of this impact, though the influence of memos varies with the qualities of the petition and other circumstances.[43] One broad effect may be to reduce the number of cases that the Court hears. On the whole, clerks who write pool memos are cautious about recommending that the Court hear a case. One reason is that they know such recommendations will be scrutinized more closely than recommendations to deny. And it would be embarrassing for a clerk to suggest that the Court take a case and have the Court do so, only to have the case disposed of with a DIG later because the clerk had missed an important fact.[44]

Two factors limit the impact of the pool on certiorari decisions. First, the great majority of petitions would elicit a denial from any justice or clerk. Justice Stephen Breyer has said that of the 150 petitions that the Court receives each week, "there are only about 10 or 12 that are even possible, that anyone would think of considering for granting."[45] Second, the justices, with help from their own clerks, undertake some independent review of cases. It is noteworthy that in a substantial proportion of the cases that the Court hears, the pool memo did not recommend that the Court accept the case.[46]

Criteria for Decision

In deciding whether to accept or deny petitions, the justices look for cases whose attributes make them desirable to hear. The Court's Rule 10 lists some of those attributes, which are based on the Court's role in enhancing the certainty and consistency of the law. Rule 10 indicates that the

Court is more interested in hearing cases if they contain important issues of federal law that the Court has not yet decided, if there is conflict between lower courts on an important legal question or conflict between a lower court's decision and the Supreme Court's prior decisions, or if a federal court of appeals has drastically departed "from the accepted and usual course of judicial proceedings" or allowed a lower court to do so.

The presence of these attributes does increase the chances that a case will be accepted, but the list in Rule 10 suggests a conception of the Court's function and of its members' interests that is unrealistically narrow. The Court's pattern of screening decisions and evidence from other sources indicate the significance of several types of considerations.

Technical Criteria. The Court will reject a petition for hearing if it fails to meet certain technical requirements. Some of these requirements are specific to the Court. For example, paid petitions must comply with the Court's Rule 33, which establishes requirements on matters such as the size of print and margins used, type of paper, format and color of the cover, and maximum length.

The Court also imposes the same kinds of technical requirements that other courts apply. One specific requirement is that petitions for hearing be filed within ninety days of the entry of judgment in the lower court, unless the time has been extended in advance. The Court routinely refuses to allow the filing of petitions that are brought after the deadline.

More fundamental are the requirements of jurisdiction and standing. The Court cannot accept a case for hearing that clearly falls outside its jurisdiction. For example, the Court could not hear a state case in which the petitioner had raised no issues of federal law in the state courts.

The rule of standing holds that a court may not hear a case unless the party bringing the case is properly before it. The most important element of standing is the requirement that a party in a case have a real and direct legal stake in its outcome. This requirement precludes hypothetical cases, cases brought on behalf of another person, "friendly suits" between parties that are not really adversaries, and cases that have become "moot" (in effect, hypothetical) because the parties can no longer be affected by the outcome.

For this reason, the Court generally must dismiss a case if the parties have reached a settlement or if the only party on one side has died. In 2010, for instance, the Court dismissed a case involving the liability of prosecutors for falsifying evidence after the two sides settled the case. The oral argument had not gone well for the prosecutors and the county that employed them, and the county then avoided an adverse decision by paying $12 million to two men who had served more than twenty years in prison for murder before disclosure of the prosecutors' actions in their case led to their release.[47]

Conflict between Courts. Chief Justice Roberts agrees with Rule 10 on the importance of conflict among lower courts in legal interpretation as a basis for accepting cases: "Our main job is to try to make sure federal law is uniform across the country."[48] Other justices have expressed a similar view, and this depiction of case selection has considerable accuracy.[49] The existence of legal conflict, typically conflicts between federal courts of appeals, greatly increases the chances that a case will be accepted. And one study found that about 70 percent of the cases that the Court decided in the 2004–2006 terms involved conflicts between lower courts.[50]

This does not mean that the Court accepts every case involving conflict between courts. There are simply too many of those cases for the Court to hear all of them. Rule 10 emphasizes the importance of the issue on which a conflict has arisen as a criterion for the Court, and that criterion undoubtedly affects the justices' choices of which conflict cases to hear. Yet the Court occasionally accepts a case to resolve a conflict on a seemingly minor issue, and it sometimes turns down cases involving fairly serious conflicts among several courts.

Importance of the Issues. Of all the cases in which litigants petition for a writ of certiorari, the great majority involve narrow issues. Frequently, the "questions presented" at the beginning of the petition ask only whether the case was wrongly decided. Those cases are easy to turn away, because the justices see no point in allocating part of the limited space on their agenda to cases in which a decision would have little effect beyond the immediate parties. Rather, the best way for the Court to maximize its impact is to decide the cases that raise the most important policy questions.

Importance is a more subjective matter than conflict between courts, so different justices may assess the importance of a case quite differently. In general, justices look for cases in which a decision would have a broad effect on courts, government, or society as a whole. In some of the cases that meet this criterion, the issues are dramatic. In others, the issues are dry and technical but nonetheless important. Even the justices may find such cases unexciting. Chief Justice William Rehnquist noted that the Court heard a steady stream of cases under the federal Employee Retirement Income Security Act. "The thing that stands out about them is that they're dreary," he said, and the Court takes such cases as a matter of "duty, not choice."[51]

Just as the Court rejects some cases that involve conflicts between lower courts, it also rejects some important cases. For example, in 2010 the Court denied certiorari in a dispute between the federal government and the tobacco industry over tobacco marketing practices even though the case had monetary stakes of hundreds of billions of dollars and raised major questions about the reach of the federal racketeering law and regulation of corporate speech.[52] The primary reason for such denials is the same reason why the Court does not resolve all conflicts between lower courts: the number of meritorious cases is considerably larger than the number the Court is willing and able to hear. Justices sometimes have more specific reasons to vote against cases with significant issues. To take two examples, they may agree with the lower-court decision or may want to delay before tackling a difficult issue.

Policy Preferences. Rule 10 does not mention justices' personal conceptions of good policy as a criterion for accepting or rejecting cases, but those conceptions have considerable effect on the Court's choices. Because the Court's agenda largely determines the scope of its work as a policymaker, members of the Court inevitably use the agenda-setting process to advance their own policy goals.

Justices can act on their policy goals primarily in two ways. First, they may vote to hear cases because they disagree with the lower-court decision they are reviewing: tentatively concluding that the lower court made an error, they want to correct it. Second, they may act strategically by voting to hear a case when they think the Court would reach a decision they favor if it decided the case on the merits and voting against certiorari when they think the Court would reach what they consider the wrong decision.

The justices' use of the first approach is made clear by the Court's decisions on the merits. The Court overturns the lower court altogether or in part in more than two-thirds of its decisions. The comparable rate for the federal courts of appeals, which lack the Court's power to screen the cases brought to it, is under 10 percent.[53] One reason for the Court's reversal rate is that it accepts so many cases in order to resolve conflicts between lower courts; in those cases, there is something like a 50–50 chance that the Court will overturn the decision it hears. Even so, the reversal rate could not be nearly as high as it is if the justices were not inclined to hear cases in which they have doubts about the validity of the lower court's decision.

The justices sometimes use the second, strategic approach as well. Elena Kagan has said that when she was a law clerk for Justice Thurgood Marshall, she and her fellow clerks would "channel" Marshall in their memos and say that "here are the cases which the Court is likely to do good things with from your perspective, and here are the ones where they are not."[54] However, it is uncertain how often the justices act strategically in their certiorari votes. Justices probably concentrate their strategic calculations on the relatively small proportion of petitions that are good candidates for acceptance on other grounds. They may also be more inclined to take the Court's prospective decisions into account when they are part of the Court's ideological minority, because members of the minority have the most reason to worry about what the Court might decide.

These two ways of acting on policy goals are likely to have the greatest impact when they reinforce each other. If a case is a good candidate for acceptance on other grounds, justices who disagree with a lower-court decision and who think that the Court would agree with them on the merits have good reason to vote for certiorari.

Identities of the Participants. Every petition for certiorari involves at least two competing parties. In most paid cases and many paupers' cases, the petitioner is represented by a lawyer. And in some cases, the petitioner is supported by one or more interest groups in amicus briefs. The identities of those participants might have an impact on the Court's decisions whether to grant certiorari.

One participant, the federal government, stands out for its success in winning hearings from the Court. Over the five terms from 2006 through 2010 the Court accepted about 80 percent of the government's requests to hear cases.[55] That success rate is enormously high in comparison with the low overall rate of success for petitioners.

This impressive record reflects the solicitor general's special relationship with the Court, discussed earlier in the chapter. As the representative of the federal government and the most frequent litigant in the Court, the solicitor general's office is viewed differently from other participants in litigation. Lawyers in the office try to accentuate this perception by taking a more neutral stance than other parties.

The large number of potential and actual cases that the office handles provides it with more specific advantages. One set of advantages derives from the office's self-restraint in bringing only a small number of those cases to the Court. Lawyers can select the cases that are the most likely to be accepted, and almost any litigant who could be so selective would enjoy a relatively high rate of success in getting its cases accepted.

Further, this self-restraint fosters a positive response from the justices when the solicitor general petitions for certiorari. For one thing, it enhances the office's credibility: the justices know that the government takes to the Court only the cases that its lawyers deem most worthy, so the justices also are inclined to view those cases as worthy. The office likely gains some gratitude from the justices as well: since its self-restraint reduces the Court's caseload, the justices may reciprocate by viewing the government's petitions in a favorable light.

The number of Supreme Court cases in which the solicitor general participates leads to another advantage. Because attorneys in the office gain so much experience, they develop considerable expertise in writing briefs and in what appeals to the justices. As a result, the government can do more than most other litigants to make cases appear worthy of acceptance.

The federal government seldom files an amicus brief on its own at the certiorari stage. When the solicitor general responds to the Court's invitation to file an amicus brief, the justices give considerable weight to the office's recommendation.

Other lawyers who frequently appear in the Supreme Court have an opportunity to develop some of the solicitor general's advantages: they can gain a high level of skill in writing petitions for certiorari, and they can gain credibility with the justices. Justice Anthony Kennedy has said that "we look at the names of counsel for lawyers we trust."[56] Indeed, there is some evidence that these lawyers and the large firms in which most of them practice fare considerably better than the average lawyer when they petition for hearings from the Court.[57]

Amicus briefs on behalf of petitioners improve the chances that a petition will be accepted. As one leading Supreme Court advocate has pointed out, an amicus brief indicates the significance of a case beyond the parties themselves.[58] And specific interest groups may have special credibility with some justices because they regularly submit high-quality briefs or because the justices respect the groups themselves.

Problematic Cases and Issues. Sometimes the Court chooses not to hear a case in order to avoid a problem. Two kinds of problems are undramatic. First, the justices may vote against hearing a case because they want to await more decisions on the issue in the lower courts, decisions that may refine the issue or give the justices a better chance to assess it. Using the standard term, Justice Clarence Thomas explained that "sometimes when we don't grant cert on a case, the reason is . . . we say it needs to percolate a little more."[59]

Second, justices sometimes see a case as a "bad vehicle" for resolution of an issue because of the factual circumstances or the presence of other issues that complicate the case. Justice Kennedy wrote an opinion to explain the Court's denial of certiorari in a 2009 case, noting that the Court might not be able to address the important bankruptcy issue that the case raised without first resolving other, unrelated issues.[60]

More dramatic is the avoidance of issues that might embroil the Court in controversy. Historically, the justices have often been willing to address such issues. And it is noteworthy that in its 2011 term the Court accepted cases involving two controversial issues in which the Court's decisions might become fodder in the 2012 presidential election campaign, the constitutional validity of the federal health care law that Congress enacted in 2010 and the power of state governments to regulate immigration.

At times, however, the justices have seemed to duck issues because they were worried about potential reactions to the Court's decision. One striking example was the Court's refusal to rule on whether it was constitutional for the United States to participate in the war in Vietnam without a declaration of war. Few issues brought to the Court have been so important, but the Court refused to hear the cases that raised this question between 1967 and 1972. Undoubtedly, some justices wanted to avoid injecting the Court into the most important and most disputed issue of national policy in that era.

The Court's mixed approach to controversial cases is illustrated by the cases involving the rights of detainees who were held as suspected terrorists at the Guantánamo Bay Naval Station. The Court accepted three cases between 2003 and 2007, even though its decisions supporting the rights of detainees in those cases—especially in *Boumediene v. Bush* (2008)—aroused considerable criticism. But the Court then denied certiorari in a series of cases that involved application of the *Boumediene* decision, and one reason may have been a reluctance to further enmesh the Court in political battles over treatment of the detainees.[61]

Summary. When Supreme Court justices vote on petitions for hearings by the Court, they act on a complex set of considerations. Inevitably, justices with different goals and perspectives respond differently to petitions. Some give a higher priority to resolving lower-court conflicts than others. Justices assess the importance of cases in various ways. And they act on quite different sets of policy preferences.

It follows that the Court's selection of cases to decide fully, like everything else it does, is affected by its membership at any given time. The great majority of petitions are unlikely to be accepted no matter who is on the Court. But the composition of the cases the Supreme Court actually accepts in a term strongly reflects the identities of the justices who serve during that term.

Setting the Size of the Agenda

In the 2006–2010 terms the Supreme Court accepted an average of 85 petitions for certiorari each term, less than half the average in the first half of the 1980s. The average number of decisions that the Court reached with full opinions also dropped in half, from 156 to 78.[62] This change is all the more striking because the number of petitions that litigants brought to the Court nearly doubled over that time. Why have those trends run in opposite directions?

An answer to that question requires some historical perspective. The number of cases brought to the Court went up dramatically over the years, in a trend that culminated in the 1960s. That growth seemed to have several sources. Outside the Court these sources included an apparent increase in "rights consciousness," which led people to bring more legal claims; the development of interest groups that assisted litigants in carrying cases through the courts; and the massive growth in the activities of the federal government, which produced new laws and legal questions. The Court itself contributed to the growth in its caseload. In particular, its sympathy for claims that government actions violated civil liberties encouraged people who felt that their rights had been violated to bring cases to the Court.

By the 1970s observers of the Court and the justices themselves argued that the larger number of cases had created problems for the Court and for federal law. For the Court the perceived problem was that the justices' ability to do their work well was compromised by the increased volume of work. For federal law the concern was that the Court was accepting a smaller proportion of petitions as their numbers grew, so important issues were going unresolved. But proposals to remedy these problems, including the creation of a new court to help the Supreme Court with its work, did not succeed.

After a period of relative stability in the Court's caseload, a second period of rapid growth began in the late 1980s and continued through the 2006 term. This second period of growth was quite different from the earlier one. As Figure 3-1 shows, it was limited to paupers' petitions. The number of paid petitions per term has been relatively stable since the early 1970s, and it has actually declined substantially since the late 1990s. In contrast, the number of paupers' petitions, which hovered around 2,000 per term from the late 1960s to the mid-1980s, grew to a high of more than 7,000 in the 2006 term, before declining by several hundred since that time.

The great majority of paupers' petitions come from prisoners, and the number of adults in prison more than quadrupled between 1980 and 2009.[63] This trend accounts for most if not all of the increase in paupers' cases. Indeed, this growth occurred even though other factors that affect criminal petitions worked in the opposite direction. The Court has become less favorable to claims brought by criminal defendants since the 1960s, and more recently both Congress and the Court have limited the use of habeas corpus actions to challenge criminal convictions.

The pattern of growth in the Court's caseload over the last two decades helps to explain why the Court is not hearing more cases than it did in the mid-1980s. Paupers' petitions are always accepted at relatively low rates, and a Court that has become less sympathetic to claims by prisoners would not find many of those petitions worthy. But why would the Court hear only half as many cases as it did before?

FIGURE 3-1
*Paid and Paupers' Cases Filed in the Supreme Court per Term,
by Five-Year Averages, 1961–2010 Terms*

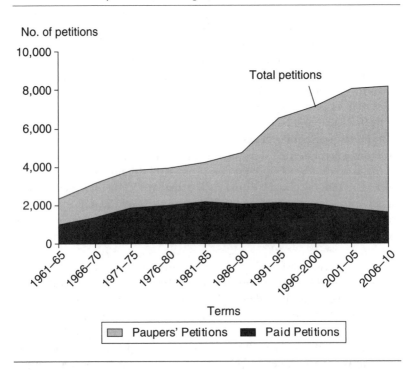

Sources: Gerhard Casper and Richard A. Posner, *The Workload of the Supreme Court* (Chicago: American Bar Foundation, 1976), 34; "Statistical Recap of Supreme Court's Workload during Last Three Terms," *United States Law Week*, various years; "Statistics" in the Supreme Court's *Journal*, various years.

Commentators and the justices themselves have offered several answers that lie outside the Court.[64] Congress in 1988 greatly reduced the range of cases that are classified as appeals (rather than petitions for certiorari), which the Court is required to decide, and the Court now hears twenty to thirty fewer appeals each term than it did before 1988. The number of conflicts between lower courts in their rulings on legal questions may have declined, and the justices and their clerks may be scrutinizing petitioners' claims of conflicts more carefully. In recent years the solicitor general's office, with its high rate of success in winning hearings for its petitions, has been bringing fewer cases to the Court. And perhaps Congress is enacting fewer major laws that require interpretation.

Other possible answers lie within the Court. On the whole, the justices who joined the Court in the late 1980s and early 1990s were less inclined to vote for certiorari than the justices they succeeded.[65] And some observers think that the justices simply like having fewer cases to decide, so that deciding cases takes less of their time. Justice Stevens said in 2007 that the Court might be "taking fewer cases than we should. But if the rate was at a level of 150 cases a year, as it was in the past, I would have left the Court long ago."[66] And once the decline occurred, the justices became accustomed to a smaller number of decisions each term, so it might be difficult for them to adjust to a reversal of the decline. Justice Scalia has said, "I don't think we can do what we were doing when I first came on the court: 150 [decisions each term]. I don't think we can do 150 well."[67]

Although the validity of specific explanations can be debated, it seems clear that the decline in the number of cases that the Court decides reflects multiple factors. Overall, the justices themselves are probably a more important factor than conditions outside the Court.[68] The biggest cuts in the number of cases accepted came long before the number of paid petitions and petitions from the solicitor general declined. And even if there are fewer major statutes and fewer conflicts between lower courts than there were in the past, there is no shortage of cases that the Court reasonably could decide.

Certainly the difficulty of gaining a hearing in the Supreme Court has increased. In its 1985 term the Court accepted for full consideration about 1 in 12 of the paid petitions filed with it. In the 2010 term that rate was 1 in 21. For paupers' petitions the decline was precipitous, from an already low 1 in 108 in 1985 to a very low 1 in 446 in 2010. Given the worsening odds and the significant costs of filing a petition for those who use lawyers' services, it is not surprising that the number of paid petitions has declined in the past decade.

Conclusion

Like other courts, the Supreme Court can decide only the cases that come to it. For that reason, people and institutions outside the Court have great influence on the Court's agenda. Ultimately, however, the Court determines which cases it hears. From the wide variety of legal and policy questions brought to the Court, the justices can choose the few they will address fully. They can also choose which issues in a case they will decide. And the justices help determine which cases are brought to them by suggesting in their opinions what kinds of legal claims they will view favorably in future cases.

The Court is sometimes criticized for its choices of cases to hear and turn aside, and in recent years it has also been criticized for the small number of cases it accepts each term. Whatever the validity of these criticisms may be, the justices employ their agenda-setting powers rather well to serve their purposes. They accept and reject cases on the basis of individual and collective goals such as avoiding troublesome issues, resolving legal conflicts, and establishing policies that the justices favor. The justices' selection of cases for full decisions helps them shape the Court's role as a policymaker. They also use that process to limit their workloads.

After the Court selects the cases to hear, of course, it decides those cases. In the next chapter, I will examine the Court's decision-making process and the forces that shape its choices.

NOTES

1. The descriptions of the *Henderson* case and of the health care cases in the Supreme Court are based on briefs and opinions in these cases. The health care cases were *Florida v. Department of Health and Human Services* (2012); *U.S. Department of Health and Human Services v. Florida* (2012); and *National Federation of Independent Business v. Sebelius* (2012).
2. "Taking Stock of the High Court Term," *National Law Journal,* August 3, 2009, 25.
3. Joseph Margulies, "A Prison beyond the Law," *Virginia Quarterly Review* 80 (Fall 2004): 39.
4. Noam Scheiber, "The Hustler," *New Republic,* April 10, 2006, 14–19.
5. The Texas redistricting case was *Perry v. Perez* (2012); the Arizona immigration case was *Arizona v. United States* (2012).
6. Mark Curriden, "The Long Shot: A Cleveland Solo's Life Is About to Change as His Practice Expands from a Spare Bedroom in His Apartment to the U.S. Supreme Court," *ABA Journal* 96 (November 2010): 52–58. The case was *Ortiz v. Jordan* (2011).
7. John Paul Stevens, *Five Chiefs: A Supreme Court Memoir* (New York: Little, Brown, 2011), 118.
8. Lyle Denniston, "Argument Recap: Disaster at the Lectern," *SCOTUSblog,* November 8, 2011, http://www.scotusblog.com/2011/11/argument-recap-disaster-at-the-lectern/. The case was *Smith v. Cain* (2012).
9. Brent Kendall, "Getting on Scalia's Good Side," *Daily Journal* Newswire article, May 12, 2008, http://pda-appellateblog.blogspot.com/2008_05_01_archive.html#4396419852952598031.
10. Adam Liptak, "As a Criminal, Mediocre; as a Jailhouse Lawyer, an Advocate Unmatched," *New York Times,* February 9, 2010, A12. The case was *Fellers v. United States* (2004).
11. Joseph W. Swanson, "Experience Matters: The Rise of a Supreme Court Bar and Its Effect on Certiorari," *Journal of Appellate Practice and Process* 9 (Spring 2007): 175–204; Tony Mauro, "High Court Vets Help Clients Win," *National Law Journal,* November 7, 2011, 11, 17.
12. Kendall, "Getting on Scalia's Good Side."
13. Tony Mauro, "After a Year on the Court, Alito Holds Forth," *Legal Times,* February 12, 2007, 12; Bryan A. Garner, "John Paul Stevens," *Scribes Journal of Legal Writing* 13 (2010): 45.

14. Timothy R. Johnson, Paul J. Wahlbeck, and James F. Spriggs II, "The Influence of Oral Arguments on the U.S. Supreme Court," *American Political Science Review* 100 (February 2006): 99–113.

15. See Nancy Morawetz, "Counterbalancing Distorted Incentives in Supreme Court Pro Bono Practice: Recommendations for the New Supreme Court Pro Bono Bar and Public Interest Practice Communities," *New York University Law Review* 86 (April 2011): 138–145.

16. Richard J. Lazarus, "Advocacy Matters before and within the Supreme Court: Transforming the Court by Transforming the Bar." *Georgetown Law Journal* 96 (May 2008): 1491.

17. See Paul M. Collins Jr., *Friends of the Supreme Court: Interest Groups and Judicial Decision Making* (New York: Oxford University Press, 2008), 24–28.

18. This discussion of the *Plata* case is based on briefs and opinions in the case, newspaper stories, and information at the website of the Prison Law Office, http://www.prisonlaw.com/.

19. On the use of amicus briefs, see Collins, *Friends of the Supreme Court*, 28–74.

20. These figures include only briefs submitted after a case was accepted for oral argument; consolidated cases were counted as a single case. The figures were compiled from listings at the *SCOTUSblog* website, http://www.scotusblog.com/.

21. Lazarus, "Advocacy Matters," 1513–1514.

22. Tony Mauro, "How 'Winning' Cases Took a Wrong Turn," *Legal Times,* July 4, 2005, 8.

23. The 1956–1965 figure is from Joseph D. Kearney and Thomas W. Merrill, "The Influence of Amicus Curiae Briefs on the Supreme Court," *University of Pennsylvania Law Review* 148 (January 2000): 754 n26.

24. This discussion draws from Adam Liptak, "Justices Offer Receptive Ear to Business Interests," *New York Times,* December 19, 2010, A1; "Robin Conrad," *National Law Journal,* June 27, 2011, 24; Adam Chandler, "Cert.-Stage Amicus Briefs: Who Files Them and to What Effect?" *SCOTUSblog,* September 27, 2007, www.scotusblog.com/wp; and National Chamber Litigation Center, *30th Anniversary Report 1977–2007* (Washington, DC: National Chamber Litigation Center, 2007).

25. See Samuel Walker, *In Defense of American Liberties: A History of the ACLU,* 2d ed. (Carbondale: Southern Illinois University Press, 1999).

26. Tony Mauro and Carrie Levine, "Raising Its Game," *National Law Journal,* August 30, 2010, 17, 20.

27. Margaret Talbot, "A Risky Proposal," *The New Yorker,* January 18, 2010, 40–51.

28. Charles R. Epp, *The Rights Revolution: Lawyers, Activists, and Supreme Courts in Comparative Perspective* (Chicago: University of Chicago Press, 1998), 44–70.

29. Most of the data on the federal government's participation that are discussed here and later in the chapter were provided by the Office of the Solicitor General.

30. This discussion is based in part on Richard L. Pacelle, Jr., *Between Law and Politics: The Solicitor General and the Structuring of Race, Gender, and Reproductive Rights Litigation* (College Station: Texas A&M University Press, 2003).

31. Ibid.

32. Tony Mauro, "Solicitor General as 'Dr. No,'" *The BLT: The Blog of Legal Times*, http://legaltimes.typepad.com/blt/2009/12/solicitor-general-as-dr-no.html, December 9, 2009.

33. One example is *Bond v. United States* (2011).

34. See David C. Thompson and Melanie F. Wachtell, "An Empirical Analysis of Supreme Court Certiorari Petition Procedures: The Call for Response and the Call for the Views of the Solicitor General," *George Mason Law Review* 16 (2009): 270–296.

35. Adam Liptak, "Obama's About-Face on Detainee Photos Leads to Supreme Court," *New York Times*, September 15, 2009, A17. The case was *Department of Defense v. American Civil Liberties Union* (2009).

36. Richard L. Pacelle, Jr., "Amicus Curiae or Amicus Praesidentis? Reexamining the Role of the Solicitor General in Filing Amici," *Judicature* 89 (May–June 2006): 317–325.

37. Mark Sherman, "Obama Legal Team Wants to Limit Defendants' Rights," Associated Press, April 23, 2009, http://www.huffingtonpost.com/2009/04/23/obama-legal-team-wants-de_n_190852.html. The case was *Montejo v. Louisiana* (2009).

38. These figures and other figures in this section on the Court's receipt and disposition of petitions are based on statistics in the Court's Journal for October Term 2010, 2, http://www.supremecourt.gov/orders/journal.aspx.

39. See Michael E. Solimine and Rafael Gely, "The Supreme Court and the Sophisticated Use of DIGs," *Supreme Court Economic Review* 18 (2010): 155–176.

40. Cases with these dissents by Justice Scalia include *Webster v. Cooper* (2009) and *Wellons v. Hall* (2010). The GVR with a 5–4 vote was in *Machado v. Holder* (2010), and the DIG with a 5–4 vote was in *Robertson v. U.S. ex rel. Watson* (2010).

41. These figures are based on analysis of the Supreme Court's reports of decisions.

42. Ryan C. Black and Christina L. Boyd, "U.S. Supreme Court Agenda Setting and the Role of Litigant Status," *Journal of Law, Economics, & Organization* 28 (June 2012): 286–312.

43. Ryan C. Black and Christina L. Boyd, "The Role of Law Clerks in the U.S. Supreme Court's Agenda-Setting Process," *American Politics Research* 40 (January 2012): 147–173.

44. David R. Stras, "The Supreme Court's Gatekeepers: The Role of Law Clerks in the Certiorari Process," *Texas Law Review* 85 (2007): 972–976; Elizabeth Francis Ward, "Clerks Avoid Getting Their DIGs In," *American Bar Association Journal* 93 (March 2007): 12–13.

45. Bryan A. Garner, "Justice Stephen G. Breyer," *Scribes Journal of Legal Writing* 13 (2010): 152.

46. Barbara Palmer, "The 'Bermuda Triangle?' The Cert Pool and Its Influence Over the Supreme Court's Agenda," *Constitutional Commentary* 18 (2001): 111; Stras, "Supreme Court's Gatekeepers," 976–980.

47. David G. Savage, "Prosecutor Conduct Case Before Supreme Court Is Settled," *Los Angeles Times*, January 5, 2010. The case was *Pottawattamie County v. McGhee* (2010).

48. Brian Lamb, Susan Swain, and Mark Farkas, eds., *The Supreme Court: A C-Span Book Featuring the Justices in Their Own Words* (New York: PublicAffairs, 2010), 13.

49. See Amanda Frost, "Overvaluing Uniformity," *Virginia Law Review* 94 (November 2008): 1631–1636.

50. Stras, "Supreme Court's Gatekeepers," 981.

51. Tony Mauro, "Court Aces," *Legal Times,* July 14, 2003, 11.

52. *Altria Group v. United States* (2010). The case is discussed in Michael Kirkland, "Under the U.S. Supreme Court: Did Big Tobacco Finally Get Burned?" *UPI.com,* August 1, 2010.

53. The proportion for the Supreme Court is based on data in the "Statistics" articles in the November issues of the *Harvard Law Review.* The proportion for the courts of appeals is based on data in Administrative Office of the United States Courts, *Judicial Business of the United States Courts: Report of the Director, 2010* (Washington, DC: Administrative Office of the U.S. Courts, n.d.), 111, 115, and the same report for earlier years.

54. "Confirmation Hearings on the Nominations of Thomas Perrelli Nominee to be Associate Attorney General of the United States and Elena Kagan Nominee to be Solicitor General of the United States," Hearing before the Senate Judiciary Committee, 111th Congress, 1st Session, February 10, 2009 (Washington, DC: U.S. Government Printing Office, 2009), 99. The transcript used the word "case" rather than "cases."

55. This figure, based on data supplied by the solicitor general's office, does not include cases that the office asked the Court to hold pending a decision in another case or cases in which the Court granted certiorari and immediately remanded the case to the lower court.

56. "Notes on Justice Kennedy," *Southern California Appellate News,* February 4, 2010, http://www.socal-appellate.blogspot.com/2010/02/notes-on-justice-kennedy.html.

57. Lazarus, "Advocacy Matters," 1515–1517, 1522–1528.

58. John J. Bursch, "Petitions for Certiorari: Understanding the Hidden Process," *Appellate Issues* 7 (February 2008), http://www.americanbar.org/groups/judicial/conferences/appellate_judges/appellate_lawyers/resources/publications.html.

59. Bryan A. Garner, "Clarence Thomas," *Scribes Journal of Legal Writing* 13 (2010): 116.

60. The case was *N.C.P. Marketing Group, Inc. v. BG Star Productions, Inc.* (2009).

61. See Linda Greenhouse, "Gitmo Fatigue at the Supreme Court," *New York Times Opinionator Blog,* April 6, 2011, http://opinionator.blogs.nytimes.com/2011/04/06/gitmo-fatigue-at-the-supreme-court/.

62. Data on the number of petitions accepted are from "Statistical Recap of Supreme Court's Workload during Last Three Terms," in *United States Law Week* (for the 1980–1984 terms) and from the Supreme Court's *Journal* (for the 2006–2010 terms). Those sources were also used for the ratios of petitions to cases accepted that are described later in this section. Data on the number of full decisions are from the "Statistics" articles in the November issues of the *Harvard Law Review.*

63. U.S. Census Bureau, *Statistical Abstract of the United States: 2012* (Washington, DC: U.S. Government Printing Office, 2011), 217.

64. Linda Greenhouse, "Case of the Dwindling Docket Mystifies the Supreme Court," *New York Times*, December 7, 2006, A1, A30; Robert Barnes, "Justices Continue Trend of Hearing Fewer Cases," *Washington Post*, January 7, 2007, A4; Adam Liptak, "Justices Opt for Fewer Cases, and Professors and Lawyers Ponder Why," *New York Times*, September 29, 2009, A20; Stevens, *Five Chiefs*, 209.

65. David R. Stras, "The Supreme Court's Declining Plenary Docket: A Membership-Based Explanation," *Constitutional Commentary* 27 (Fall 2010): 151–161.

66. Pamela A. MacLean, "9th Circuit Reversal Rate Is Misleading," *National Law Journal*, July 30, 2007, 14.

67. Lamb, Swain, and Farkas, *The Supreme Court*, 55.

68. Kevin M. Scott, "Shaping the Supreme Court's Federal Certiorari Docket," *Justice System Journal* 27 (2006): 191–207.

Chapter 4

Decision Making

Once the Supreme Court determines which cases to hear, the justices get to the heart of their work—reaching decisions in those cases. This chapter examines how and why the Court makes its decisions.

Components of the Court's Decision

A Supreme Court decision on the merits has two components: the immediate outcome for the parties to the case and a statement of general legal rules. In cases that the Court fully considers, it nearly always presents the two components in an opinion. In the great majority of cases, at least five justices subscribe to this opinion. As a result, it constitutes an authoritative statement by the Court.

Opinions for the Court vary in form, but an opinion usually begins with a description of the background of the case before it reached the Court. The opinion then turns to the legal issues, discussing the opposing views on those issues and describing the Court's conclusions about them. A summary of the outcome for the parties ends the opinion.

Except in the few cases the Court hears under its original jurisdiction, the Court describes the outcome in relation to the lower-court decision it is reviewing. The Court can affirm the lower-court decision, leaving that court's treatment of the parties undisturbed. Alternatively, it can modify or reverse the lower-court decision. In general, a reversal overturns the lower-court decision altogether or nearly so, and modification is a more limited, partial overturning. Frequently, the Court "vacates" (makes void) the lower-court decision, an action whose effect is similar to that of reversal.

When the Court does disturb a lower-court decision, it sometimes makes a final judgment. More often, it remands the case to the lower court, sending it back for reconsideration. The Court's opinion provides guidance on how the case should be reconsidered. For example, the opinion in a tax case may say that a court of appeals adopted the wrong interpretation of the federal tax laws and the lower court should reexamine the case on the basis of a different interpretation. The Court's opinion in a 2011 case used typical language: "The judgment of the Nevada Supreme Court is reversed, and the case is remanded for further proceedings not inconsistent with this opinion."[1]

In most cases, the outcome has little impact beyond the parties themselves. Rather, what makes most decisions consequential is the statement of legal rules that apply to the nation as a whole. When the Court's opinion resolves the legal issues in a case, it is not just providing guidance to a specific lower court in a specific case. It is also laying down rules that any court must follow in a case to which they apply and that can affect the behavior of people outside of court. As a result, a decision may have a substantial effect on thousands or even millions of people who were not parties in the case.

The Court chooses which legal rules it establishes in a case, just as it chooses the outcome for the parties. A ruling for one of the parties often could be based on any of several different rules or sets of rules. That reality is underlined when the Court affirms a lower-court decision on a legal ground different from the one that the lower court used.[2] The rules chosen by the Court largely determine the long-term impact of its decision. If the Court overturns the death sentence for a particular defendant, it might base that decision on an unusual error in the defendant's trial, so that the decision would affect few other defendants. Alternatively, the Court could declare that the death penalty is unconstitutional under all circumstances and thereby make a fundamental policy change.

The Decision-Making Process

When the Court accepts a case for a decision on the merits, it initiates the decision-making process for that case. This process varies from case to case, but it typically involves several stages.

Presentation of Cases to the Court

The written briefs that the Court receives when it considers whether to hear a case usually give some attention to the merits of the case. Once a case has been accepted for oral argument and decision, attorneys for the parties submit new briefs that focus only on the merits. In the preponderance of cases that reach this stage, interest groups submit amicus curiae briefs stating their own arguments on the merits.

Paul Clement presents his oral argument in one segment of the cases on the federal health care law of 2010 that the Court heard in March 2012.

Most of the material in these briefs concerns legal issues. The parties muster evidence to support their interpretations of relevant constitutional provisions and statutes. In their briefs they frequently offer arguments about policy as well, seeking to persuade the justices that support for their position constitutes not only good law but good public policy.

Material in the briefs is supplemented by attorneys' presentations in oral argument before the Court. Attorneys for the parties sometimes share their time with the lawyer for an amicus, usually the federal government. In most cases each side is provided half an hour for its argument. One exception was the set of three cases involving challenges to the 2010 federal health care law, for which the Court allocated a total of six hours over three days in 2012.[3] When a lawyer's time expires, a red light goes on at the lectern. Chief Justice William Rehnquist enforced the time limit strictly, but John Roberts is sometimes more lenient. In *Arizona v. United States* (2012), in which the federal government challenged a state immigration law, Roberts allowed the argument to go twenty minutes longer than scheduled.

The justices are quite vocal during the arguments. During the Court's 1998-2006 terms, the justices averaged 133 questions and comments per case, more than two a minute.[4] In a 2011 argument, one of the lawyers got only partway through the ritual opening, "Mr. Chief Justice, and may it please the Court," before Elena Kagan asked the first question.[5] In the current Court most of the justices are active questioners, so much so that they frequently interrupt each other. Samuel Alito has reported that it can be difficult to get a question in without interrupting a lawyer in mid-sentence.[6] Chief Justice Roberts said in 2009 that "it is a little too much domination" of the argument time by the justices, while admitting, "I'm as guilty as anyone."[7] In one argument that year, Roberts intervened after Stephen Breyer responded to two questions from Antonin Scalia, remind-ing the justices that "we direct our questions to counsel."[8]

The least vocal justice by far is Clarence Thomas, who has asked no questions during oral arguments since 2006. In Thomas's view, the Court should give lawyers a chance to make their arguments, and the justices have opportunities after the arguments to express their own views to each other.[9] He has also suggested that there is no point to aggressive question-ing of lawyers when the justices usually know their position in a case before the argument. "So why do you beat up on people if you already know?"[10]

For the justices, oral argument has two broad functions. First, it allows them to gather information about the strengths and weaknesses of the parties' positions and about other aspects of the case that interest them. Second, and perhaps more important, the argument provides them an opportunity to shape their colleagues' perceptions of a case. To a consid-erable degree, questions and comments to lawyers are really directed at other justices. In particular, justices try to expose weaknesses in the argu-ments of the side whose position they oppose. This is one reason for a pattern that observers of the Court have noticed: on the whole, justices ask more questions of the side they ultimately vote against, and their ques-tions to that side tend to be more negative in tone.[11]

Antonin Scalia demonstrates these tendencies especially well. Scalia asks tough questions of lawyers when he disagrees with their position, and he also tries to help attorneys for the side he favors. In a 2011 argument, Scalia was dissatisfied with the answer that a lawyer was giving to a ques-tion by Ruth Bader Ginsburg, and he interrupted with his own answer. The grateful lawyer responded, "Justice Scalia, you said it much more artfully, but that's exactly the point I was trying to make."[12]

Justices have indicated that oral argument often shapes their percep-tion of cases and occasionally shifts their judgment about which side to support.[13] Once in a while, the argument seems to have a decisive effect. In *United States v. Jones* (2012), federal agents had installed a GPS device on a car and tracked the car's location for a month without a valid war-rant. The federal government's lawyer responded to questions by saying that if the government tracked all nine Supreme Court justices for a month with GPS devices it had installed on their cars, its actions would not constitute a search and thus would be subject to no legal restrictions.

"After that," a commentator said when the Court announced its decision, "it seemed to be mainly a question of how the government would lose, not whether. And this week, sure enough, the tally was Jones 9, Big Brother 0."[14]

Tentative Decisions

After oral argument the Court discusses each case in one of its conferences later the same week. The chief justice begins the discussion of a case, which continues with the other justices from most senior to most junior. The justices indicate their vote in the case and the reasons for their positions.

Chief Justice Rehnquist enforced tight limits on conference discussion of cases. Those limits reflected his view that discussion would have little impact, since the justices typically come to the conference with strong views about cases. He concluded that "it is very much the exception" for justices' minds to be changed in conference.[15]

The discussion is looser under Chief Justice Roberts. Justice Thomas has reported that "now, there's more back-and-forth, more discussion."[16] But the discussion remains structured. As Roberts described it, "Nobody speaks twice until everyone has spoken once."[17] And as he noted, sometimes the justices decide that there is no need for any further discussion after the first comments from each justice. It remains true that, as Justice Scalia put it, the discussion of a case in conference "is not really an exercise in persuading each other, it's an exercise in stating your views while the rest of us take notes."[18]

After each two-week sitting, the writing of the Court's opinion in each case is assigned to a justice. If the chief justice voted with the majority, the chief assigns the opinion. In other cases, the most senior associate justice in the majority makes the assignment.

Reaching Final Decisions

The justice who was assigned the Court's opinion writes an initial draft, guided by the views expressed in conference. The justice's clerks often do most of the drafting. Once this opinion is completed and circulated, a justice who was in the majority at conference usually signs on to it.[19] Sometimes, however, justices hold back rather than signing on, either because they have developed doubts about their original vote or because they disagree with some of the language in the draft opinion. The language is important because justices are reluctant to join an opinion when they disagree with its reasoning. Indeed, Justice Scalia reported in 2003 that he could not recall any instance in which he had done so.[20] Members of the original minority also read the draft opinion for the Court. They might decide to sign on to the opinion because their view of the case has changed, or they might see a possibility of signing on if the opinion is modified.

Justices who do not immediately sign on may indicate fundamental disagreement with the opinion. Exaggerating somewhat, Justice Thomas has described such responses: "Dear Clarence, I disagree with everything in your opinion except your name. Cheers."[21] But justices often indicate that they would be willing to join an opinion if certain changes are made. Justices who voted with the majority are especially likely to ask for changes. Their memos initiate a process of explicit or implicit negotiation in which the assigned justice tries to gain the support of as many colleagues as possible. At the least, that justice wants to maintain the original majority for the outcome supported by the opinion and to win a majority for the language of the opinion, so that it becomes the official statement of the Court. This negotiation process operates primarily through written memos. But the justices sometimes interact directly, and law clerks often gather information from clerks for other justices to help identify what revisions are needed to gain a colleague's support for an opinion.[22]

In this effort the justice who was assigned the Court's opinion often competes with other justices, who write alternative opinions supporting the opposite outcome or arguing for the same outcome with a different rationale. Most of the time assigned justices succeed in winning a majority for their opinions, though sometimes with substantial alterations. More often than not, however, they fail to win the unanimous support of their colleagues. As shown in Table 4-1, which summarizes attributes of the Court's decisions in the 2010 term, such unanimity was achieved only 26 percent of the time.

Occasionally, no opinion gains the support of a majority. This occurred once in the 2010 term, and in three other cases there was a majority for only part of an opinion. Without a majority opinion, there is no authoritative statement of the Court's position on the legal issues in the case. But the opinion on the winning side with the greatest support—the "plurality opinion"—may specify the points for which majority support exists.

On rare occasions the justices find themselves unable to reach a final decision in a case before the term ends. They then schedule the case for a second set of oral arguments, usually in the following term. The Court took this route in two landmark cases, *Brown v. Board of Education* (1954) and *Roe v. Wade* (1973).

In *Citizens United v. Federal Election Commission* (2010), a case involving a challenge to federal regulation of funding for political campaigns, the Court ordered a second set of arguments on the question of whether the Court should overrule a 1990 decision and part of a 2003 decision that had upheld regulations of campaign funding. The Court did overrule

TABLE 4-1
Selected Characteristics of Supreme Court Decisions, 2010 Term

Characteristic	Number	Percentage
Number of decisions	81	NA
Vote for Court's decision[a]		
Unanimous	37	46
Nonunanimous	44	54
Support for Court's opinion		
Unanimous for whole opinion	21	26
Unanimous for part of opinion	6	7
Majority but not unanimous	50	62
Majority for only part of opinion	3	4
No majority for opinion	1	1
One or more concurring opinions[b]	42	52
One or more dissenting opinions[c]	43	53
Total number of opinions		
Concurring	49	NA
Dissenting	50	NA

Source: The decisions included are those decided with opinions and listed in the front section of *United States Supreme Court Reports, Lawyers' Edition,* Volumes 178–180.

Note: NA = not applicable.

a. "Decision" refers to the outcome for the parties. Partial dissents are not counted as votes for the decision.
b. Some concurring opinions are in full agreement with the Court's opinion.
c. Opinions labeled "concurring and dissenting" are treated as dissenting opinions.

those decisions, a step that Justice Stevens in dissent portrayed as inappropriate: "Our colleagues' suggestion that 'we are asked to reconsider *Austin* and, in effect, *McConnell*,' . . . would be more accurate if rephrased to state that 'we have asked ourselves' to reconsider those cases."[23]

Concurring and Dissenting Opinions

In most cases an opinion gains a majority but lacks unanimous support. Disagreement with the majority opinion can take two forms. First, a justice may cast a dissenting vote, which disagrees with the result reached by the Court as it affects the parties to a case. If a criminal conviction is reversed, for example, a justice who believes it should have been affirmed will dissent. Second, a justice may concur with the Court's decision, agreeing with the result in the specific case but differing with the rationale expressed in the Court's opinion. Table 4-1 shows that both kinds of disagreement are common, and in most terms dissenting opinions are even more numerous than they were in the 2010 term.

A justice who disagrees with the majority opinion nearly always writes or joins in a dissenting or concurring opinion. When the conference vote is not unanimous, the senior dissenting justice assigns the dissenting opinion. This opinion is written at the same time as the assigned opinion for the majority, and often one goal is to persuade enough colleagues to change their positions that a minority becomes a majority.

That goal is no longer relevant after the Court reaches its final decision, but issuing a dissenting opinion can serve several other purposes. For one thing, dissenting opinions give justices the satisfaction of expressing unhappiness with the result in a case and justifying their disagreement. Dissenting opinions sometimes have more concrete purposes as well. Through their arguments, dissenters may try to set the stage for a later Court to adopt their view. In the short term, a dissenting opinion may be intended to subvert the Court's decision by pointing out how lower courts can interpret it narrowly or by urging Congress to overturn the Court's reading of a statute. This is one reason why majority opinions sometimes respond to dissents.

When more than one justice dissents, the dissenters usually join in a single opinion—most likely the one originally assigned. But often there are multiple dissenting opinions, each expressing the particular view of the justice who wrote it but sometimes indicating agreement with another opinion.

A concurring opinion that disagrees with the majority opinion on the legal rationale for a decision is labeled a "special concurrence." In some cases the disagreement is quite limited. In some other cases the majority and concurring opinions offer fundamentally different rationales for the outcome they favor. In *Graham v. Florida* (2010) the Court overturned a sentence of life in prison without the possibility of parole for a defendant who was convicted of two offenses related to a robbery. The majority opinion ruled that under the Eighth Amendment's prohibition of cruel and unusual punishments, a defendant who was convicted of a crime other than murder could not be sentenced to life without parole if the crime had been committed when the defendant was a juvenile. The concurring opinion by Chief Justice Roberts agreed that Graham's sentence should be overturned because of the specific circumstances of his case, but Roberts strongly disagreed with the majority's absolute prohibition of life without parole for juvenile offenders.

Another type of concurring opinion, a "regular concurrence," is written by justices who join the majority opinion, indicating that they agree with both the outcome for the litigants and the legal rules that the Court establishes. Under those circumstances, why would justices write separate opinions? Most often, they offer their own interpretation of the majority opinion as a means to influence lower courts and other audiences, as well as the Court itself in future cases. For instance, Justice Alito wrote a concurrence in a 2011 case to influence how a court of appeals should analyze the case after the Court's remand, and Justice Breyer wrote a concurrence in another 2011 case to influence how the lower federal courts applied the Court's decision to other cases.[24] Occasionally, as in a 2011 opinion by Justice Scalia, a regular concurrence addresses the arguments in a dissenting opinion.[25] The value to justices of expressing their individual views about a case are illustrated by *Doe v. Reed* (2010), in which justices on the majority side of an 8–1 decision wrote three regular concurring opinions and two special concurrences.

The Styles of Opinions

Majority opinions tend to be formal in style, primarily because they represent the Court as a whole. Still, they sometimes show a degree of flair. In *Federal Communications Commission v. AT&T* (2011), Chief Justice Roberts wrote an opinion for a unanimous Court holding that AT&T and other corporations do not have the benefit of protection for "personal privacy" under the federal Freedom of Information Act. In the last sentence of the opinion, Roberts said that "we trust that AT&T will not take it personally."[26] Not surprisingly, an analysis of majority opinions indicates that the justices differ in their writing styles. But the opinions written by a single justice also vary in style across cases and time, a pattern that reflects the role of law clerks in drafting opinions.[27]

Legal scholars and other readers of majority opinions sometimes complain that they are not as clear as they might be. A lack of clarity sometimes results from the author's effort to gain support from colleagues. One study found that the larger the number of justices who sign on to a majority opinion, the less clear the opinion is; building a large coalition may require some obscurity to patch over disagreements. The study also found considerable variation in clarity across justices.[28] Clarity aside, the average majority opinion since 1970 has been considerably longer than it was in the Court's earlier history. As of 2010, nine of the Court's ten longest opinions had come since 1970, four of them since 2006.[29]

Because concurring and dissenting opinions are individual expressions rather than statements for the Court, they usually reveal more about the author's views and often express those views in more colorful language. Dissenting opinions sometimes state their disagreement with the majority in strong terms, and occasionally concurring opinions do so as well. Among the current justices, Justice Scalia writes such sharply worded opinions most often. To take one example, a 2011 dissent pointed to the series of Court decisions interpreting a statutory provision: "Today's opinion produces a fourth ad hoc judgment that will sow further confusion. Insanity, it has been said, is doing the same thing over and over again, but expecting different results."[30] But Scalia is not the only justice who writes strong dissenting opinions. In a 2011 case, for instance, Justice Sotomayor charged that the majority "invents new principles of pre-emption law out of thin air" and that its decision led to a good many "absurd consequences."[31]

Announcing the Decision

The decision-making process for a case ends when all the opinions have been put in final form and all justices have determined which opinions they will join. The Supreme Court is unusual in that it announces its decisions in a court session, in what one commentator called "ceremonial showtime."[32] Typically, the justice who wrote the majority opinion reads a portion of the opinion. Occasionally—on average, about four times a term between 1999 and 2009—the authors of dissenting opinions also read portions of their opinions. Their doing so reflects unusually strong disagreement with the Court's decision.[33]

The length of time required for a case to go through all the stages from filing in the Court to the announcement of a decision varies a good deal. The cases that the Court decided in June 2011 were filed as early as May 2009 and as late as December 2010. The Court's decision often comes many years after the incident that triggered the case.

After the Court decides a case—or declines to hear it—the losing party may petition for a rehearing. Such petitions are rarely granted. However, the Court's major decision on the rights of detainees at the Guantánamo Bay Naval Station, *Boumediene v. Bush* (2008), came after it had granted a rehearing and reversed its original denial of certiorari in the case.

Influences on Decisions: Introduction

Of all the questions that might be asked about the Supreme Court, the one that has intrigued people most is how the Court's decisions are best explained. Cases present the justices with choices: which party to support, what rules of law to establish. On what bases do they make their choices?

This question is difficult to answer. Like policymakers elsewhere in government, Supreme Court justices act on multiple considerations; those considerations are intermixed and their relative importance varies among justices and cases.[34] Because of this complexity, people who study the Court disagree sharply about how best to explain the Court's decisions.

The rest of this chapter is devoted to this question. No conclusive answer is possible. But some insight can be gained by examining four broad forces that shape the Court's decisions: the state of the legal rules the Court interprets, the justices' personal values, interaction among the justices, and the Court's political and social environment. The sections that follow consider each of these forces.

The State of the Law

Every case requires the Supreme Court to interpret the law, usually in the form of constitutional provisions or federal statutes. In this sense a justice's job differs from that of a legislator; justices interpret existing law rather than write new law. For this reason, the state of the existing law is a good starting point for explanation of the Court's decisions.

The Law's Significance in Decisions

When nominees to the Supreme Court testify before the Senate Judiciary Committee, they regularly describe their prospective role on the Court as one of simply interpreting the law. In 2005 John Roberts told the committee that "judges and justices are servants of the law, not the other way around. Judges are like umpires. Umpires don't make the rules; they apply them." Four years later, Sonia Sotomayor said that "the task of a judge is not to make law, it is to apply the law," and in her decisions the law was "commanding the result in every case." Responding to a senator's questions in 2010, Elena Kagan said that "at the end of the day, what the judge does is to apply the law" and in reaching decisions "it's law all the way down."[35]

Nominees make such statements in part to reassure senators and to fend off questions about their personal views. But even after their confirmation, justices typically speak of their job in the same way. In 2007, for instance, Justice Thomas offered an analogy similar to the one that Chief Justice Roberts had offered: "We're like referees. We're neutral. And we use the rules given to us."[36]

Common though it is, the justices' depiction of their job as simply applying the law evokes considerable disagreement. Scholars have pointed to two realities that conflict with that depiction.

One reality is what might be called the legal ambiguity of the cases the Court decides. In at least the great majority of cases the Court chooses to hear, the proper interpretation of the Constitution or a federal statute is uncertain—often quite uncertain. As a result, a good case can be made for either side on the basis of the applicable legal rules. Taking a different perspective from the one that she presented at her confirmation hearing, Justice Sotomayor in 2011 offered her own interpretation of the analogy between justices and umpires:

The baseball rules tell you what the strike zone is, but the umpire has to use judgment about where the ball hit in that strike zone. And for those of you who have ever played umpire, you know a lot of those balls are right on the line, so did it tilt that way or this way?[37]

The second reality is that justices care about more than the law. Most important, they often hold strong preferences about the policy issues involved in cases. Inevitably, most justices have views, often intense views, on matters such as the merits of the federal health care law that President Obama sponsored and the desirability of affirmative action in college admissions. Understandably, they are happier if their position in a case is consistent with their conception of good policy. Thus, unlike umpires, members of the Supreme Court have rooting interests in the cases they decide.

Facing ambiguous legal issues and caring about the policy issues in the case, justices may act consciously to reach decisions that accord with their policy preferences. But even if justices try only to interpret the law properly, they will tend toward the interpretation that is most consistent with their preferences. One of Justice Felix Frankfurter's law clerks described that process well in talking about Frankfurter:

He felt very intensely about lots of things, and sometimes he didn't realize that his feelings and his deeply felt values were pushing him as a judge relentlessly in one direction rather than another. I'm sure that you can put these things aside consciously, but what's underneath the consciousness you can't control.[38]

Thus, it is understandable that in most cases the justices disagree among themselves about the outcome for the litigants, the legal rules to adopt, or both. The primary reason for those disagreements is the ambiguity of the law, which causes justices with different preferences to reach different conclusions.

Because of this reality, some observers of the Court take a position directly opposite to the one that justices usually express, arguing that the state of the law has essentially no impact on justices' choices.[39] This argument can be defended, but there is good reason to conclude that legal considerations do have an impact on justices' choices. Even when decisions on either side of a case could be justified under the law, the law may weigh more heavily on one side than on the other. If justices care about making good law, they will be drawn toward the side that seems to have a stronger legal argument.

And there is excellent reason to think that justices do care about making good law. They have been trained in a tradition that emphasizes the law as a basis for judicial decisions. They are evaluated informally by a peer group of judges and legal scholars who care about their ability to reach well-founded interpretations of the law. Perhaps most important, they work in the language of the law. The arguments they receive in written briefs and oral arguments are primarily about the law, and so are the arguments they make to each other in draft opinions and memoranda.[40]

Indeed, some aspects of justices' behavior indicate that the state of the law does affect their choices.[41] Sometimes they take positions that seem to conflict with their conceptions of good policy. In a 2008 opinion, for instance, Justice Stevens voted to uphold New York's system for election of judges but cited former justice Thurgood Marshall's aphorism that "the Constitution does not prohibit legislatures from enacting stupid laws."[42] Sometimes the justices in the majority are sufficiently unhappy with the consequences of their interpretation of a statute that they ask Congress to consider rewriting the statute to override their decision—that is, to establish a policy that the justices feel powerless to adopt themselves because of their reading of the law. While the law is hardly the dominant force in decision making, it exerts a real impact on the Court's decisions.

Means of Interpretation

The role of the law in the Court's decisions can be probed further by considering the techniques that justices use to interpret provisions of the law, techniques that are important in themselves. Most fit into a few broad approaches, which differ somewhat depending on whether the Court is interpreting the Constitution or federal statutes.

Plain Meaning. In the most basic approach, judges analyze the literal meaning of the words in the law, an approach that is often called textualism. Nearly everyone agrees that interpretation of a legal provision should begin with a search for what is called the "plain meaning" of constitutional and statutory provisions. Some justices, such as Antonin Scalia, strongly emphasize the text of the law they are interpreting as a basis for their decisions. The emphasis on plain meaning in the current Court is reflected in the frequency with which justices cite dictionary definitions of words in statutes and the Constitution.[43]

The plain meaning of a legal provision is not always obvious, and this is especially true in the cases that the Supreme Court considers. Many of the Court's decisions involve interpretation of the Constitution, and the Constitution is written in broad language that often has no plain meaning. This is true, for instance, of the "due process of law" clause in the Fourteenth Amendment. The First Amendment states that "Congress shall make no law . . . abridging the freedom of speech," but justices and commentators have disagreed about the meaning of "freedom of speech" and even of "speech."

Federal statutes are typically less vague than the Constitution, but often their provisions have uncertain meanings. The statutory cases that the

Court decides tend to involve issues on which Congress has not spoken clearly. In these cases justices can do their best to ascertain the most reasonable interpretation of the words in a statute, but there may be considerable room for disagreement. In a 2011 case, for instance, Justice Breyer's majority opinion and Justice Scalia's dissent reached conflicting conclusions about the meaning of the phrase "filed any complaint" in a civil rights law.[44]

Even when a legal provision seems to have a clear meaning, the justices do not always adhere to it. That is especially true in constitutional law. Over time the Court has accepted several interpretations of the Constitution that seem to depart from the language of its provisions. The due process clause of the Fifth Amendment requires only that the federal government follow proper procedures in taking "life, liberty, or property," but the Court interprets it to prohibit discrimination.[45] It interprets the same language in the Fourteenth Amendment as a protection of freedom of expression and freedom of religion.[46] And for more than a century the Court has read the Eleventh Amendment's prohibition of lawsuits against states "by citizens of another state" to prohibit most lawsuits against a state by the state's own residents as well.[47]

Why have justices adopted and adhered to these seemingly inaccurate interpretations? The primary reason is that doing so advances values that are important to them, values such as protecting freedom of speech. The general acceptance of these "constitutional fictions" shows that no justice always adheres to the plain meaning of the law.

Intent of Framers or Legislators. When the plain meaning of a legal provision is unclear, justices can seek to ascertain the intentions of the people who wrote the provision. Evidence concerning legislative intent can be found in congressional committee reports and floor debates, which constitute what is called the "legislative history" of a statute or a constitutional amendment. For provisions of the original Constitution, evidence is found in reports of deliberations at the Constitutional Convention of 1787 and other sources.

Sometimes the intent of Congress or the framers of the Constitution is fairly clear. Frequently, however, it is not. The body that adopted a provision may not have spoken on an issue; the members of Congress who wrote the broad language of the Fourteenth Amendment could hardly indicate their intent about all the issues that have arisen under that amendment. And evidence about intent may be contradictory, in part because of conflicting efforts to influence the courts. Committee reports, seemingly a good indicator of what members of Congress had in mind, often represent the views of congressional staff more than those of the members.

Justices disagree about the use of legislative intent in interpreting statutes. The leading opponent is Justice Scalia, who views legislative history as illegitimate; he argues that it is the language of the statute, not legislators' intent, that governs. Further, he sees legislative history as an uncertain and easily distorted guide to congressional intent. Accordingly, Scalia does not refer to legislative history himself and distances himself from its use by his colleagues. Scalia has gained some support for his view from other justices, primarily other conservatives, and the Court's use of legislative history declined after he joined the Court.[48] But some justices, such as Stephen Breyer, continue to favor the use of legislative history.

A somewhat different debate about interpretation of the Constitution involves plain meaning as well as legislative intent. Some people argue that the Court should adhere to the meaning of constitutional provisions at the time they were adopted, a meaning reflected in the way that words in the Constitution were understood at that time. Others believe the Court should interpret the Constitution according to the current meaning of its language and its underlying values. Taking the first position, Justice Scalia criticized judges and justices who "have invented this notion of a living Constitution, where the interpretation of the Constitution could change." Taking the second position, Justice Ginsburg argued that "no one would say that the Constitution means today what it meant when it was written."[49]

To a considerable extent, this is an ideological debate, with liberals wanting the freedom to adopt broad interpretations of constitutional rights. The debate has been especially heated on capital punishment. The Court's decisions prohibiting the death penalty for people who are mentally retarded (in 2002), for murders committed when the defendant was not yet eighteen years old (in 2005), and for sexual assaults of children (in 2008) were based on the majority's view that the prohibition of "cruel and unusual punishments" in the Eighth Amendment should be interpreted on the basis of current values. The conservative dissenters in each case focused on the meaning of "cruel and unusual" when the Eighth Amendment was written and strongly criticized the majority for its approach to interpretation of the Constitution.[50]

Precedent. The Supreme Court's past decisions, its precedents, provide another guide to decision making. A basic doctrine of the law is stare decisis (let the decision stand). Under this doctrine a court is bound to adhere to the rules of law established by courts that stand above it. No court stands above the Supreme Court, but stare decisis includes an expectation that courts will generally adhere to their own precedents.

Technically, a court is expected to follow not everything stated in a relevant precedent but only the rule of law that is necessary for decision in that case—what is called the holding. In *District of Columbia v. Heller* (2008), the Court ruled that the Second Amendment protects the right of individuals to possess guns, and it struck down a Washington, DC, law on the ground that the law infringed that right. That was the holding of the case. The Court's opinion also described some types of gun regulations that were "presumptively lawful." Because those regulations were not involved in this case, that part of the Court's opinion was "dictum," which has no legal force. The distinction between holding and dictum is not always so clear, however.

The rule of adhering to precedent would not eliminate ambiguity in legal interpretation even if the justices followed it strictly. Most cases before the Supreme Court concern issues that are at least marginally different from those decided in past cases, so precedents do not lead directly to a particular outcome. Indeed, justices often "distinguish" a precedent, holding that it does not govern the current case. They may also narrow a precedent without overturning it altogether. In some instances these methods effectively undercut a precedent. One legal scholar referred to decisions in the last decade that limited the scope of decisions such as *Miranda v. Arizona* (1966) as "stealth overruling" of those precedents.[51]

The Court explicitly abandons some precedents, and it has done so at an unusually high rate since 1960. By one count, the Court overruled precedents only ninety-four times between 1790 and 1959 but did so seventy-six times in the twenty years from 1960 through 1979. The pace has slowed since then, but the sixty-four decisions overruling precedents between 1980 and 2010, about two per year, is still a much higher rate than in the period prior to 1960.[52] These counts are approximate because the Court is not always clear about whether it has overruled a precedent, and sometimes the justices themselves disagree about that question.

The number of times the Court overrules precedents is a small fraction of the times when it follows them. The same is true of individual justices. But most of the time when justices follow a precedent, its validity is not in question, or they simply agree with it. What do justices do when they confront a precedent with which they strongly disagree?

One way to identify such disagreement is when a justice dissents from a legal rule at the time the Court first establishes it. Most of the time, justices continue to reject that precedent in later cases, engaging in what one legal scholar called "perpetual dissents."[53] Similarly, justices are more likely to vote to override precedents that run counter to their ideological positions. In a 2009 decision and a 2010 decision in which the Court overrode liberal precedents, the Court was divided 5–4, with the four most liberal justices in dissent. In both cases the Court had asked the parties to address the question of whether it should overrule the precedents in question, a step that suggested the eagerness of some justices to eliminate what they saw as undesirable rules of law.[54]

In the current era every justice votes to overrule some precedents. Clarence Thomas is especially inclined to do so because he believes there is no reason to maintain a specific precedent or a line of Court doctrine if it is faulty. Exaggerating somewhat, Justice Scalia has said of Thomas that "he does not believe in *stare decisis*, period."[55] Indeed, Thomas has written a good many opinions in which he argues that a precedent in constitutional law should be overruled or at least reconsidered. Scalia has joined some of these opinions and authored similar ones himself.

All this may suggest that precedents carry no weight. Yet justices have a degree of reluctance—some more than others—to overturn precedents directly. The Court as a whole adheres to a good many precedents that no longer accord with the majority view among the justices. And justices sometimes announce in an opinion that they are following a relevant precedent even though they disagree with it. As Justice David Souter wrote in a 2009 opinion, "I am not through regretting that my position in" a 2003 case "did not carry the day. But it did not, and I agree that the precedent of that case calls for the result reached here." More dramatically, Justice Stevens in 2008 wrote an opinion announcing that he had come to the view that the death penalty was unconstitutional. But Stevens added that his conclusion did not "justify a refusal to respect precedents that remain a part of our law," and he voted to reject a challenge to Kentucky's method of execution.[56] Further, there is evidence that precedents shape justices' positions in cases by establishing the analytic frameworks that they use.[57]

The extent to which precedents influence justices is uncertain and a matter of dispute among commentators. However, precedents clearly have some effect. The rule of stare decisis does not control the Court's decisions, but it does structure and shape them. The same is true of the law in general: it channels justices' choices, often in subtle ways, but it also leaves them considerable freedom in making those choices.

Justices' Values

If the law leaves justices free to make choices largely on other bases, the most likely basis is their own values. And of those values the most salient are justices' policy preferences.

The importance of policy preferences is reflected in the process of selecting justices. Presidents and their advisers work hard to identify nominees who share the administration's views on major issues of legal policy. Interest groups support or oppose nominees on the basis of their perceived values. And senators are increasingly willing to vote against confirmation of a nominee whose ideological position seems distant from their own positions. All these people act on the assumption that justices' policy preferences have a powerful impact on the votes they cast and the opinions they write.

The Influence of Policy Preferences

It is difficult to ascertain the actual effect of justices' policy preferences on their behavior as decision makers, simply because their preferences cannot be observed directly. But some evidence strongly suggests that preferences exert a strong influence on justices' choices. There is considerable consistency between justices' expressions of personal views outside the Court and their votes and opinions in cases. Certainly this is true of the justices who speak and write most frequently about judicial issues, such as Stephen Breyer, Antonin Scalia, and Clarence Thomas. Further, justices' votes and opinions tend to be consistent with the positions they took on similar issues before their appointment.

Some scholars argue that justices' policy preferences are essentially a complete explanation of the Court's decisions.[58] In contrast, I think that justices' preferences exert their effects in combination with other important forces, especially the law. But policy preferences provide the best explanation for differences in the positions that the nine justices take in the same cases, because no other factor varies so much from one justice to another.

Justices' attitudes on policy issues result from the same influences that shape political attitudes generally. Family socialization, religious training, and career activities all can help mold the values of people who become Supreme Court justices. Justice John Paul Stevens directly acknowledged the effects of his own experiences. He described the impact of his military experience in World War II and the criminal conviction of his father for embezzlement (later overturned by the Illinois Supreme Court) on his attitudes toward issues of legal policy. And in a 2007 opinion Stevens brought his childhood recollection of Prohibition in Illinois to bear on the "war on drugs."[59] To a degree, the differences in justices' backgrounds and in what they learn from their experiences account for the differences in their attitudes about legal issues.

Justices' policy preferences could shape their behavior on the Court in two different ways. Justices might simply take positions in cases that best reflect their views of good policy. Alternatively, they might act strategically, departing from the positions they most prefer when doing so could advance the policies they favor. In Chapter 3 I discussed strategy in the selection of cases: justices might vote whether to hear cases on the basis of their predictions about how the Court would rule on those cases. In decisions on the merits strategic justices might write opinions that do not fully reflect their

Clarence Thomas, speaking as chair of the Equal Employment Opportunity Commission in the 1980s. Justices' policy preferences are shaped by their experiences prior to joining the Court.

own views in order to win the support of other justices. To take another example, the Court collectively could modify the legal rules it establishes in a case to reduce the chances that Congress will override the Court's decision and substitute a policy that most justices see as undesirable.

It is not clear to what extent justices behave strategically and what forms their strategies take.[60] But it appears that strategic considerations seldom move justices very far from the positions they most prefer. For this reason, the impact of justices' policy preferences can be considered initially without taking strategy into account. In the two sections that follow I will consider strategy aimed at other justices and at the Court's political environment.

The Ideological Dimension

On most issues that come to the Court, the opposing positions can be labeled as liberal and conservative. For this reason, justices' preferences, and the votes and opinions that reflect those preferences, may be understood in ideological terms.

Defining Liberal and Conservative Positions. The positions from which justices can choose are most easily defined on civil liberties issues. In this field, with some exceptions such as gun rights, the position more favorable to legal protection for liberties is considered liberal. Thus, the liberal position gives relatively heavy weight to people's right to equal treatment by government and private institutions, to procedural rights of criminal defendants and others who deal with government, and to substantive rights such as freedom of expression and privacy. In contrast, the conservative position gives relatively great weight to values that compete with these rights, such as effective law enforcement and national security.

Liberal and conservative positions on economic issues are somewhat more difficult to define. But the liberal position is basically more favorable to economic "underdogs" and to government policies that are intended to benefit underdogs. In contrast, the conservative position is more favorable to businesses in conflicts with labor unions and less favorable to government regulation of business practices.

Some cases that come before the Supreme Court, such as boundary disputes between states, do not have obvious liberal and conservative sides. On some other issues, including aspects of free expression, ideological lines in American society and thus in the Court have become more complicated. Still, most issues that the Court decides do have clearly defined conservative and liberal sides.

Ideology and the Justices' Positions. If opposing positions in most cases can be identified as liberal or conservative, the justices' voting patterns can be described in terms of the frequency with which they support the conservative side and the liberal side. Table 4-2 shows the ideological patterns of votes for the eight justices who served in both the 2009 and 2010 terms. The table shows that every justice cast a good many votes on both sides: each of the eight justices took liberal positions at least one-third of the time and conservative positions at least one-third of the time. But the justices also differed considerably in their proportions of liberal and conservative votes.

When justices respond differently to the same cases, the primary reason is differences in their policy preferences. Thus, one can conclude from Table 4-2 that Justice Alito is considerably more conservative than Justice Sotomayor. One piece of evidence for this conclusion is that the relative positions of the justices on a liberal-to-conservative scale tend to remain fairly stable from term to term. It is also true that the justices' relative positions tend to be similar across different issues. This similarity, however, is far from absolute. A justice who has one of the most liberal voting records on conflicts between business and labor might have a relatively conservative record on criminal justice.

Justices' relative ideological positions are reflected in the frequency with which they join the same opinions in a case. In the Court's 2010 term the mean rate of agreement on opinions between pairs of justices was 66

TABLE 4-2
Percentages of Liberal Votes
Cast by Justices, 2009–2010 Terms

Justice	Liberal votes
Sotomayor	59.9
Ginsburg	56.7
Breyer	56.5
Kennedy	42.1
Roberts	41.4
Scalia	39.2
Thomas	36.3
Alito	34.5

Source: Analysis of data in The Supreme Court Database (http://scdb.wustl.edu/).

Note: Cases are included if they were decided on the merits with full opinions and if votes could be classified as liberal or conservative. Criteria for classifying votes are those used in the database. Justice Stevens, who served only in the 2009 term, cast liberal votes 64.4 percent of the time; Justice Kagan, who served only in the 2010 term and who participated in about two-thirds of the cases in that term, cast liberal votes 55.6 percent of the time.

percent. The mean rate of agreement among the four most liberal justices was 83 percent; for the four most conservative justices it was 77 percent. In contrast, the mean rate of agreement between the four most liberal justices and the four most conservative justices was 54 percent.[61] To a small degree, rates of agreement on opinions may reflect self-conscious alliances or personal relationships, but they are primarily the result of similar policy preferences.

The general patterns of agreement and disagreement between the justices are reflected in the lineups of justices in individual cases. In the 2010 term, for instance, fourteen of the sixteen 5–4 decisions found either the four most liberal justices or the four most conservative justices dissenting, with Justice Kennedy joining one side or the other to create the majority in each case. (In ten of those fourteen cases, Kennedy joined the conservative side.)[62]

But divisions on the Court often diverge from ideological lines. In *Bullcoming v. New Mexico* (2011), for instance, the five-justice majority included three of the most liberal justices and two of the most conservative. That decision also illustrates how justices' ideological stances can vary across issues: Antonin Scalia and Clarence Thomas, relatively unfavorable to most kinds of constitutional claims by criminal defendants, are much more favorable to claims made under defendants' Sixth Amendment right to confront witnesses against them, including the claim that the defendant made in the *Bullcoming* case.

Observers of the Court regularly label justices not just in relative terms but in absolute terms as well: Justice Thomas is called a conservative, Justice Ginsburg a liberal. Because justices' votes in cases reflect several different forces, this conclusion does not follow directly from the patterns of votes. This is especially true because the proportions of liberal and conservative votes that a justice casts in a particular period reflect the mix of cases that the Court decides in that period. A justice with a strongly liberal voting record in one era might not have as liberal a record in a different era.

Still, the role of justices' policy preferences in their votes and opinions is sufficiently strong that those ideological labels seem appropriate. A justice who casts a preponderance of votes that can be characterized as conservative almost surely holds conservative views on most issues. Indeed, most justices who were perceived as strongly liberal or strongly conservative at the time of their appointment establish records on the Court that are consistent with those perceptions.[63]

Court Policy and Policy Change

If the positions of individual justices reflect their policy preferences, the collective decisions of the Court must also reflect the mix of preferences among the justices. When most of the justices are conservative, the Court will tend to make conservative decisions and move legal doctrine in a conservative direction.

The proportions of liberal and conservative decisions fluctuate from term to term, and that is even more true of the liberal-conservative balance in the Court's most visible decisions. Observers of the Court often make a good deal of this fluctuation, but it generally reflects the particular mix of cases that the Court decides each term rather than a shift in the Court's collective ideological position. Sometimes, however, that collective position does change, in the sense that the Court would decide the same cases differently from the way it would have decided them in an earlier term. As a result, there is change in the Court's policies in a specific policy area or in a broader field such as civil liberties.

If the Court's collective positions reflect the policy preferences of individual justices more than anything else, the primary source of changes in Court policies must be a shift in the preferences of the justices as a group. These shifts could come from change in the preferences of people already serving on the Court or from change in the Court's membership. In practice, both are significant but the second is more important.

Changes in Individual Preferences. Close observers of the Supreme Court often try to predict how the Court will decide a pending case; typically, they do rather well in their predictions. The primary reason is that individual justices tend to take stable positions on the issues that arise in various policy areas. The views that a justice expressed in past cases about when cars can be searched or when mergers of companies violate the antitrust laws are a good guide to the justice's stance in a future case. In turn, the Court's collective position on such issues generally remains stable as long as its membership remains unchanged.

But as members of the Court, justices are exposed to new influences and confront issues in new forms. The result may be a change in their policy preferences on specific issues. For instance, a few justices have reported that the process of deciding death penalty cases over the years has affected their views on the desirability of capital punishment.

It is difficult to ascertain whether justices have shifted in their overall ideological positions over time, but it is clear that most justices retain the same basic positions throughout their career. The liberal Ruth Bader Ginsburg and the conservative Clarence Thomas are good examples. When a justice's position shifts relative to that of the Court as a whole, it is usually because new appointments have moved the Court's ideological center while the justice has retained the same general views. This seemed to be true of John Paul Stevens, who was initially near the center of the Court but had the most liberal record of any justice in the second half of his Court career.

Justice Harry Blackmun was one of the few justices whose basic views seemed to change fundamentally. Blackmun came to the Court in 1970 as a Nixon appointee, and early in his tenure he aligned himself chiefly with the other conservative justices. He and Chief Justice Warren Burger, boyhood friends from Minnesota, were dubbed the "Minnesota Twins." In the 1973 term, Blackmun agreed with Burger on opinions in 84 percent of the Court's decisions and with the liberal William Brennan in only 49 percent.[64] Blackmun gradually moved toward the center of the Court, and from the 1980 term onward he usually had higher agreement rates with Brennan than with Burger. In 1985, Burger's last term, it was 30 percentage points higher. In the last few terms before his 1994 retirement, Blackmun had become one of the two most liberal justices on the Court.

This shift to the Court's left resulted in part from the replacement of liberal colleagues with conservatives, but Blackmun's own positions clearly became more liberal. Although the reasons for this change are uncertain, it appears that his experiences in dealing with cases that came to the Court—especially *Roe v. Wade*, in which he wrote the Court's opinion—were important.[65]

Perhaps more common than individual shifts are changes in the views of the justices as a group in a particular issue area. These changes typically result from developments in American society that shape the views of the population as a whole. One example concerns the legal status of women. The liberal Warren Court gave unprecedented support to the goal of equality under the law, but it did not strike down legal rules that treated women and men differently. In contrast, the more conservative Burger Court handed down a series of decisions promoting legal equality for men and women. Today, even the most conservative justices use a fairly rigorous standard to evaluate laws that treat women and men differently, a standard that no justice supported in the 1960s. The most fundamental cause of this change was the direct and indirect effect of the feminist movement on the Court's agenda and, even more, on justices' views about women's social roles. This example underlines the potential for significant changes in justices' collective views on policy issues.

Membership Change. In *Citizens United v. Federal Election Commission* (2010), the Supreme Court overruled two of its precedents that had allowed certain regulations of funding for political campaigns. In his dissenting opinion, Justice Stevens argued that "in the end, the Court's rejection of *Austin* and *McConnell* comes down to nothing more than its disagreement with their results. Virtually every one of its arguments was made and rejected in those cases, and the majority opinion is essentially an amalgamation of resuscitated dissents. The only relevant thing that has changed since *Austin* and *McConnell* is the composition of this Court."[66]

Whether or not Justice Stevens's general criticism of the decision was justified, he was surely right about the reason why the Court rejected the two precedents. In doing so, he underlined the importance of membership change. If the Court's policies are largely a product of the justices' preferences, and if those preferences tend to be stable, then the most common source of significant policy change is the arrival of new justices on the Court.

As the *Citizens United* decision illustrates, a change in the Court's membership sometimes alters its positions on specific issues. The overturning of a recent precedent usually results from the replacement of justices who helped create that precedent with others who disagree with it. Even when the Court maintains a precedent, a shift in membership may result in a narrower interpretation of the precedent. Retired justice Sandra Day O'Connor has said that the law "shouldn't change just because the faces on the court have changed,"[67] but frequently it does.

More broadly, shifts in the Court's overall ideological position through new appointments typically lead to change in the general content of its policies. The Court's civil liberties policies since the 1950s demonstrate this effect of membership change. The proportion of cases in which parties with civil liberties claims won in the Court peaked at 79 percent during the late Warren Court, in the 1962–1968 terms. That proportion fell below 45 percent in the 1970s, and it has remained at that lower level ever since. If change in the content of cases over time is taken into account, the Court's support for civil liberties claims has declined further with additional appointments by Republican presidents, reaching its lowest point over the past half-century in the Roberts Court.[68]

The early Warren Court was closely divided between liberals and conservatives on civil liberties issues. From 1958 until 1961 there was a relatively stable division between a four-member liberal bloc and a moderate-to-conservative bloc of five. By the standards of the 1920s and 1930s, the Court's decisions were quite liberal, but parties with civil liberties claims won only a little more than half their cases between 1958 and 1961.

President Kennedy's 1962 appointments created a liberal majority; a law clerk during the 1962 term referred to it as "a turning point in the modern history of the Supreme Court."[69] The Johnson appointments later in the decade maintained that majority. The 1962 through 1968 terms were probably the most liberal period in the Court's history. The Court established strikingly liberal positions in a variety of policy areas, and the proportion of pro–civil liberties decisions increased substantially.

Between 1969 and 1992 every appointment to the Court was made by a Republican president, and all but Ford sought to use their appointments to make the Court more conservative. Thus, the Court gained a distinctly more conservative set of justices. The effect of these membership changes on the Court's civil liberties policies was somewhat ambiguous. The Court adhered to some policies of the Warren Court and even took new liberal directions on a few issues such as women's rights. Yet, on the whole, the Burger Court was distinctly less supportive of civil liberties than the Court of the 1960s, and the early Rehnquist Court was even less supportive than the Burger Court.

Ruth Bader Ginsburg and Steven Breyer, selected by President Clinton, were the first appointees of a Democratic president since 1967. Best characterized as moderate liberals, they did not change the Court's ideological balance a great deal. The same has been true so far of President Obama's appointees Sonia Sotomayor and Elena Kagan, who succeeded two Republican appointees with relatively liberal records. In contrast, President George W. Bush's appointments of John Roberts and Samuel Alito moved the Court further to the right, where it has remained. That shift underlines the ability of presidents to shape the Supreme Court through the selection of justices.

Role Values

Policy preferences are not the only values that can affect the Court's decisions. Justices may also be influenced by their role values, their views about what constitutes appropriate behavior for the Supreme Court and its members. In any government body, whether it is a court or a legislature, members' conceptions of how they should carry out their jobs structure what they do.

A variety of role values can shape justices' behavior, including their views about the importance of consensus and about the legitimacy of "lobbying" colleagues on decisions. But the role values with the greatest potential impact are justices' beliefs about the considerations they should take into account in reaching their decisions and the acceptability of active intervention in the making of public policy.

It is clear that several different considerations affect justices' votes and opinions. The relative weight of these considerations depends in part on what justices think they ought to do. In particular, justices have to balance their strong policy preferences on many issues with the expectation of others (and themselves) that they will seek to interpret the law accurately.

Some evidence suggests that justices differ in the relative weights they give to these legal and policy considerations.[70] However, these differences are not as sharp as they sometimes appear. For example, at any given time, some justices vote more often than others to uproot some of the Court's precedents. To a degree, this difference reflects differing attitudes toward precedent. But more important are justices' attitudes toward the policies embodied in particular precedents. As noted earlier, justices are more inclined to overrule a precedent when the precedent runs counter to their general ideological position.

Active intervention in policymaking is often viewed negatively. Justices who seem eager to engage in that intervention are criticized as "activists," and those who seem less prone to do so are praised as "restrained." But activism, like the treatment of precedent, does not seem to differ all that much among justices.

The most visible form of active intervention in policymaking is striking down federal statutes. The historical patterns are illuminating. During the 1920s and early 1930s, the laws that the Court struck down were primarily government regulations of business practices. Conservative justices were the most willing to strike down such laws, and liberals on the Court and elsewhere argued for judicial restraint. In contrast, in the 1960s and 1970s, the Court struck down primarily laws that conflicted with civil liberties. Liberals were most likely to act against these laws and conservatives to call for judicial restraint.

Since the 1980s the Court has overturned a wide variety of federal laws. No justice has stood out for a willingness or unwillingness to strike down laws. Rather, justices have responded to the ideological content of the statutes in question. The same is true of the decisions in which the Court strikes down state laws on constitutional grounds.[71] In this respect the justices' decisions on whether to declare laws unconstitutional are similar to their decisions on whether to overrule precedents.

All this is not to say that justices' role values have no impact on their behavior. Undoubtedly, such values help to structure the ways in which justices perceive their jobs. But justices' conceptions of good public policy have a more fundamental impact on their choices.

Group Interaction

In the preceding section I spoke of justices as if they acted entirely on their own. But when justices make choices, they do so as part of a Court that makes collective decisions and as part of American government and society. Justices who seek to make good policy might act strategically by taking their colleagues and other institutions into account. Whether or not justices act strategically, they can be influenced in a variety of ways by other justices and by their political and social environment. This section examines the justices as a group, and the next section considers the Court's environment.

A Quasi-Collegial Body

In historical accounts of the Supreme Court some of the most dramatic events concern interactions among the justices in major cases. Newly appointed Chief Justice Earl Warren, engaging in what Justice Douglas called "a brilliant diplomatic process," moved the Court from sharp division to a unanimous decision in *Brown v. Board of Education* (1954).[72] The Court's decision in *Planned Parenthood v. Casey* (1992) reflected close collaboration among three justices on a joint opinion that determined the Court's position, with one of the three shifting position after the Court's initial vote and thereby preventing the Court from overturning *Roe v. Wade*.[73] In *Bush v. Gore* (2000), which ensured that George W. Bush would become president, the Court's decision came after intense interplay among the justices over the short period in which the Court considered the case.[74]

Those episodes are consistent with the image of the Court that many people hold, one in which justices constantly lobby each other over the cases before them and decisions reflect the persuasive powers of certain justices. For the most part, however, that image is false. For one thing, except for oral argument and conferences, there is only limited face-to-face interaction among justices in the decision-making process. Instead, they communicate chiefly in writing.

More fundamentally, the justices' influence on each other occurs within constraints—constraints that result from their strongly held views on many issues. When they apply their general positions on an issue to a specific case, the resulting judgment about that case may be too firm for colleagues to sway. As Justice Rehnquist wrote early in his tenure, when justices who have prepared themselves "assemble around the conference table on Friday morning to decide an important case presenting constitutional questions that they have all debated and written about before, the outcome may be a foregone conclusion."[75]

But justices' independence from each other should not be overstated. They have powerful incentives to work together, even if doing so requires them to modify their positions in cases. One reason is institutional: justices want to achieve opinions that at least five members endorse so that the Court lays down authoritative legal rules. And to give more weight to the Court's decisions, they generally would like to reach greater consensus.

A second reason is more personal: justices' interest in winning majority support for their positions creates a strong incentive to work with colleagues. Justices want the Court to adopt the legal rules they favor, and at least some justices get satisfaction from being on the winning side. Thus, justices have good reason to engage in efforts at persuasion. They also have reason to be flexible in the positions they take in cases, because flexibility can help them win colleagues' support for rules that are close to the ones they prefer.

These incentives are reflected in the negotiation process that was described in the first section of this chapter.[76] The most common course of events in a case is for a justice to write a draft opinion for the Court and then gain the support of a majority for that opinion with no difficulty. But other justices frequently ask for changes in the draft opinion, and most of the time justices who make these requests indicate that they cannot join the opinion unless the changes are made. The opinion author usually makes these changes.

Pamela Corley's analysis of Justice Harry Blackmun's papers from the late 1980s provides a sense of how this process works.[77] Blackmun's drafts of opinions for the Court frequently attracted memos from other members of the conference majority who disagreed with something in the draft. Blackmun nearly always made changes in the opinion in response to those memos. As a result, the colleagues who requested changes in the original draft usually joined Blackmun's final opinion; they wrote concurring opinions in only about 20 percent of those cases. The negotiations sometimes got complicated. In one case, Blackmun received conflicting suggestions from Antonin Scalia and Anthony Kennedy, and ultimately Scalia and Kennedy came up with a compromise that they and Blackmun could all accept. Not surprisingly, Blackmun became much less willing to accommodate colleagues when he had already secured majority support for his opinion.

Whether or not colleagues request changes in opinions for the Court, those opinions frequently are revised during the decision process. In the Burger Court, in slightly more than half of all cases the author of the Court's opinion circulated at least three drafts of the opinion.[78] Although successive drafts may differ only on minor matters, they sometimes proclaim quite different legal rules.

Beyond the content of opinions, the votes of individual justices on the case outcome can shift between the Court conference and the final decision. In the Burger Court, 7.5 percent of the justices' individual votes to reverse or affirm were switched from one side to the other, and at least one switch occurred in 37 percent of the cases. Most vote switches increase the size of the majority, as the Court works toward consensus. During the Burger Court, the justices who initially voted with the majority switched their votes 5 percent of the time, but those who initially voted with the minority switched 18 percent of the time.[79] Occasionally, however, shifts of position turn an initial minority into a majority. This occurred in about 7 percent of the cases decided by the Burger Court.[80]

The effects of interactions among the justices should not be exaggerated. After all, in the great majority of cases the side that won in the Court's first vote on the merits of the case wins in the final vote as well. Most of the majority opinions that the Court issues look similar to the original drafts of those opinions. But votes and opinions do change; the Court's decisions are often more than simply an adding together of the positions with which each justice began.

The similarity between the original draft and the final opinion in most cases suggests that the majority opinion author largely determines the legal rules that the Court lays down in its opinion. But as I have noted, sometimes the opinion changes a good deal as a result of interactions among justices. And even the original draft reflects the author's recognition of what other justices will find acceptable. Thus, it might be that the majority opinion author has little more influence than the other justices over the Court's doctrinal position in a case. Research on this issue so far has reached different conclusions, but as a whole it supports the view shared by most observers of the Court: the opinion author does have special influence over the content of the Court's opinion, but that influence falls well short of complete control.[81]

The group life of the Court has broader effects on its decisions as well. Interactions among the justices create general patterns of influence within the Court, and the extent of conflict among its members affects its ability to reach consensus. Both of these effects merit consideration.

Patterns of Influence

Because the justices' influence on each other is inherently limited, the influence of any specific justice also has limits. Justice O'Connor said, "I work with eight very strong-willed colleagues. I don't think that any of us exerts much power over the others."[82] Other members of the Court have expressed similar views.

Yet the justices do exert some influence over their colleagues, and inevitably some are more influential than others. In general, the primary requisites for influence are the same as in any other group: an interest in exerting influence and skill in doing so.

What we know now about justices who served in past eras underlines the importance of both these considerations. For instance, Justice William O. Douglas, who served for a record thirty-six years between 1939 and 1975, had relatively little influence because he made only limited efforts to achieve it. Douglas's long-time colleague Felix Frankfurter actively sought influence over his colleagues, and his eminence as a legal scholar should have put him in a good position to persuade his colleagues to his positions. But his weak interpersonal skills, especially his inability to hide his lack of respect for colleagues, worked against him. William Brennan, who served from 1956 to 1990, shared Frankfurter's strong interest in exerting influence, but he was far more skilled in working with colleagues. This skill helped Brennan in his efforts to forge a liberal majority for the expansion of civil liberties in the Warren Court and to limit the Court's conservative shift in the Burger Court.

Another source of influence is a justice's position on the ideological spectrum. The vote of a "swing" justice at the ideological center of the Court often will determine which side wins in cases that closely divide the Court along ideological lines. In itself, this does not mean that the swing justice is influential, because every justice in a 5–4 majority contributes to that result with one vote.

Still, swing justices do have a degree of influence because their positions are seen as relatively unpredictable and their support as crucial to the outcome of many cases. Lawyers work to devise arguments that appeal to the swing justice, and colleagues also work hard to win the support of that justice. Since 2006 Anthony Kennedy has clearly been the swing justice, because four justices are well to his ideological left and four others to his right. On a series of major decisions on issues such as abortion and the death penalty, he has created liberal or conservative majorities with his vote. As a result, lawyers and colleagues show considerable deference to him. One observer of the Court suggested in 2009 that "two blocs of four justices seem to spend much of their energy competing for the affections of the one in the middle"—Justice Kennedy.[83] In a 2009 oral argument, all four of the

Justice Anthony Kennedy, testifying before the House Appropriations Committee in 2011. As the justice who stands at the Court's ideological center, Kennedy receives considerable attention from lawyers and his colleagues.

liberal justices referred to questions that Kennedy had raised earlier in the argument, and Justice Breyer twice cited hypothetical examples that Kennedy had presented in a 2007 opinion.[84] Reporting on another oral argument, another observer reported that "as Kennedy speaks, Breyer nods so vigorously, I want to call in a chiropractor."[85]

With Kennedy or any other contemporary justice, it is very difficult to make the estimates of influence that are possible for justices from past eras, after accounts of the Court's workings have come out. For instance, some evidence suggests that Justice Scalia has had limited influence on his colleagues because of his unwillingness to compromise and his strongly worded attacks on other justices' positions in his opinions.[86] Yet he may well exert substantial influence on his colleagues through the force of his arguments on issues such as the use of legislative history to interpret statutes. What we do know is that today, as in most past eras, there are substantial limits to the influence of any member of the Court over the other justices.

The Chief Justice

Compared with other justices, the chief justice has both advantages and limitations in achieving influence over colleagues. One limitation stems from administrative duties, which reduce the time that the chief can spend on cases. More fundamental is the difficulty of leading colleagues who strongly resist control. When a reporter asked, "You can't tell Justice Scalia what to do?" Chief Justice Roberts responded, "You know, I don't think anybody can tell Justice Scalia what to do." More broadly, Roberts has said that "the chief's ability to get the Court to do something is really quite restrained."[87] Balanced against these limitations are the chief's formal powers, which provide at least a moderate advantage over the other justices in exerting influence.

The Chief Justice's Powers. The chief presides over the Court in oral argument and in conference. In conference the chief can direct discussion and frame alternatives, roles that may shape the outcome of the discussion. Most important, the chief ordinarily speaks first on a case in conference. Another power involves the discuss list, the set of petitions for hearing that the Court considers fully. The chief, aided by clerks, makes up the initial version of the discuss list. This task gives the chief the largest role in determining which cases are set aside without group discussion.

Opinion Assignment. Perhaps the most significant power of the chief justice is opinion assignment. The chief is in the majority and thus assigns the Court's opinion in the preponderance of cases. In making assignments chief justices balance different considerations.[88]

Administrative considerations relate to spreading the workload and opportunities among the justices. Chief justices generally try to make sure that each colleague gets about the same number of opinions for the Court, taking into account assignments from senior associate justices. And as Chief Justice Roberts put it, "You want to make sure everyone has their fair share of interesting cases and has their fair share of what we call the dogs, the uninteresting cases."[89] Chiefs may also take into account the workload of opinion writing that a justice already faces at a given time, a criterion that was especially important to Chief Justice Rehnquist. He wrote in 2001, "As the term goes on I take into consideration the extent to which the various justices are current in writing and circulating opinions that have previously been assigned." [90]

Other considerations relate to the substance of the Court's decisions. Because the legal rules proclaimed by the Court depend in part on who writes its opinion, chief justices tend to favor themselves and colleagues who are close to them ideologically when assigning opinions in the cases they care most about. The chief might also act to help the conference majority remain a majority. When there is a close vote at conference, the chief often assigns the opinion to a relatively moderate member of that majority. One reason is that a moderate may be in a good position to write an opinion that will maintain the majority and perhaps win over justices who were initially on the other side. Justice Ginsburg has pointed out a second, practical reason for assigning an opinion to the justice who is wavering the most in a 5–4 vote: if that justice shifts to the other side, he or she will remain in the majority and can still write the Court's opinion.[91]

Because chief justices favor ideological allies in assigning important opinions, in effect they reward the justices who vote with them the most often. They might also use the assignment power more directly to reward and punish colleagues. Chief Justice Roberts said in 2006 that "you can always give all the tax opinions to a justice, if you want to punish them."[92] Roberts added that he had not yet taken that kind of action. But according to Justice Blackmun, Chief Justice Burger might assign one of the "crud" opinions "that nobody wants to write" to a justice who was "in the doghouse" with Burger.[93]

Still more considerations can come into play. Justice Stevens gained the impression that Chief Justice Burger would assign himself opinions favoring freedom of expression claims in an effort to garner favorable reactions from the press. But in cases in which the Court ruled against those claims, Burger would assign the opinions to Byron White.[94] And Stevens confessed that when assigning cases as senior associate justice, he sometimes assigned himself an interesting case to keep the chief justice from assigning him a case from the same sitting that he wanted to avoid.[95]

Variation in Leadership. What particular chief justices make of their formal powers and the strength of their leadership vary a good deal. These differences result from several conditions, including the chief's interest in leading the Court, the chief's skill as a leader, and the willingness of the associate justices to be led.

Warren Burger was ambitious for leadership. He had some success in securing administrative changes in the federal courts and procedural changes in the Court itself. But he was not especially influential in the decision-making process.

Burger's limited impact on the Court's decisions stemmed largely from his own qualities and predilections. Colleagues chafed at what they considered a poor style of leadership in conference, and they disliked Burger's occasional practice of casting "false" votes so that he could assign the Court's opinion.[96] He was also accused of bullying his colleagues. One scholar concluded that Potter Stewart "loathed" Burger,[97] and other colleagues also disliked his leadership style. Apparently, they were not alone; Justice Marshall's messenger reported that when Burger retired, "it was just like Christmas morning."[98] But Burger also faced obstacles that were beyond his control. Perhaps most important, as a strong conservative he had the disadvantage of standing near one end of the Court's ideological spectrum.

William Rehnquist became chief justice in 1986 after serving on the Court for fifteen years. He brought important strengths to the position, especially his well-respected intellectual abilities and a pleasant manner of interaction with people.

Having served in the Burger Court as an associate justice, Rehnquist learned—in one observer's words—"how *not* to be Chief Justice."[99] In any event, Rehnquist was an effective chief justice, and his leadership was widely praised even by justices who did not share his conservative views on most judicial issues.[100] Reflecting his preferences, the Court's discussions of cases at conference were shorter and tighter than they had been in the recent past. Rehnquist's leadership was one source of the sharp decline in the number of cases accepted by the Court. In decision making he enhanced his influence by taking strong positions with an affable style.

John Roberts's effectiveness as chief justice will become clear only with time. Still, both colleagues and observers of the Court have already attested to his strengths. "With regard to all of his special responsibilities" as chief justice, Justice Stevens said, "John Roberts is an excellent chief justice." [101]

Yet Roberts's tenure thus far underlines the limits to the influence of the chief justice. From the start, he has emphasized his goal of achieving greater consensus in the Court's decisions, with more unanimous decisions and fewer separate opinions.[102] But this is a difficult task, because justices are accustomed to expressing their own views and feel reluctant to join opinions that diverge from those views. Justice Alito expressed agreement with Roberts's desire for unanimity, but not if it meant "endorsing something you don't believe in."[103] Justice Scalia's reaction was more pointed: "Lots of luck."[104] Indeed, in Roberts's first six terms the proportion of unanimous decisions was only 1 percentage point higher than it was in the Rehnquist Court, and the proportion of 5–4 and 5–3 decisions was 3 percentage points higher.[105] As this result indicates, even the most effective chief justice can achieve only limited influence over a set of highly independent colleagues.

Harmony and Conflict

In the Supreme Court, as in other work groups, some conditions favor harmonious relations among the justices but other conditions foster conflict. Harmony makes the Court a more pleasant place to work in, and it also helps the justices to achieve consensus in decisions. And justices who seek the support of colleagues for the positions they prefer want to maintain good relations with those colleagues. Still, all the sources of strife that exist in other groups can operate in the Court as well. The justices care a great deal about many of the issues they address in their decisions, issues on which they disagree with each other, and they often work under considerable pressure.

The justices' interest in achieving harmony is reflected in some of the ways the Court operates, especially the conduct of the Court's conferences. We would expect justices to express anger with each other at conferences at least occasionally, yet some of the justices serving in recent years have said that they have never observed such behavior. "I just finished my eighteenth term," Clarence Thomas said in 2009, "and I still haven't heard the first unkind word in that room."[106]

The harsh language in some concurring and dissenting opinions suggests a different picture. One study found significant numbers of opinions that charged colleagues with personal bias in a case or with making arguments they did not actually believe, although such opinions were exceptions to the general practice of putting disagreements in gentler terms.[107] Harsh opinions may reflect, or create, friction between justices. But a former law clerk for John Paul Stevens has reported that Antonin Scalia's frequent strong attacks on Stevens's opinions did not seem to bother Stevens, whose responses usually fell "somewhere between amusement and delight. . . . Never anger, not that I saw."[108] And Sonia Sotomayor said that based on her reading of the justices' opinions, she "was always a little bit dubious" about their claims that their disagreements were not personal. But after joining the Court, Sotomayor said, "I no longer am." She reported that "it is the level of respect and affection that surprised me."[109]

The character of relationships among the justices has varied over time. The current Court clearly is more harmonious than some of its predecessors, in which the justices' anger at each other came out openly at conferences and enmities among them impaired the Court's work. Noting that difference, in 2007 commentator Jeffrey Toobin pointed to what he saw as a second attribute of interpersonal relations in the current Court:

The justices are polite to and respectful of each other. . . . Yet there are few real friendships among them, either. They spend little time together outside of the Court. They do not shoot the breeze in each others' offices. This was not true at other times in the Court's history. There were times when several justices hated each other, and there were times when there were close friendships; neither has been true over the last two decades at the Court.[110]

There does seem to be at least one close friendship, between Antonin Scalia and Ruth Bader Ginsburg, a friendship that is noteworthy because of the ideological distance between them.[111] And Elena Kagan, also distant in views from Scalia, has joined him on hunting trips.[112] But Toobin's overall characterization of the Court accords with the perceptions of other observers. It may be that the personal distance among justices today helps to limit personal conflict. Whatever the reasons may be, the current

Court is more harmonious than several past Courts, in which some pairs of justices were actually unable to work with each other. The absence of such deep conflicts undoubtedly improves the functioning of the Court.

The Court's Environment

In comparison with Congress and the president, the Supreme Court is more isolated from the world around it and more insulated from the influence of that world. The isolation is reflected in the relatively limited contact between the justices and other participants in politics, such as members of Congress and representatives of interest groups. The primary source of insulation is the justices' life terms; no matter whom they displease, they can be removed from office only through impeachment proceedings, a quite unlikely prospect.

But the Court's isolation and insulation are far from total. Of course, justices interact with people outside the Court. Some interact a good deal with news reporters, the general public, and people who are active in politics, and these interactions have become more common in recent years. Certainly justices are aware of events and developments in American society. And even with life terms, they have reasons to care about what people think of them and their Court, reasons that range from concern about the Court's effectiveness as a policymaker to an interest in their personal standing in the legal community. Thus, the Court's environment—the world outside the Court—might affect the justices' choices as decision makers, and the potential influence of that environment merits consideration.

Mass Public Opinion

Supreme Court justices would seem to be especially free from influence by the general public. The public has no direct control over the Court, and the great majority of the Court's decisions are essentially invisible to the public. Yet some observers of the Court have argued that the justices pay attention to public opinion. As these observers see it, the justices listen to the public primarily because public support strengthens the Court's ability to secure acceptance of its decisions from public officials who are responsible for carrying out those decisions and who can limit or overturn them.

It is not clear that justices need to worry about maintaining public support. The Court is viewed more positively by the public than are the other branches of government, and even highly unpopular decisions have little long-term effect on public support for the Court as an institution. Yet justices themselves sometimes refer to the Court's need to act in ways that maintain its legitimacy with the general public, and they may perceive that the Court's public standing is more fragile than it actually is.

Further, justices might simply feel more comfortable when the Court's decisions and their own positions in cases garner approval from the general public. Justice John Paul Stevens wrote the Court's 2006 opinion that supported cities' right to take over residential areas for development projects through their eminent domain powers. Five years later, and a year after his retirement, Justice Stevens gave a law school lecture in which he acknowledged the great unpopularity of that decision and sought to refute the criticisms it had received. Clearly, disapproval of the decision continued to bother him.[113]

If the justices do take public opinion into account when they decide cases, one effect might be to draw them to support the majority view in the public on cases and issues that many people know and care about. Major decisions on questions such as constitutional protection for gun rights and the states' power to enforce immigration laws attract considerable attention, and the justices might be swayed consciously or unconsciously to take what they perceive as the more popular side. Most individual decisions that interpret the procedural rights of criminal defendants garner little public attention, but in deciding those cases justices still might recognize and respond to public skepticism about the value of interpreting defendants' rights broadly.

Some observers argue that the justices collectively do fall in step with public opinion on major issues. "Time and time again," one legal scholar has said, the Court's decisions "plainly reflect the tug of public views."[114] Yet the Court sometimes makes highly unpopular decisions, even when reactions to earlier decisions have made it clear that a decision will arouse strong disapproval. That has been the case, for instance, with its rulings on school prayer and flag burning.[115] It is very difficult to determine whether a concern with public opinion has deterred the Court from making such unpopular decisions even more often.

Another possible effect of concern with public opinion is more subtle but also more pervasive. It might be that as the general public moves left or right on an ideological scale, the Court moves along with it to avoid straying too far from public opinion in its decisions as a whole. Indeed, some studies have found a tendency for the Court and the public to move in the same ideological direction over time. But even if that tendency exists, it is uncertain whether the justices are being pulled along by the public or whether the justices and the public are responding in the same way to developments in government and society.[116]

The same is true of the justices' decisions in particular areas of public policy. To take one example, since the 1980s the Court has addressed a wide range of cases involving conflicts between individual liberties and the government's interest in controlling illegal drugs. For the most part, the Court has approved the government policies in question. It might be that the justices have sought to align themselves with a public that strongly supports the government's "war on drugs." But it is at least as likely that most justices simply shared the views of the public.

That point applies to specific decisions as well. It is noteworthy that on issues for which opinion surveys are available, the Court's decisions agree with the majority of the public more often than not.[117] But potential decisions that most people would dislike usually run contrary to the justices' own preferences. Almost surely, the tendency for the Court to take positions that most people favor reflects a similarity of attitudes between the public and the Court more than public influence on the Court.

Justices' interest in maintaining public support for the Court might manifest itself in other ways. Perhaps they seek to minimize the number of laws they strike down to avoid the appearance of judicial activism. Perhaps Chief Justice Roberts's decisive vote to uphold the most controversial provision of the 2010 federal health care law in 2012 reflected his concern about the effect on the Court's image if it struck down a major law on a party-line vote. But such effects of public opinion are likely to operate only at the margins. On the whole justices seem largely independent of the public, and certainly they are quite independent in comparison with elected officials.

Elite Opinion: Friends and Acquaintances, the Legal Community, and the News Media

Whether or not the justices respond to public opinion, they can be influenced by more specific sets of relevant people. One set is the justices' personal friends and acquaintances. We would expect the justices, like other people, to pay attention to the views of those who are most important to them. If most of the people who are close to a justice share a strong point of view about certain issues that come before the Court, they may exert a subtle influence on the justice to take positions consistent with that point of view.

The legal community is important as a professional reference group. Justices draw many of their acquaintances from this community. Most justices interact a good deal with practicing lawyers, law professors, and lower-court judges, and most of the justices' public appearances are before legal groups. Lawyers are also the primary source of expert evaluations of the Court, often presented in the law reviews that law schools publish. Scrutiny by the legal community helps to make legal considerations important to the justices in reaching decisions. And if a particular view of legal issues is dominant among lawyers or in a segment of the bar with which a justice identifies, the justice may be drawn toward that dominant view.

Law reviews can have another kind of impact as well. Because law review articles are often discussed in briefs, they constitute one source of the information that enters into the Court's decisions. Justices frequently cite law review articles in support of their positions, and on occasion the material in articles may affect their positions.

The news media may also be important to the justices. The media are the public's primary source of information about the Court, so they can shape public attitudes toward the justices. And whether or not the news media influence public views of the Court, justices understandably prefer to be depicted positively rather than negatively in news reports. For these reasons, justices pay attention to coverage of the Court. In 2006, for instance, Justice Kennedy criticized newspaper editorial writers for their coverage, asking members of a legal group to suggest "that they read the opinions before they write their editorials."[118] These considerations may explain the justices' increased willingness to give interviews to reporters for the print media and to appear on television.

Most of the people in the justices' personal circles, the legal community, and the news media are from elite groups in American society. To the extent that these elites have a distinctive point of view, they may move justices toward that point of view. Indeed, some conservative commentators have argued that the desire to win praise from legal scholars, reporters who write about the Court, and other elites caused some Republican appointees to the Court to become more liberal during their tenure as justices.[119]

But political polarization in recent years has created distinct groupings of legal scholars and news outlets, among others, on both the left and the right. Justices who seek approval from elite groups could gain widespread approval from either liberal or conservative segments of the elite, reinforcing their own ideological leanings. It may be, then, that justices today respond to quite different subsets of the political and social elites in the United States. In any event, this segment of society almost surely has greater influence on the justices than does the public as a whole.[120]

Litigants and Interest Groups

Simply by bringing cases to the Supreme Court, litigants, interest groups, and the lawyers who represent them influence the Court's policies. Once the Court has accepted a case, litigants and interest groups may influence its decision on the merits through advocacy in written briefs and oral arguments.

Certainly, justices pay attention to the material provided by litigants and interest groups. Opinions for the Court address the arguments raised by the parties to the case, they make use of language in the parties'

Justice Antonin Scalia at the 25th Anniversary celebration for the Federalist Society, a conservative group in the legal community. Justices may be reinforced in their views by groups that share those views.

briefs,[121] and they often refer to amicus briefs. Controlling for other factors, the number of amicus briefs on each side has a meaningful effect on the outcome of cases.[122] One reason is that new information and arguments presented by amici sometimes persuade the justices. In a 2009 case involving the placement of private monuments in public parks, for instance, amicus briefs seemed to persuade the justices that local governments would face great difficulties if they lost control over the choice of monuments.[123] When justices question lawyers closely during oral argument, they are often looking for responses to strong arguments by the other side. Therefore, the way lawyers frame arguments in a case can affect the justices' thinking and ultimately their decisions.

Justices may react to the identities of the litigants or amici themselves rather than just the arguments they present. Individual justices may have positive or negative attitudes toward particular interest groups or companies, but the federal government is probably in the best position to benefit from favorable perceptions of the justices. The government enjoys a high rate of success as a party and amicus in the Court's decisions on the merits, 73 percent in the 2006–2010 terms.[124] In part, that success rate reflects the agreement of conservative justices with the government's positions on issues such as criminal justice. Another source of the government's success is the expertise of the advocates in the solicitor general's office. But the justices' sympathies for the government's interests may also play a part.

Thus, the identities of the participants in cases may influence the Court, and the arguments they make certainly have an effect. But neither influence is as strong as justices' preexisting attitudes toward the issues they address. Whatever influence the federal government has over the Court, the government wins the justices' support far more often when its arguments accord with their ideological positions than when the two conflict.[125]

Congress and the President

Policymakers elsewhere in government take actions that affect the Court and the impact of its policies. Because of this effect, justices may take those policymakers into account when they reach decisions. The president and Congress are especially important to the Court, so they have the greatest potential influence on the Court's decisions.

Congress. Congressional powers over the Court range from overriding the Court's interpretations of statutes to controlling salary increases for the justices. Because of this array of powers, justices have some reason to consider congressional reactions to their decisions. Relations with Congress can affect their prestige and their comfort. And justices who think strategically in a broad sense, who care about the impact of the Court's policies, want to avoid congressional actions that undercut those policies.

If justices do act strategically toward Congress, one potential form of strategy involves decisions that interpret federal statutes. These decisions are more vulnerable than the Court's interpretations of the Constitution because Congress and the president can override them simply by enacting a new statute. Indeed, Congress considers such overrides quite frequently, and it actually enacts them fairly often.

For this reason, justices might try to calculate whether their preferred interpretation of a statute would be sufficiently unpopular in Congress to produce an override. If so, justices would modify their interpretation to make it more acceptable to members of Congress and thereby avoid an override. By making this implicit compromise with Congress, the justices could get the best possible result under the circumstances—not the interpretation of a statute that they favor the most but one that is closer to their preferences than the new statute that Congress would enact to override the Court's decision. It may be, however, that most justices are not bothered much when Congress overrides their decisions. Or justices might find it so difficult to predict overrides that little can be gained by trying to make those predictions.

It is not yet clear how often justices pursue this strategic approach.[126] One possibility is that they do so selectively, when they perceive that a decision disfavored by Congress is a very good candidate for an override. If so, to take one example, justices might be wary of handing down highly conservative statutory decisions on issues such as civil rights when the president is a Democrat and both houses of Congress have solid Democratic majorities.

Occasionally, a conflict between the Court and Congress goes much deeper than disagreement over the meaning of statutes. During a few periods in the Court's history, its general line of policy aroused so much dissatisfaction in Congress that there was a serious threat of concrete action against the Court itself. It may be that at least some justices take care to avoid creating such conflicts. It is more likely that justices act to reduce the threat of negative congressional action in periods when serious conflicts actually arise.

The first such period was the early nineteenth century, when Chief Justice John Marshall's Court faced congressional attacks because of its policies. As the Court's dominant member, Marshall was careful to limit the frequency of decisions that would further anger the Court's opponents. In the late 1930s the Court's shift from opposition to support of New Deal legislation may have reflected an effort by one or two justices to end a serious confrontation with the other branches. In the late 1950s members of Congress reacted to the Court's expansions of civil liberties by seeking to override its policies and limit its jurisdiction. A few justices shifted their positions on some contentious issues. As a result, the Court reversed some of its collective positions and thereby helped to quiet congressional attacks on the Court.

The period since the 1950s has featured strong attacks on the Court by members of Congress in response to decisions on a variety of civil liberties issues, including school desegregation, legislative districting, abortion, school prayer, and flag burning. On each of these issues, members have denounced the Court and introduced bills to overturn the Court's decisions, to limit its jurisdiction over the issue, or both. There have also been proposals to attack the Court more broadly, such as constitutional amendments that would limit the justices' tenure to a set number of years. However, Congress has adopted no measures that would take strong action against the Court, such as narrowing of its jurisdiction or a constitutional amendment to overturn a decision.

Despite the absence of strong action against the Court, it is possible that the attacks in themselves have had some effect on the Court's decisions.[127] Yet the Court has adhered to many of the policies that aroused these attacks. Although it changed some of these policies when new appointments made the Court more conservative, there have been no clear retreats in response to congressional pressure since the 1950s—even when that pressure coincided with heavy criticism of the Court from other quarters.

The President. Presidents have multifaceted relationships with the Supreme Court, and these relationships provide several sources of potential influence. Two of these sources, discussed already, are the power to appoint justices and the government's major role in Supreme Court litigation. The appointment power gives presidents considerable ability to determine the Court's direction. The president helps to shape the federal government's litigation policy and thereby influences the Court's decisions through appointment of the solicitor general and occasional intervention in specific cases.

Presidents have other ways to influence the justices. The most important derives from the president's impact on other institutions. Because of their visibility and prestige, presidents may shape the public's view of the Court and its decisions. They also influence responses to the Court's decisions by Congress and the federal bureaucracy. For these reasons, justices have an incentive to keep the peace with the president.

It is difficult to say how much effect this incentive has had. To the extent that presidents have fared well in the Court, that success seems to result chiefly from other factors such as their appointment power and the tendency of the other branches to defer to the president in foreign policy. But it may be that at the margins, some justices favor the president in some decisions because they take the president's powers over the Court into account.

Conclusion

Of all the considerations that influence the Supreme Court's decisions, the justices' policy preferences appear to be the most important. The application of the law to the Court's cases is usually ambiguous, and constraints from the Court's environment are generally weak. As a result, justices have considerable freedom to take positions that accord with their own conceptions of good policy. For this reason, the Court's membership has the greatest impact on the Court's direction.

If justices' preferences explain a great deal, they do not explain everything. The law and the political environment rule out some possible options for the Court, and they influence the justices' choices among the options that remain. The group life of the Court affects the behavior of individual justices and the Court's collective decisions. In particular, justices frequently adjust their positions in cases to win support from colleagues and help build majorities. Factors other than policy preferences are reflected in results that might seem surprising—strikingly liberal decisions from conservative Courts and the maintenance of precedents even when most justices no longer favor the policies they embody.

Thus, what the Court does is a product of multiple and intertwined forces. These forces can be discussed one at a time, but ultimately they operate together in complicated ways to shape the Court's decisions. Efforts to understand why the Court does what it does must take into account the complexity of the process by which the justices make their choices.

NOTES

1. *Nevada Commission on Ethics v. Carrigan*, 180 L. Ed. 2d 150, 161 (2011).
2. An example is *McNeill v. United States* (2011).
3. The cases were *Florida v. Department of Health and Human Services* (2012); *U.S. Department of Health and Human Services v. Florida* (2012); and *National Federation of Independent Business v. Sebelius* (2012).
4. Timothy R. Johnson, Ryan C. Black, and Justin Wedeking, "Pardon the Interruption: An Empirical Analysis of Supreme Court Justices' Behavior during Oral Arguments," *Loyola Law Review* 55 (2009): 331–351.
5. *Hosanna-Tabor Evangelical Lutheran Church v. Equal Employment Opportunity Commission*, 10-553, Transcript of oral argument, October 5, 2011, 45.
6. Brian Lamb, Susan Swain, and Mark Farkas, eds., *The Supreme Court: A C-Span Book Featuring the Justices in Their Own Words* (New York: PublicAffairs, 2010), 157.
7. "Remarks by Chief Justice John Roberts at the Fourth Circuit Court of Appeals' Judicial Conference," Federal News Service, June 27, 2009.
8. *Harrison v. Bell*, 07-8521, Transcript of oral argument, January 12, 2009, 40.
9. Lamb, Swain, and Farkas, *The Supreme Court*, 93–94.
10. Jay Reeves, "Thomas to Other Supreme Court Justices: Hush!" Associated Press, October 23, 2009.
11. Timothy R. Johnson, Ryan C. Black, Jerry Goldman, and Sarah A. Treul, "Inquiring Minds Want to Know: Do Justices Tip Their Hands with Questions at Oral Argument in the U.S. Supreme Court?" *Washington University Journal of Law & Policy* 29 (2009): 241–261; Ryan C. Black, Sarah A. Treul, Timothy R. Johnson, and Jerry Goldman, "Emotions, Oral Arguments, and Supreme Court Decision Making," *Journal of Politics* 73 (April 2011): 572–581.
12. *Lafler v. Cooper*, 10-209, Transcript of oral argument, October 31, 2011, 13.
13. Lamb, Swain, and Farkas, "The Supreme Court," 61, 132.
14. Garrett Epps, "Justice Scalia Turns to 18th-Century Wisdom for Guidance on GPS," *The Atlantic* online, January 24, 2012, http://www.theatlantic .com/technology/archive/2012/01/justice-scalia-turns-to-18th-century-wisdom-for-guidance-on-gps/251883/.
15. William H. Rehnquist, *The Supreme Court*, New ed. (New York: Knopf, 2001), 258.
16. Lamb, Swain, and Farkas, *The Supreme Court*, 94.

17. Ibid., 25.
18. Ibid., 63.
19. The process of responding to draft majority opinions is described in Forrest Maltzman, James F. Spriggs II, and Paul J. Wahlbeck, *Crafting Law on the Supreme Court: The Collegial Game* (New York: Cambridge University Press, 2000), 62–72.
20. Ralph A. Rossum, *Antonin Scalia's Jurisprudence: Text and Tradition* (Lawrence: University Press of Kansas, 2006), ix.
21. Kevin Merida and Michael A. Fletcher, "Thomas v. Blackmun: Late Jurist's Papers Puncture Colleague's Portrait of a Genteel Court," *Washington Post*, October 10, 2004, A15.
22. Clare Cushman, *Courtwatchers: Eyewitness Accounts in Supreme Court History* (Lanham, MD: Rowman & Littlefield, 2011), 198–199.
23. *Citizens United v. Federal Election Commission*, 175 L. Ed. 2d 753, 818 (2010).
24. The cases were *Milner v. Department of the Navy* (2011) and *Microsoft Corporation v. i4i Limited Partnership* (2011), respectively.
25. *Connick v. Thompson* (2011).
26. *Federal Communications Commission v. AT&T Inc.*, 179 L. Ed. 2d 132, 142 (2011).
27. Jeffrey S. Rosenthal and Albert H. Yoon, "Judicial Ghostwriting: Authorship on the Supreme Court," *Cornell Law Review* 96 (2011): 1307–1343.
28. Ryan J. Owens and Justin P. Wedeking, "Justices and Legal Clarity: Analyzing the Complexity of U.S. Supreme Court Opinions," *Law & Society Review* 45 (2011): 1027–1061.
29. Ryan C. Black and James F. Spriggs II, "An Empirical Analysis of the Length of U.S. Supreme Court Opinions," *Houston Law Review* 45 (2008): 632–638; Adam Liptak, "Justices Long on Words but Short on Guidance," *New York Times*, November 18, 2010, A22.
30. *Sykes v. United States*, 180 L. Ed. 2d 60, 82 (2011).
31. *PLIVA, Inc. v. Mensing*, 180 L. Ed. 2d 580, 597, 611 (2011).
32. Walter Dellinger, "Showtime for the Supremes," *Slate Magazine*, June 28, 2004, http://www.slate.com/.
33. Jill Duffy and Elizabeth Lambert, "Dissents from the Bench: A Compilation of Oral Dissents by U.S. Supreme Court Justices," *Law Library Journal* 102 (2010): 7–37; William D. Blake and Hans J. Hacker, "'The Brooding Spirit of the Law': Supreme Court Justices Reading Dissents from the Bench," *Justice System Journal* 31 (2010): 1–25; Timothy R. Johnson, Ryan C. Black, and Eve M. Ringsmuth, "Hear Me Roar: What Provokes Supreme Court Justices to Dissent from the Bench?" *Minnesota Law Review* 93 (May 2009): 1560–1581.
34. See Richard L. Pacelle Jr., Brett W. Curry, and Bryan W. Marshall, *Decision Making by the Modern Supreme Court* (New York: Cambridge University Press, 2011).
35. U.S. Senate, *Confirmation Hearing on the Nomination of John G. Roberts, Jr. to be Chief Justice of the United States*, 109th Cong., 1st sess., 2005, 55; U.S. Senate, *Confirmation Hearing on the Nomination of Hon. Sonia Sotomayor, to be an Associate Justice of the Supreme Court of the United States*, 111th Cong., 1st sess., 2009, 59; U.S. Senate, *The Nomination of Elena Kagan to be an Associate Justice of the Supreme Court of the United States*, 111th Cong., 2nd sess., 2010, 103.
36. Chris Dickerson, "Thomas Talks Courts, Sports at Marshall," *West Virginia Record*, September 12, 2007.

37. Sonia Sotomayor, "Landon Lecture," Kansas State University, January 27, 2011, http://www.k-state.edu/media/newsreleases/landonlect/sotomayortext127.html. See William Blake, "Umpires as Legal Realists," *P.S.: Political Science & Politics* 45 (April 2012): 271–276.

38. Norman I. Silber, *With All Deliberate Speed: The Life of Philip Elman* (Ann Arbor: University of Michigan Press, 2004), 51.

39. Jeffrey A. Segal and Harold J. Spaeth, *The Supreme Court and the Attitudinal Model Revisited* (New York: Cambridge University Press, 2002), chap. 2.

40. Walter Murphy, *Elements of Judicial Strategy* (Chicago: University of Chicago Press, 1964), 44n. See Jack Knight and Lee Epstein, "The Norm of Stare Decisis," *American Journal of Political Science* 40 (November 1996): 1018–1035.

41. Evidence of the impact of law is discussed and presented in Stefanie A. Lindquist and David E. Klein, "The Influence of Jurisprudential Considerations on Supreme Court Decision Making: A Study of Conflict Cases," *Law & Society Review* 40 (2006): 135–161; and Michael A. Bailey and Forrest Maltzman, *The Constrained Court: Law, Politics, and the Decisions Justices Make* (Princeton, N.J.: Princeton University Press, 2011), chaps. 4, 5.

42. *New York State Board of Elections v. Lopez Torres,* 552 U.S. 196, 209 (2008).

43. Jeffrey L. Kirchmeier and Samuel A. Thumma, "Scaling the Lexicon Fortress: The United States Supreme Court's Use of Dictionaries in the Twenty-First Century," *Marquette Law Review* 94 (Fall 2010): 77–261.

44. *Kasten v. Saint-Gobain Performance Plastics Corporation* (2011).

45. *Bolling v. Sharpe* (1954).

46. *Gitlow v. New York* (1925); *Cantwell v. Connecticut* (1940).

47. *Hans v. Louisiana* (1890).

48. James J. Brudney and Corey Ditslear, "The Decline and Fall of Legislative History? Patterns of Supreme Court Reliance in the Burger and Rehnquist Eras," *Judicature* 89 (January–February 2006): 220–229.

49. Carl Smith, "Quizzing Justice," *The Reflector* (Mississippi State University), January 25, 2008; Sally Friedman, "Supreme Court Justice Ginsburg Advocates Women Pursuing Law," *Philadelphia Bulletin,* March 11, 2008. An apparent typographical error in the Scalia quotation was corrected.

50. The decisions were *Atkins v. Virginia* (2002); *Roper v. Simmons* (2005); and *Kennedy v. Louisiana* (2008).

51. Barry Friedman, "The Wages of Stealth Overruling (With Particular Attention to *Miranda v. Arizona*)," *Georgetown Law Journal* 99 (November 2010): 1–63.

52. Congressional Research Service, *The Constitution of the United States of America: Analysis and Interpretation* (Washington, DC: Government Printing Office, 2004), 2392–2399; *2008 Supplement* (Washington, DC: Government Printing Office, 2008), 169; Kenneth Jost, "The 2008-2009 Term Analyzed" and "The 2009-2010 Term Analyzed," *Supreme Court Yearbook,* Online ed. (Washington, DC: CQ Press, 2009 and 2010, respectively). In many of these decisions, the Court overruled multiple precedents.

53. Harold J. Spaeth and Jeffrey A. Segal, *Majority Rule or Minority Will: Adherence to Precedent on the U.S. Supreme Court* (New York: Cambridge University Press, 1999); Allison Orr Larsen, "Perpetual Dissents," *George Mason Law Review* 15 (2008): 447–478.

54. The decisions were *Montejo v. Louisiana* (2009) and *Citizens United v. Federal Election Commission* (2010).

55. Ken Foskett, *Judging Thomas: The Life and Times of Clarence Thomas* (New York: Morrow, 2004), 281.

56. The decisions were *United States v. Navajo Nation*, 556 U.S. 287, 302 (2009) and *Baze v. Rees*, 553 U.S. 35, 87 (2008), respectively.

57. Mark J. Richards and Herbert M. Kritzer, "Jurisprudential Regimes in Supreme Court Decision Making," *American Political Science Review* 96 (June 2002): 305–320; Brandon L. Bartels, "The Constraining Capacity of Legal Doctrine on the U.S. Supreme Court," *American Political Science Review* 103 (August 2009): 474–495.

58. A good example is Segal and Spaeth, *Supreme Court and the Attitudinal Model Revisited* (Cambridge, MA: Cambridge University Press, 2002).

59. Diane Marie Amann, "John Paul Stevens, Human Rights Judge," *Fordham Law Review* 74 (2006): 1582–1583; Ken Kobayashi, "Justice Stevens Recalls War Years in Honolulu," *Honolulu Advertiser*, July 20, 2007; Jeffrey Rosen, "The Dissenter," *New York Times Magazine*, September 23, 2007, 54; *Morse v. Frederick*, 551 U.S. 393, 447–448 (2007).

60. For two competing positions, see Lee Epstein and Jack Knight, *The Choices Justices Make* (Washington, DC: CQ Press, 1998); and Saul Brenner and Joseph M. Whitmeyer, *Strategy on the United States Supreme Court* (New York: Cambridge University Press, 2009).

61. Data on rates of agreement are from "The Statistics," *Harvard Law Review* 125 (November 2011): 364.

62. Ibid., 368.

63. Jeffrey A. Segal, Lee Epstein, Charles M. Cameron, and Harold J. Spaeth, "Ideological Values and the Votes of Justices Revisited," *Journal of Politics* 57 (August 1995): 812–823.

64. Figures on agreement between Blackmun and his colleagues are taken from the annual statistics on the Supreme Court term in the November issues of *Harvard Law Review*, vols. 85–100 (1972–1987). See also "The Changing Social Vision of Justice Blackmun," *Harvard Law Review* 96 (1983): 717–736.

65. See Linda Greenhouse, *Becoming Justice Blackmun: Harry Blackmun's Supreme Court Journey* (New York: Times Books, 2005).

66. *Citizens United v. Federal Election Commission*, 175 L. Ed. 2d 753, 829 (2010).

67. Hope Yen, "O'Connor: Supreme Court Rulings Shouldn't Differ Based on Who Sits on Court," Associated Press, May 20, 2007.

68. The percentages of pro–civil liberties decisions are based on analysis of data in The Supreme Court Database, http://scdb.wustl.edu/. The unit of analysis is the case citation. Civil liberties cases are those in issue areas 1–6. The technique for taking change in the content of cases into account is described in Lawrence Baum, "Measuring Policy Change in the U.S. Supreme Court," *American Political Science Review* 82 (September 1988): 905–912.

69. Richard A. Posner, "A Tribute to Justice William J. Brennan, Jr.," *Harvard Law Review* 104 (November 1990): 13.

70. Bailey and Maltzman, *The Constrained Court*, chaps. 4, 5.

71. Lori A. Ringhand, "Judicial Activism," *Constitutional Commentary* 24 (2007): 48–63.

72. See Richard Kluger, *Simple Justice: The History of* Brown v. Board of Education *and Black America's Struggle for Equality* (New York: Knopf,

1976), 582–699. The quotation is from William O. Douglas, *The Court Years, 1939–1975: The Autobiography of William O. Douglas* (New York: Random House, 1980), 115.

73. David G. Savage, "The Rescue of Roe vs. Wade," *Los Angeles Times*, December 13, 1992, A1, A28, A29.

74. David Margolick, "Bush's Court Advantage," *Vanity Fair*, December 2003, 144–162; Jan Crawford Greenburg, *Supreme Conflict: The Inside Story of the Struggle for Control of the United States Supreme Court* (New York: Penguin Press, 2007), 174–177.

75. William H. Rehnquist, "Chief Justices I Never Knew," *Hastings Constitutional Law Quarterly* 3 (Summer 1976): 647.

76. See Maltzman, Spriggs, and Wahlbeck, *Crafting Law on the Supreme Court.*

77. Pamela C. Corley, "Bargaining and Accommodation on the United States Supreme Court: Insight from Justice Blackmun," *Judicature* 90 (January–February 2007): 157–165.

78. Maltzman, Spriggs, and Wahlbeck, *Crafting Law on the Supreme Court,* 116.

79. Forrest Maltzman and Paul J. Wahlbeck, "Strategic Policy Considerations and Voting Fluidity on the Burger Court," *American Political Science Review* 90 (September 1996): 587.

80. Segal and Spaeth, "Supreme Court and the Attitudinal Model Revisited," 286.

81. Chris W. Bonneau, Thomas H. Hammond, Forrest Maltzman, and Paul J. Wahlbeck, "Agenda Control, the Median Justice, and the Majority Opinion on the U.S. Supreme Court," *American Journal of Political Science* 51 (October 2007): 890–905; Jeffrey R. Lax and Kelly T. Rader, "Bargaining Power in the Supreme Court" (New York: Department of Political Science, Columbia University, 2011).

82. Sandra Day O'Connor, *The Majesty of the Law* (New York: Random House, 2003), 195.

83. Linda Greenhouse, "Every Justice Creates a New Court," *New York Times,* May 27, 2009, A25.

84. *Ricci v. DeStefano,* 07-1428, Transcript of oral argument, April 22, 2009, 12, 14, 15, 20, 22, 24, 49, 50.

85. Dahlia Lithwick, "Button It," *Slate Magazine,* October 11, 2006, http://www.slate.com/.

86. Joan Biskupic, *American Original: The Life and Constitution of Supreme Court Justice Antonin Scalia* (New York: Farrar, Strauss, & Giroux, 2009), 131, 132, 277, 354.

87. Jan Crawford Greenburg, "Interview with Chief Justice Roberts," November 28, 2006, http://abcnews.go.com/Nightline/story?id=2661589&page=12#.T6d1bVJYK9s; Jeffrey Rosen, "Roberts's Rules," *The Atlantic,* January/February 2007, 105.

88. This discussion of criteria for opinion assignment is based largely on the findings for the 1953–1990 period in Forrest Maltzman and Paul J. Wahlbeck, "A Conditional Model of Opinion Assignment on the Supreme Court," *Political Research Quarterly* 57 (December 2004): 551–563; Forrest Maltzman and Paul J. Wahlbeck, "May It Please the Chief? Opinion Assignments in the Rehnquist Court," *American Journal of Political Science* 40 (May 1996): 421–443; and Paul J. Wahlbeck, "Strategy and Constraints on Supreme Court Opinion Assignment," *University of Pennsylvania Law Review* 154 (2006): 1729–1755.

89. Greenburg, "Interview with Chief Justice Roberts."

90. Rehnquist, "Supreme Court," 260.

91. Bill Barnhart and Gene Schlickman, *John Paul Stevens: An Independent Life* (DeKalb: Northern Illinois University Press, 2010), 230.

92. Greenburg, "Interview with Chief Justice Roberts."

93. Ruth Marcus, "Alumni Brennan, Blackmun Greet Harvard Law Freshmen," *Washington Post*, September 6, 1986, 2.

94. John Paul Stevens, *Five Chiefs: A Supreme Court Memoir* (New York: Little Brown, 2011), 236.

95. Adam Liptak, "As Justices Get Back to Business, Old Pro Reveals Tricks of the Trade," *New York Times*, October 4, 2011, A15.

96. See Timothy R. Johnson, James F. Spriggs II, and Paul J. Wahlbeck, "Passing and Strategic Voting on the U.S. Supreme Court," *Law and Society Review* 39 (June 2005): 349–377.

97. David J. Garrow, *Liberty and Sexuality: The Right to Privacy and the Making of* Roe v. Wade (New York: Macmillan, 1994), 558.

98. John C. Jeffries Jr., *Justice Lewis F. Powell, Jr.* (New York: Scribner's, 1994), 545.

99. Linda Greenhouse, "How Not to Be Chief Justice: The Apprenticeship of William H. Rehnquist," *University of Pennsylvania Law Review* 154 (2006): 1367, emphasis in original.

100. Jeffrey Rosen, "Rehnquist the Great?" *Atlantic Monthly*, April 2005, 79–80.

101. Stevens, *Five Chiefs*, 210.

102. Rosen, "Roberts's Rules," 105–113.

103. Tony Mauro, "Alito Recaps First Year on High Court," *The Legal Intelligencer*, February 7, 2007, 4.

104. Jan Crawford Greenburg, "Justices Scalia and Breyer: Little in Common, Much to Debate," *ABC News*, December 6, 2006, www.abcnews.go.com/Politics/print?id=2704898.

105. These findings are based on analysis of The Supreme Court Database, http://scdb.wustl.edu/.

106. See Lamb, Swain, and Farkas, *The Supreme Court*, 95.

107. David A. Yalof, Joseph Mello, and Patrick Schmidt, "Collegiality Among U.S. Supreme Court Justices? An Early Assessment of the Roberts Court," *Judicature* 95 (July–August 2011): 12–19.

108. Jamal Greene, "Justice Stevens' Temperance," *Judicature* 94 (July–August 2010): 11.

109. Robert Barnes, "The Un-Routine Sets Apart Sotomayor's First Term," *Washington Post*, July 11, 2010, A1.

110. Ben Winograd, "'Ask the Author' with Jeffrey Toobin: Part 2," *SCOTUSblog*, September 19, 2007, www.scotusblog.com/wp/?s=ask+the+author+with+jeffrey+toobin.

111. Joan Biskupic, "Justices Strike a Balance," *USA Today*, December 26, 2007, 1D.

112. Bill Mears, "Kagan Talks About Her Faith, the Court, and Her Hunting Trips,"CNN.com, October 19, 2011, http://www.cnn.com/2011/10/19/politics/scotus-kagan/.

113. John Paul Stevens, "*Kelo*, Popularity, and Substantive Due Process," Albritton Lecture, University of Alabama School of Law, November 16, 2011, http://www.supremecourt.gov/publicinfo/speeches/speeches .aspx. The decision was *Kelo v. City of New London* (2005).

114. Barry Friedman, *The Will of the People: How Public Opinion Has Influenced the Supreme Court and Shaped the Meaning of the Constitution* (New York: Farras, Straus, & Giroux, 2009), 371. A contrary view is presented in Richard H. Pildes, "Is the Supreme Court a 'Majoritarian' Institution?" *Supreme Court Review*, 2010, 103–158.

115. See Nathaniel Persily, Jack Citrin, and Patrick J. Egan, eds., *Public Opinion and Constitutional Controversy* (New York: Oxford University Press, 2008).

116. See Micheal W. Giles, Bethany Blackstone, and Richard L. Vining Jr., "The Supreme Court in American Democracy: Unraveling the Linkages between Public Opinion and Judicial Decision Making," *Journal of Politics* 70 (April 2008): 293–306; and Christopher J. Casillas, Peter K. Enns, and Patrick C. Wohlfarth, "How Public Opinion Constrains the U.S. Supreme Court," *American Journal of Political Science* 55 (January 2011): 74–88.

117. Thomas Marshall, *Public Opinion and the Rehnquist Court* (Albany: State University of New York Press, 2008).

118. Charles Lane, "Kennedy's Assault on Editorial Writers," *Washington Post*, April 3, 2006, A17.

119. Thomas Sowell, "Blackmun Plays to the Crowd," *St. Louis Post Dispatch*, March 4, 1994, 7B; Michael Barone, "Justices Have Typically Felt Little Compunction about Overturning Laws and Making Public Policy," *Chicago Sun-Times*, July 13, 2005, 55.

120. Lawrence Baum and Neal Devins, "Why the Supreme Court Cares about Elites, Not the American People," *Georgetown Law Journal* 98 (August 2010): 1515–1581.

121. Pamela C. Corley, "The Supreme Court and Opinion Content: The Influence of Parties' Briefs," *Political Research Quarterly* 61 (September 2008): 468–478.

122. Paul M. Collins Jr., *Friends of the Supreme Court: Interest Groups and Judicial Decision Making* (New York: Oxford University Press, 2008), chap. 4.

123. Marci A. Hamilton, "Pleasant Grove City v. Summum: The Supreme Court's Puzzling, Fascinating New Free Speech Decision," FindLaw, March 5, 2009, http://writ.news.findlaw.com/hamilton/20090305.html.

124. This percentage is based on data provided by the Office of the Solicitor General. Cases in which there was not a clear win or loss for the government are excluded.

125. See Rebecca E. Deen, Joseph Ignagni, and James Meernik, "Individual Justices and the Solicitor General: The Amicus Curiae Cases, 1953–2000," *Judicature* 89 (September–October 2005): 68–77.

126. For contrasting arguments and evidence, see Segal and Spaeth, "Supreme Court and the Attitudinal Model Revisited," 326–356; and Bailey and Maltzman, *The Constrained Court*, chap. 6.

127. Tom S. Clark, *The Limits of Judicial Independence* (New York: Cambridge University Press, 2011).

Chapter 5

Policy Outputs

The last two chapters examined the processes that shape the Supreme Court's policies. In this chapter I consider the substance of those policies by discussing several questions. What kinds of issues does the Court address? How active is the Court as a policymaker? Finally, what is the ideological content of its policies? I conclude the chapter by developing an explanation for historical patterns in the Court's outputs.

Areas of Activity: What the Court Addresses

During any given term, the Supreme Court resolves a broad range of issues in fields as varied as antitrust, environmental protection, and freedom of speech. In this sense the Court's agenda is highly diverse. But the Court generally devotes most of its efforts to a few types of policy. To a considerable degree, then, the Court is a specialist.

The Court's Current Activity

The content of the Court's agenda can be illustrated with the cases that it heard in the 2010 term. It is useful to begin by describing the issues in a fairly representative sample of cases decided during that term.

1. Under federal sentencing laws, can a district judge impose or lengthen a prison term in order to help rehabilitate the defendant? (*Tapia v. United States*, 2011)

2. Under Title VII of the Civil Rights Act of 1964, is it illegal for an employer to fire an employee in retaliation for a discrimination complaint by the employee's fiancée? (*Thompson v. North American Stainless*, 2011)

3. Did a regulation made by the Federal Reserve Board require a bank to inform a credit card holder before raising the interest rate on his balance when the increase was based on a provision in his card-holder agreement? (*Chase Bank USA, N.A., v. McCoy*, 2011)

4. When a police search is illegal, because of a new rule that the Supreme Court established after the search was conducted, should the evidence obtained from the search be excluded from use at the defendant's trial? (*Davis v. United States*, 2011)

5. Does the National Childhood Vaccine Injury Act preempt and thus rule out lawsuits against vaccine manufacturers for injuries or deaths that result from defects in a vaccine's design? (*Bruesewitz v. Wyeth LLC*, 2011)

6. Does a Nevada law that prohibits public officials from voting or taking a position on a matter on which they have a conflict of interest violate officials' constitutional right to freedom of speech? (*Nevada Commission on Ethics v. Carrigan*, 2011)

7. Is a Treasury Department regulation that treats medical residents as full-time employees who must pay taxes on their income a reasonable interpretation of the federal Tax Code? (*Mayo Foundation v. United States*, 2011)

8. When ceilings on the prices that drug manufacturers charge health care facilities are written into contracts between the manufacturers and the Department of Health and Human Services, can health care facilities sue to enforce those ceilings? (*Astra USA, Inc. v. Santa Clara County*, 2011)

9. In determining whether a juvenile suspect was in custody and thus whether the *Miranda* rules for questioning of suspects apply, should the age of the suspect be taken into account? (*J. D. B. v. North Carolina*, 2011)

10. Do the Clean Air Act and action by the Environmental Protection Agency under the Act preclude states from filing lawsuits under the federal common law to limit carbon dioxide emissions from electric power plants? (*American Electric Power Company, Inc. v. Connecticut*, 2011)

Table 5-1 provides a more systematic picture of the Court's agenda in the 2010 term by summarizing the characteristics of the 81 decisions with full opinions in that term. The Court's decisions were closely connected with the other branches of government. The federal government or one of its agencies was a party in about one-quarter of all cases. State governments were parties in the majority of other cases, so that two in three cases had at least one government party. Moreover, most of the disputes between private parties were based directly on government policy in fields such as environmental protection and civil rights.

TABLE 5-1
Characteristics of Decisions by the Supreme Court
with Full Opinions, 2010 Term

Characteristic	Number	Percentage
Number of decisions	81	NA
Cases from lower federal courts	71	88
Cases from state courts	9	11
Original cases	1	1
Federal government party[a]	22	27
State or local government party[a]	33	41
No government party	26	32
Constitutional issue decided[b]	28	35
No constitutional issue decided	53	65
Civil liberties issue present[c]	44	54
No civil liberties issue	37	46
Criminal cases[d]	27	33
Civil cases	54	67

Source: The cases listed were those decided with opinions and listed in the front section of *United States Supreme Court Reports, Lawyers' Edition,* vols. 178–180.

Note: NA = not applicable. Consolidated cases decided with one set of opinions were counted once.

a. Cases with both a federal government party and another government party were listed as federal government. Government as party includes agencies and individual government officials.
b. In several additional cases the parties raised constitutional issues, or those issues were present in the underlying case. Cases involving federal preemption of state laws are not treated as constitutional.
c. Includes cases in which the Court did not decide the civil liberties issue directly.
d. Includes actions brought by prisoners to challenge the legality of their convictions but excludes cases concerning rights of prisoners.

The 2010 term was similar to other recent terms in that the majority of cases involved interpretations of federal statutes. Observers of the Court tend to focus on its interpretations of the Constitution, but the Court devotes most of its collective energy to statutory interpretation.

As has been true for several decades, the Court's single biggest area of activity in the 2010 term was civil liberties. As in earlier discussions, the term *civil liberties* refers here to three general types of rights: the right to fair procedure in dealings with government, the right to equal treatment by government and by private institutions, and certain substantive rights protected against government violations such as freedom of expression and freedom of religion. By that definition, about half of the Court's decisions fell into this area.

Related to the Court's civil liberties emphasis is its work in criminal law and procedure. One-third of the 2010 decisions resulted from criminal prosecutions. Since the 1950s criminal cases have consistently made up a substantial proportion of the Court's agenda. In many of the criminal cases the Court addresses civil liberties issues by interpreting constitutional protections of procedural rights.

The list of representative cases from the 2010 term illustrates two other areas in which the Court is active. After civil liberties, the most common subject of cases is economic issues. Most civil liberties cases are based on constitutional questions, but economic cases generally involve statutory interpretation. Most of these cases arise from government regulation of economic activity, such as labor relations, antitrust, and environmental protection.

Another major subject of Court activity is federalism, the division of power between federal and state governments. Federalism overlaps with other categories, and most federalism cases involve economic issues. This subject has been especially prominent in the past two decades.

Taken together, civil liberties, economic policy, and federalism cover a large portion of the issues that arise in American government. Still, the Court's emphasis on those issues constitutes something of a specialized focus. Most striking is its concentration on civil liberties. Although civil liberties is a broad category, the fact that half the Court's decisions concern this single kind of issue indicates the Court's specialization.

Change in the Court's Agenda

The Court's agenda is not static. Even over a few terms, the Court's attention to specific categories of cases sometimes increases or decreases considerably. The shape of its agenda as a whole has changed more slowly, but the changes have been fundamental.[1]

Changes in Specific Portions of the Agenda. Sometimes an issue that has occupied a very small place on the Court's agenda, or no place at all, becomes more prominent. More often than not, this change comes from new federal legislation. Before federal law prohibited employment discrimination, for instance, people who felt that they had been subjected to discrimination had little basis for bringing cases to court. The series of statutes that Congress enacted beginning in 1963 provided that basis, and the resulting cases created a substantial number of legal questions that the Court chose to resolve. Since the first of these statutes was adopted, the Court has heard more than 130 cases on employment discrimination.

Another example concerns employee pension plans. Until 1980 the Court decided few cases involving those issues. Since then these cases have been common. The source of this change is simple: Congress enacted the Employee Retirement Income Security Act of 1974 (ERISA). This regulation of pension plans raised a variety of legal questions that the courts had to address. The justices have seen a need to resolve many of these questions themselves, even though they have limited interest in the complex issues that arise under ERISA. As a result, the Court has heard more than fifty cases interpreting ERISA.

The Court itself can open up new areas on its agenda with decisions that create legal rights or add to existing rights. The Court's decision in *Batson v. Kentucky* (1986) allowed criminal defendants to challenge the use of peremptory challenges by prosecutors on the ground that the challenges were used in a racially discriminatory way. Since then, the Court has decided a series of cases about who has the right to raise a *Batson* claim and how judges should determine whether a challenge was used with discriminatory intent. A similar process has occurred with *Strickland v. Washington* (1984), which set up new standards to determine whether a criminal defendant was effectively denied the right to counsel by a lawyer's poor performance.

Just as issues can rise on the Court's agenda, they can also recede. Often, a new statute or Court decision raises a series of issues that the Court resolves during a particular period, but after that wave of cases the Court can move away from that field. In *Benton v. Maryland* (1969) the Court ruled that the constitutional protection against double jeopardy for criminal offenses applied to the states. This decision opened the way for state cases with double jeopardy issues to reach the Court, and the Court decided more than fifty cases in that field in the 1970s and 1980s. But with so many issues resolved, the Court has heard only occasional double jeopardy cases since then.

Changes in the Agenda as a Whole. Beyond changes in specific areas, the overall pattern of the Court's agenda may change over a period of several decades. The current agenda reflects a fundamental change that occurred between the 1930s and 1960s. In the half-century up to the 1930s, the largest part of the Court's agenda was devoted to economic issues. Also important but clearly secondary were cases about federalism. Issues of procedural due process constituted a small proportion of the agenda, and relatively few cases addressed other areas of civil liberties.

Over the next three decades, the Court evolved into an institution that gave most of its attention to individual liberties. The proportion of decisions dealing with civil liberties grew from 8 percent of the agenda in the 1933–1937 terms to 59 percent in the 1968–1972 terms.[2] Issues involving the rights of criminal defendants became far more numerous, and other civil liberties issues such as racial equality took a large share of the agenda. At the same time, some kinds of economic cases declined precipitously. In 1933–1937 one of every three cases involved federal taxation or economic disputes between private parties. By 1968–1972 those two areas accounted for only 6 percent of the Court's agenda. Federalism also took a reduced share of the agenda, falling from 14 percent in 1933–1937 to 5 percent in 1968–1972.

Many forces contributed to this change, from public opinion to federal legislation. Interest groups that supported civil liberties cases played a key role by bringing relevant cases to the Court. But actions by the Court itself had the most direct effect. Perhaps most important, the justices became more interested in protecting civil liberties and thus in hearing claims that government policies infringed on liberties. Partly because they had to make room for civil liberties cases, the justices gave more limited attention to other fields. They continued to hear a good many cases involving economic issues, but economics declined considerably as part of the Court's work.

The Court's agenda has changed in some respects since the 1960s. Within the civil liberties field, cases involving criminal law and procedure have taken a larger share of the agenda, while issues of equality and First Amendment rights have declined. Meanwhile, federalism cases have become somewhat more common. But on the whole, the broad contours of the agenda have remained stable. In particular, as the agenda for the 2010 term illustrates, the Court continues to hear more cases in civil liberties than in any other field. Thus, the Court's work still reflects the changes in its agenda that occurred between the 1930s and the 1960s.

A Broader View of the Agenda

The Supreme Court's current agenda distinguishes the Court from other policymakers. In some respects the Court's agenda resembles the agendas of other appellate courts, especially state supreme courts and federal courts of appeals. All these courts give considerable attention to government parties and government policies. Nearly all appellate courts hear large numbers of criminal cases, and most give much of their attention to cases with economic issues. Where the Court stands out is in the prominence of civil liberties issues on its agenda. Except for the rights of criminal defendants, most other appellate courts hear few cases about civil liberties.

Like the Court, the president is something of a specialist. But the president's agenda has its own emphases, foreign policy and management of the economy. In contrast, the Court makes few decisions about foreign policy, and with occasional exceptions such as the health care cases of 2012,[3] its decisions on economic policy barely touch issues of government policy that shape the economy as a whole.

In contrast, Congress is a generalist that spreads its activity across a very broad set of issues. One result is that the congressional agenda covers virtually all the types of policy that the Supreme Court deals with. But Congress gives relatively little attention to some of the issues that are central to the Court, especially in civil liberties. And Congress gives high priority to several fields that are less important to the Court, ranging from foreign policy to agriculture.

These differences provide some perspective on the Court's role by underlining the limited range of its work. Its jurisdiction is broad, but the bulk of its decisions are made in only a few policy areas. The Court's specialization affects its role as a policymaker. By deciding as many civil liberties cases as it does, the Court can do much to shape law and policy in this area. In contrast, the Court's more limited activity in some major areas, especially foreign policy, severely narrows its potential impact in those fields.

Even in the areas in which it is most active, the Court addresses only certain types of issues. In criminal justice, for instance, the Court does much to define the rights of criminal defendants and the scope of federal criminal statutes. But its cases do not affect the funding of criminal justice agencies, and they have little to do with decisions to prosecute.

One effect of the Court's narrow focus is that it does not deal with most of the issues that are high on the agendas of government and the public. The conduct of the wars in Iraq and Afghanistan proceeded with essentially no involvement by the Court. The major decisions on revival of the economy have been made in the other branches of government. In this respect as well, the health care cases of 2012 stand out as an important exception to the general rule.

These realities should caution against exaggerating the Supreme Court's power as a policymaker. Although the importance of its role can be debated, the limited range of its activities inevitably limits its power. The Court could not possibly be dominant as a policymaker except in federalism, civil liberties, and some limited areas of economic policy. For reasons that are discussed later in this chapter and in Chapter 6, even in those areas the Court is far from dominant.

The Court's Activism

The Court's level of attention to various areas of policy helps determine where it is likely to play a significant role. But its impact also depends on

Ben Bernanke, chair of the Federal Reserve Board, testifying before a Senate committee in 2011. The Court generally has little impact on the role of government in managing the economy.

what it rules in those policy areas. Of particular importance is how much it engages in activism.

The term *judicial activism* has multiple meanings, and people most often use the term simply as a negative label for decisions they dislike. What I mean by activism is that a court makes significant changes in public policy, especially in policies that the other branches have established. The most prominent form of activism involves the use of judicial review, the power to overturn acts of other policymakers on the ground that they violate the Constitution.

Overturning Acts of Congress

The most familiar use of judicial review comes in Supreme Court decisions holding that federal statutes are unconstitutional. Such a ruling represents a clear assertion of power by the Court, because it directly negates a decision by another branch of the federal government.

According to one count, shown in Table 5-2, by the end of 2011 the Court had overturned 166 federal laws completely or in part.[4] (When different provisions of a statute were struck down in different decisions, each decision is counted once.) This number in itself is noteworthy. On the one hand, it indicates that the Court has made considerable use of its review power. On the other hand, the laws struck down by the Court constitute a minute fraction of the laws that Congress has adopted. And when

TABLE 5-2
Number of Federal Statutes and State and Local Statutes
Held Unconstitutional by the Supreme Court, 1790–2011

Period	Federal statutes	State and local statutes
1790–1799	0	0
1800–1809	1	1
1810–1819	0	7
1820–1829	0	8
1830–1839	0	3
1840–1849	0	10
1850–1859	1	7
1860–1869	4	24
1870–1879	7	36
1880–1889	4	46
1890–1899	5	36
1900–1909	9	40
1910–1919	6	119
1920–1929	15	139
1930–1939	13	92
1940–1949	2	61
1950–1959	4	66
1960–1969	18	151
1970–1979	19	195
1980–1989	16	164
1990–1999	24	62
2000–2009	15	36
2010–2011	3	4
Total	166	1,307

Sources: Congressional Research Service, *The Constitution of the United States of America: Analysis and Interpretation, 2002 Edition* and *2008 Supplement* (Washington, DC: Government Printing Office, 2004, 2008); updated for 2009–2011 by the author.

Note: State and local laws include those that the Supreme Court held to be preempted by federal statutes.

the Court rules on whether a federal statute is unconstitutional, about five times out of six it upholds the statute.[5]

A closer look at the decisions striking down federal laws provides a better sense of their significance.[6] One question is the importance of the statutes that the Court overturns. The Court has struck down some statutes of major importance. One example was the Missouri Compromise of 1820, limiting slavery in the territories, which the Court declared unconstitutional in the *Dred Scott* case in 1857. Another was the New Deal economic legislation that the Court overturned in several decisions in 1935 and 1936.[7] In contrast, many of the Court's decisions declaring statutes invalid have been unimportant to the policy goals of Congress and the president, either because the statutes were minor or because they were struck down only as they applied to particular circumstances.

A related question is the timing of judicial review. The Court's decisions striking down federal statutes fall into three groups of nearly equal size: those that came within four calendar years of a statute's enactment, those that came five to twelve years after enactment, and those that occurred more than twelve years later. Congress sometimes retains a strong commitment to a statute from an earlier period. But often few members care much when an older law is overturned, because the statute has become less relevant over time or because the members of Congress have become less favorable to the provision that was struck down.

For these reasons the Court's frequent use of its power to invalidate congressional acts is somewhat misleading. Any decision that strikes down a federal statute might seem likely to produce major conflict between the Court and Congress, but that is not necessarily the case. Conflict is most likely when the Court invalidates an important congressional policy within a few years of its enactment, but most decisions striking down statutes do not meet both those criteria. Some decisions overturning legislation receive little attention, and some others are actually welcomed by presidents and members of Congress.[8]

As Table 5-2 shows, the Court has not overturned federal statutes at a constant rate. It struck down only two statutes before 1865. It then began to exercise its judicial review power more actively, overturning thirty-five federal laws between 1865 and 1919. Two more increases, even more dramatic, followed: the Court struck down fifteen federal laws during the 1920s and twelve from 1934 through 1936.

The period between 1918 and 1936 featured the highest level of conflict between the Court and Congress. The Court overturned twenty-nine federal laws, many of them quite significant. Between 1918 and 1928 the Court invalidated two child labor laws and a minimum wage law, along with several less important statutes. Then, between 1933 and 1936 a majority of the Court engaged in a frontal attack on the New Deal program, an attack that ended with the Court's 1937 shift in position.

The Court used its judicial review power sparingly in the quarter-century after 1936. But it overturned ninety-five statutes between 1963 and 2011, far more than in any previous period of the same length and more than half of the total for the Court's entire history. This recent period can be divided into three parts.

Among all the statutes that the Court declared unconstitutional between 1963 and 1994, most were of limited significance. As a result, the decisions striking them down received little attention from the mass media or the general public. However, a few of those statutes were quite important. *Buckley v. Valeo* (1976) and several later decisions invalidated major provisions of the federal campaign funding laws of the 1970s on First Amendment grounds and thereby made it impossible for Congress to regulate campaign finance comprehensively. In *Immigration and Naturalization Service v. Chadha* (1983), the Court struck down a relatively minor provision of an immigration law. But its ruling indicated that the legislative veto, a mechanism widely used for congressional control of the executive branch, violated the constitutional separation of powers.

Between 1995 and 2002 the Court invalidated thirty-two federal laws, a record number for an eight-year period. During that period too, most of these laws were relatively minor. The biggest exception was the statute that gave presidents the power to veto individual items in budget bills, a major addition to presidential power, which the Court struck down in *Clinton v. City of New York* (1998).

Over those eight years, the Court also handed down ten decisions that limited the power of Congress to regulate state governments. In these decisions the Court gave narrow interpretations to the commerce clause and the Fourteenth Amendment as bases for federal power, while giving a broad interpretation to the Eleventh Amendment as a limit on lawsuits against states. In *Board of Trustees v. Garrett* (2001), for example, the Court ruled that Congress could not authorize people with disabilities to seek monetary damages from states in lawsuits for discrimination. This set of decisions constituted a substantial change in the federal-state balance. But it did not create serious conflict with Congress, because the Republican majorities in Congress during that period were not inclined to assert federal power against the states in the areas in which the Court limited that power.

The frequency of overturnings declined considerably after 2002. In the nine years that followed, the Court issued only eight decisions striking down federal laws. But as a group, these decisions were highly consequential. In *United States v. Booker* (2005), the Court invalidated the provision that made the federal sentencing guidelines mandatory, thereby upsetting the sentencing system that had operated in the federal courts for nearly two decades and establishing a sentencing system that differed significantly. Four other decisions held that various provisions of the Bipartisan Campaign Reform Act of 2002 were unconstitutional. Taken together, these decisions largely blunted the second major effort by Congress to regulate funding of political campaigns.[9]

With these decisions, the Court had considerable impact in two major areas of federal policy. The *Booker* decision changed the pattern of sentences for federal crimes and thus affected the outcomes for a great many defendants. The Court's decisions on campaign funding spurred major changes in campaigns for federal policy and thus helped to determine which candidates were elected to Congress and the presidency in the years from 2010 on.

Overturning State and Local Laws

The Supreme Court's exercise of judicial review over state and local laws has less of an activist element than its use of that power over federal laws. When the Court strikes down a state law, it does not put itself in conflict with the other branches of the federal government. Indeed, it may be supporting their powers over those of the states. Still, the Court is invalidating the action of another policymaker. For that reason, this form of judicial review is significant.

From 1790 to 2011, by one count, the Court overturned 1,075 state statutes and local ordinances as unconstitutional. It ruled that another 232 state and local laws were invalid because they were preempted by federal law under the constitutional principle of federal supremacy. As shown in Table 5-2, the total of 1,307 state and local laws struck down is about eight times the number for federal statutes. The disparity is even greater than that figure suggests, because many decisions that overturned specific state and local laws also applied to similar laws in other locations.

As with federal laws, the rate at which the Court invalidates state and local laws has tended to increase over time, and it was far higher in the twentieth century than in the nineteenth. The rate of overturnings was very high between 1909 and 1937, and that rate was even higher from the 1960s through the 1980s. In that period the Court declared unconstitutional an average of seventeen state and local laws per year. The rate of invalidations has been much lower since 1990, and in the first decade of the twenty-first century it returned to the pace of the late nineteenth century.

Although the Court struck down relatively few state laws before 1860, its decisions during that period were important because they limited state powers under the Constitution. For example, under Chief Justice John Marshall (1801–1835) the Court weakened the states with decisions such as *McCulloch v. Maryland* (1819), which denied the states power to tax federal agencies, and *Gibbons v. Ogden* (1824), which reduced state power to regulate commerce.

The state and local laws the Court has overturned in more recent periods have been a mixture of the important and the minor. In the aggregate the Court's decisions have given it a significant role in shaping state policy. During the late nineteenth century and the first one-third of the twentieth, the Court struck down a great deal of state economic legislation, including many laws regulating business practices and labor relations. The net effect was to slow a major tide of public policy.

Some of the Court's decisions since the mid-1950s have also impinged on major elements of state policy. A series of rulings helped to break down the legal bases of racial segregation and discrimination in the southern states. In 1973 the Court overturned the broad prohibitions of abortion that existed in most states, thereby requiring a general legalization of abortion; later decisions struck down several new laws regulating abortion and indirectly invalidated many other abortion laws. And through a long series of decisions, the Court limited state power to regulate the economy in areas that Congress has preempted under its constitutional supremacy. In doing so, the Court shifted power further toward the federal government and away from the states.

Other Targets of Judicial Review

The Supreme Court can declare unconstitutional any government policy or practice, not just laws enacted by legislatures. The number of nonstatutory policies and practices that the Court has struck down is probably much larger than the number of laws it has overturned. On constitutional grounds the Court has overruled actions taken by federal cabinet departments, local school boards, and state courts, among other policymakers.

The Court is especially active in overseeing criminal procedure under the Constitution, and it frequently holds that actions by police officers or trial judges violate the rights of defendants. In 2011, for instance, the Court declared unconstitutional the admission of a forensic laboratory report into evidence in a criminal case without testimony by the analyst who carried it out and the jailing of an indigent person for civil contempt without providing him with a lawyer or procedural safeguards that substitute for a lawyer.[10] And there has been a long series of decisions holding that police searches and questioning of suspects violated constitutional protections under certain conditions.

Of particular interest is the Court's review of presidential orders and policies. Decisions of presidents or officials acting on their behalf can be challenged on the grounds that they are unauthorized by the Constitution or that they violate a constitutional rule. It is impossible to specify how frequently the Court strikes down presidential actions as unconstitutional, because it is often unclear whether an action by the executive branch should be considered "presidential." But such decisions by the Court seem to be relatively rare, though the Court arguably has become more willing to challenge presidential policies in the past few decades.[11]

Over its history, the Court has invalidated a few major actions by presidents. In *Ex parte Milligan* (1866), it held that President Abraham Lincoln had lacked the power to suspend the writ of habeas corpus for military prisoners during the Civil War. And in *Youngstown Sheet and Tube Co. v. Sawyer* (1952), it declared that President Harry Truman had acted illegally during the Korean War when he ordered the federal government to seize and operate major steel mills because their workers were preparing to go on strike. Between 2004 and 2008 the Court issued four decisions that established procedural protections for Guantánamo detainees. Those decisions did not hold that any decisions by President George W. Bush were unconstitutional, but they overruled some of the president's policies relating to terrorism.[12]

Judicial Review: The General Picture

The Supreme Court's record of judicial review is complicated. The Court has been more activist in some eras than in others. The overall level of activism has increased over time, in part because of growth in the amount of government activity that is available to challenge. The Court has struck down far more state and local policies than federal policies.

Altogether, the justices have made considerable use of the power of judicial review. Yet the justices also have been quite selective in using their power to strike down laws. Partly as a result, the great majority of public policies at all levels of government have continued without interference from the Court. Thus, important as judicial review has been, it has not given the Court anything like a dominant position in the national government.

Statutory Interpretation

Historically and currently, most of the Supreme Court's decisions interpret federal statutes rather than constitutional provisions. Statutory interpretation may seem routine, but it can involve activism. For one thing, the Court's statutory decisions often determine whether an administrative agency has interpreted a statute correctly in the process of implementing it. If the Court concludes that an agency has erred, it strikes down the agency's action as contrary to the statute. More broadly, the Court often puts its own stamp on a statute through its interpretations of that statute over the years. It has done so in fields such as antitrust, labor relations, and environmental protection.

This process is exemplified by Title VII of the Civil Rights Act of 1964, the most important of the federal statutes that prohibit employment discrimination. As with many other statutes, Congress laid out the broad outlines of the law and left it to the other branches to fill in the gaps. Over the years the Court has resolved many major issues. For example, it has established and revised the guidelines that trial courts use to determine whether an employer has engaged in discrimination.[13] It ruled that a company's policies could violate Title VII on the basis of their impact, even if the employer did not intend to discriminate.[14] It held that sexual harassment may constitute sex discrimination under Title VII and set up rules to determine when an employer is legally responsible for harassment.[15] And most recently, it limited the use of class action lawsuits to challenge

Betty Dukes (left) with two of her lawyers. The Court's decision in *Wal-Mart Stores v. Dukes* (2011) on the use of class actions to challenge employment discrimination illustrates how it shapes policy through statutory interpretation.

a company's employment practices.[16] Through these and other rulings, the Court has shaped federal policy on employment discrimination.

The Content of Policy

So far, I have examined the areas in which the Supreme Court concentrates its efforts and the extent of its activism. A third aspect of the Court's role as a policymaker is the content of its policies. This content can best be understood in terms of its ideological direction and its beneficiaries. Dividing the Court's history into eras is arbitrary, but it is useful to think of the period since the late nineteenth century as containing three eras.

The 1890s to the 1930s

Over several decades the Supreme Court is certain to shift its position on some broad issues. That was true of the period that began in the 1890s and ended in the 1930s. But in ideological terms the Court of that era was predominantly conservative. Most of its activism was on behalf of advantaged interests such as business corporations. In contrast, it did little to protect disadvantaged interests such as racial minority groups.

Scrutinizing Economic Regulation. In 1915 the Supreme Court decided *South Covington & Cincinnati Street Railway Co. v. City of Covington.* The company, which ran streetcars between Covington, Kentucky, and Cincinnati, Ohio, challenged several provisions of a Covington ordinance regulating its operations. The Court struck down some provisions on the ground that they constituted a burden on interstate commerce between Ohio and Kentucky. The Court also declared invalid a regulation stipulating that the temperature in the cars never be permitted to go below 50 degrees Fahrenheit—"We therefore think . . . this feature of the ordinance is unreasonable and cannot be sustained"—apparently on the ground that the regulation violated the Fourteenth Amendment by depriving the company of its property without due process of law.

The *South Covington* case illustrates some important attributes of the Court's decisions from the 1890s to the late 1930s. During that period the Court dealt primarily with economic issues. Most important, it ruled on challenges to growing government regulation of business practices.

In those cases the Court frequently ruled in favor of government, rejecting most challenges to federal and state policies and giving broad interpretations to some government powers.[17] But the Court limited government regulatory powers in important respects, and over time its limits on regulation tightened. This development is reflected in the number of laws involving economic policy that the Court struck down each decade: 43 from 1900 to 1909, 114 from 1910 to 1919, and 133 from 1920 to 1929.[18] The Court's attacks on government regulation peaked in the mid-1930s, when it struck down most of the major statutes in President Franklin Roosevelt's New Deal program to deal with the Great Depression.

The theme of limiting government regulatory powers was reflected in the Court's constitutional doctrines. At the national level the Court gave narrow interpretations to congressional powers to tax and regulate interstate commerce. In contrast, the Court gave a broad reading to the general limitation on federal power in the Tenth Amendment, using that provision to prohibit some federal actions on the ground that they interfered with state prerogatives. At the same time the Court limited state powers in the economic sphere. It ruled in 1886 that corporations were "persons" with rights protected by the Fourteenth Amendment.[19] It also interpreted the Fourteenth Amendment requirement that state governments provide due process of law as an absolute prohibition of regulations that interfered unduly with the liberty and property rights of businesses. The Court's ruling against the streetcar temperature regulation was one of many such decisions.

The Court's Beneficiaries. The Court's mixed record in economic cases meant that there was no dominant beneficiary of its decisions. But to the extent that the Court limited government regulatory powers, the business community—especially large businesses—benefited from the Court's policies during this period. Of the regulatory legislation that the Court overturned or limited, much was aimed at the activities of large businesses. The railroads were the most prominent example. Although the Court allowed a good deal of government control over railroads, it also struck down a large body of railroad regulation.[20] In the decade from 1910 to 1919, the Court overturned forty-one state laws in cases brought by railroad companies. Major corporations such as railroads might be considered the clientele of the Court from the 1890s to the 1930s.

Large corporations did not simply benefit from the Court's policies; they helped to bring them about.[21] Beginning in the late nineteenth century, the corporate community employed much of the best legal talent in the United States to challenge the validity of regulatory statutes. The effective advocacy of these attorneys helped lay the groundwork for the Court's policies favoring business.

Corporate interests came to the judiciary because of their defeats elsewhere in government. On the whole, Congress and the state legislatures were friendly to business interests, but they did enact a good many regulations of private enterprise. In scrutinizing these regulations closely, the Court served as a court of last resort for corporations politically as well as legally.

Civil Liberties: A Limited Concern. Some of the Court's decisions limiting government regulation of business were based on constitutional protections of civil liberties. The Court decided relatively few cases involving the liberties of individuals in that era, but it gave some attention to that field.[22] Overall, the justices provided less protection for individual liberties than for the economic rights of businesses. The Court's limited support for racial equality was exemplified by *Plessy v. Ferguson* (1896), in which it promoted racial segregation by ruling that state governments could mandate "separate but equal" facilities for different racial groups. The Court reached some decisions that favored the rights of criminal defendants, but it held that only a small subset of the procedural rights for criminal defendants in the Bill of Rights was incorporated into the due process clause of the Fourteenth Amendment and thus was applicable to proceedings in state courts.[23] Late in that era the Court ruled that the due process clause protected freedom of speech and freedom of the press from state violations. But in a series of decisions it held that the federal government could prosecute people whose expressions allegedly endangered military recruitment and other national security interests.[24]

A Long-Standing Position. The Court's conservatism during that period was not new; the dominant themes of the Court's work in earlier periods were also conservative. The Court provided considerable support for the rights of property holders and much less support for civil liberties outside the economic sphere.

Because of this history, observers of the Supreme Court in the New Deal period had reason to conclude that the Court was a fundamentally conservative body. Indeed, this was the position of two distinguished observers in the early 1940s. The historian Henry Steele Commager argued in 1943 that, with one possible exception, the Court had never intervened on behalf of the underprivileged; in fact, it frequently had blocked efforts by Congress to protect the underprivileged.[25] Two years earlier, Attorney General Robert Jackson, a future Supreme Court justice, reached this stark conclusion: "Never in its entire history can the Supreme Court be said to have for a single hour been representative of anything except the relatively conservative forces of its day."[26] Jackson may have exaggerated for effect, but he captured an important theme in the Court's history.

1937 to 1969

Even before Commager and Jackson described this record of conservatism, however, the Court was beginning a shift in its direction, which one historian called "the Constitutional Revolution of 1937." That revolution, he said,

altered fundamentally the character of the Court's business, the nature of its decisions, and the alignment of its friends and foes. From the Marshall Court to the Hughes Court, the judiciary had been largely concerned with questions of property rights. After 1937 the most significant matters on the docket were civil liberties and other personal rights. . . . While from 1800 to 1937 the principal critics of the Supreme Court were social reformers and the main supporters people of means who were the principal beneficiaries of the Court's decisions, after 1937 roles were reversed, with liberals commending and conservatives censuring the Court.[27]

Acceptance of Government Economic Policy. In the first stage of the revolution, the Court abandoned the limits it had placed on government intervention in the economy. That step came quickly. In a series of decisions beginning in 1937, majorities accepted the constitutional power of government—especially the federal government—to regulate and manage the economy. This shift culminated in *Wickard v. Filburn* (1942), in which the Court held that federal power to regulate interstate commerce extended so far that it applied to a farmer who grew wheat for his own livestock.

This collective change of heart proved to be of long duration. The Court consistently upheld major economic legislation against constitutional challenges, striking down only one minor provision of the federal laws regulating business from the 1940s through the 1960s.[28] Supporting federal supremacy in economic matters, the Court invalidated many state laws on the ground that they impinged on the constitutional powers of the federal government or that they were preempted by federal statutes. But in other respects it gave state governments more freedom to make economic policy.

The Court continued to address economic issues involving interpretations of federal statutes. In some instances it overrode decisions of regulatory agencies such as the National Labor Relations Board, holding that those decisions misinterpreted the statutes they applied. Some of these interventions were significant, but the Court did not challenge the basic economic programs of the federal government.

Support for Civil Liberties. In a 1938 decision, *United States v. Carolene Products Co.*, the Court signaled that there might be a second stage of the revolution. The case was one of many in which the Court upheld federal economic policies. But in what would become known as "footnote 4," Justice Harlan Fiske Stone's opinion for the Court argued that the Court was justified in taking a tolerant view of government economic policies while it gave "more exacting judicial scrutiny" to policies that infringed on civil liberties.

This second stage took a long time to develop. The Court gave more support to civil liberties in the 1940s and 1950s than it had in earlier eras, but it did not make a strong and consistent commitment to the expansion of individual liberties. This stage of the revolution finally came to full fruition in the 1960s. Civil liberties issues dominated the Court's agenda for the first time. The Court's decisions expanded liberties in many areas, from civil rights of racial minority groups to procedural rights of criminal defendants to freedom of expression.

As in the preceding era, the Court's policy position was reflected in the constitutional doctrines it adopted. Departing from its earlier view, the Court of the 1960s ruled that nearly all the rights of criminal defendants in the Bill of Rights were incorporated into the Fourteenth Amendment and therefore applied to state proceedings. In interpreting the equal protection clause of the Fourteenth Amendment, the Court held that it would give government policies "strict scrutiny" if the groups that the policies disfavored were especially vulnerable or if the rights involved were especially important.

The Court's sympathies for civil liberties were symbolized by *Griswold v. Connecticut* (1965), which established a new constitutional right to privacy. A majority of the justices discovered that right in provisions of the Bill of Rights nearly two centuries after those provisions were written.

FIGURE 5-1
*Number of Economic and Civil Liberties Laws (Federal, State, and Local)
Overturned by the Supreme Court by Decade, 1900–2009*

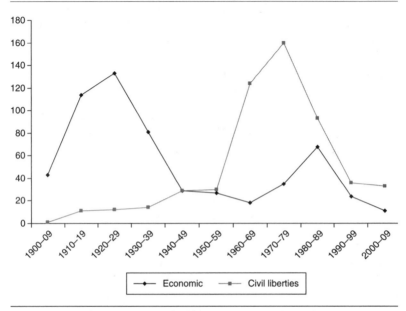

Sources: Congressional Research Service, *The Constitution of the United States of America:
Analysis and Interpretation, 2002 Edition* and *2008 Supplement* (Washington, DC: Government
Printing Office, 2004, 2008); updated for 2009 by the author.

Note: Civil liberties category does not include laws supportive of civil liberties.

The Court's direction after 1937 is illustrated by the pattern of decisions declaring laws unconstitutional. Figure 5-1 shows the number of
economic statutes and statutes limiting civil liberties that the Court overturned in each decade of the twentieth century and the first decade of the
twenty-first. The number of economic laws the Court struck down
declined precipitously between the 1920s and the 1940s and fell even
lower in the 1960s. In contrast, the number of statutes struck down on civil
liberties grounds became substantial in the 1940s and 1950s and rose
sharply in the 1960s. The reversal of these trends in the 1980s is also noteworthy, and I will discuss its implications later in this section.

The Court's Beneficiaries. The groups that the Court's policies benefited
most were those that gained from expansions of legal protections for civil
liberties. Among them were socially and economically disadvantaged
groups, criminal defendants, and people who took unpopular political

stands. In 1967, during the Court's most liberal period, an unsympathetic editorial cartoonist depicted the Court as a Santa Claus whose list of gift recipients included communists, pornographers, extremists, drug push-ers, criminals, and perverts.[29] Whatever may be the accuracy of that char-acterization, it underlines the change in the Court. Like the Court's policies favoring corporations in an earlier era, this support reflected effective litigation efforts by groups such as the NAACP Legal Defense Fund and the American Civil Liberties Union.

The segment of the population that the Court supported most strongly was black citizens, especially in the fields of education and voting rights. The Court also made efforts to protect the civil rights movement when southern states attacked it in the late 1950s and 1960s.

The Court was generally more favorable to liberties than were the other branches of government. Congress did not adopt a strong statute attacking racial discrimination until 1964, ten years after *Brown v. Board of Education.* The Court's support for some other liberties diverged even more from the positions of the other branches. The procedural rights of criminal defen-dants had few advocates in the executive and legislative branches. Congress did much to attack leftist political groups such as the Communist Party. As it had done when it favored business interests, the Court provided relief for groups that fared less well elsewhere in government.

The Era Since 1969

It is even more difficult to characterize the Supreme Court's policies in the recent past than in more distant eras, and that certainly is true of the period since the end of the Warren Court in 1969. Perhaps the best char-acterization is that the Court has moved slowly, unevenly, but substantially in a conservative direction.

Mixed Positions on Civil Liberties. To some extent in the Burger Court, and to a greater extent since then, the Court has narrowed legal protections for individual liberties. The Court's shift is reflected in the rate of success for parties bringing civil liberties claims. Comparisons over time are inexact, because the kinds of cases that the Court hears evolve, but those comparisons provide a general sense of changes in the Court's position. As discussed in Chapter 4, the proportion of decisions that favored civil liberties claims dropped precipitously between the 1960s and the 1970s, and it has remained at that lower level since then. Figure 5-1 shows that the number of laws struck down on the ground that they violated constitutional protections of civil lib-erties increased in the 1970s but declined dramatically after that.

The reduction in support for civil liberties came most quickly on the rights of criminal defendants. Beginning in the early 1970s, the Court has narrowed the *Miranda* rules for police questioning of suspects and the *Mapp* rule disallowing the use of evidence obtained through illegal searches. The Court's policies on capital punishment have been complicated: the Court struck down existing death penalty laws in *Furman v. Georgia* (1972), upheld a new set of laws in *Gregg v. Georgia* (1976), and since then has had a mixed record on a wide array of issues about when the death penalty can be imposed. In conjunction with Congress the Court limited the use of habeas corpus petitions as a means for criminal defendants to challenge their convictions after their original appeals ran out.

On issues of equality, the Court moved in a conservative direction more slowly and unevenly. The Burger Court was the first to strike down laws under the equal protection clause on the ground that they discriminated against women. It also held that northern-style school segregation, in which schools were not explicitly segregated by law, could violate equal protection. It generally gave broad interpretations to federal laws against discrimination but limited constitutional challenges to discrimination in private institutions that are connected to government. The Rehnquist and Roberts Courts have interpreted federal antidiscrimination laws more narrowly. The Rehnquist Court also approved the termination of court orders that maintained racial integration of public schools and limited the power of the federal government to enforce antidiscrimination laws against states. However, the Rehnquist Court continued to strengthen legal protections against sex discrimination in some important respects.

Freedom of expression is the only field in which the Court has directly overruled major Warren Court decisions favoring civil liberties—specifically, on the definition of obscenity.[30] The Burger and Rehnquist Courts narrowed some other First Amendment protections as well. But this is the field in which the Court in the current era has given the greatest support to civil liberties. One example is its protections for commercial speech such as advertising. The Court also struck down much of a broad congressional statute regulating campaign finance on First Amendment grounds in *Buckley v. Valeo* (1976), and it did the same to a later statute in *Citizens United v. Federal Election Commission* (2010) and other decisions.

Conservatism on Economic Issues. The Court since 1969 has not reversed its expansion of government powers to regulate the economy, though it has narrowed federal power to regulate interstate commerce in some respects. Most recently, in *National Federation of Independent Business v. Sebelius* (2012), five justices agreed that the commerce power did not extend to a mandate that people buy health insurance, though the Court upheld that mandate under the federal power to levy taxes.

But in its interpretations of federal statutes, the Court has taken positions that are markedly, and increasingly, more conservative. The proportion of economic decisions that can be classified as liberal was 75 percent in the 1962–1968 terms. That proportion dropped to 52 percent in the Burger Court (1969–1985 terms), 47 percent in the Rehnquist Court (1986–2004 terms), and 38 percent in the first six terms of the Roberts Court.[31]

This decrease reflects policy changes in several economic fields, changes that are clearest in the Roberts Court. Since 1969 the Court has narrowed the application of antitrust laws to business practices, it has given more support to employers in labor law, and for the most part it has interpreted environmental laws narrowly. In several decisions, most recently in *CompuCredit Corp. v. Greenwood* (2012), it has upheld the enforcement of contract provisions that require consumers to bring their disputes against companies to arbitration rather than going to court.

The Court has also reached a number of decisions in which it barred individuals' lawsuits against businesses or the enforcement of state regulations of business on the ground that they are preempted by federal laws in the same fields and thus invalid. The Court took such action in three cases in 2011.[32] The Court's decisions limiting the amount of punitive damages that winning parties can be awarded have their impact primarily on plaintiffs who are individuals.

The Court's Beneficiaries. As in the early twentieth century, but perhaps to a greater degree, the primary beneficiary of the Court's policies in the current era has been the business community. The Court's conservative policies on economic issues have been favorable to the interests of businesses. This is true of both its substantive decisions in areas such as labor-management relations and its decisions and rules of procedure affecting the ability of litigants to bring cases to court.[33] This support extends to the civil liberties field: some of the Court's expansions of protection for freedom of expression have come in cases brought by businesses. This was true, for instance, of the 2011 cases in which the Court struck down state laws prohibiting the sale or rental of violent video games to juveniles and prohibiting the sale of certain information about doctors' drug prescriptions.[34] The percentage of decisions favorable to business interests has grown over the current era, and the same is true of the smaller set of cases that were important enough to business interests for the U.S. Chamber of Commerce to participate as a party or amicus.[35]

As in an earlier era, this favorable record is partly a product of effective litigation by businesses and business groups. Beginning in the 1970s the Chamber of Commerce developed a strong litigation arm to advocate for business interests. The lawyers in the private sector who have become regular and effective advocates in the Supreme Court serve primarily business clients.

Rachel Brand, chief counsel for regulatory litigation at the National Chamber Litigation Center. The success of the U.S. Chamber of Commerce in the Roberts Court underlines the Court's relatively conservative positions on economic issues.

The Court has not been uniformly favorable to business in the current era, even in the Roberts Court. As in other eras, the Court's recent policies are too mixed in theme to allow easy generalizations. Still, both the Court's major beneficiary and its dominant ideological direction clearly differ from those of the preceding period.

Explaining the Court's Policies

In the preceding sections I described the Supreme Court's agenda, the extent of its activism, and the content of its policies in three historical periods. Each is summarized in Table 5-3.

The substantial changes in these aspects of the Court's policies over time underline the need to explain them. What forces can account for patterns in Supreme Court policies, especially their ideological content? Elaborating on ideas presented earlier in the book, I will suggest some explanations for those patterns.

The Court's Environment

Freedom from External Pressures. The life terms of Supreme Court justices give them considerable freedom from the rest of government and the

TABLE 5-3
Summary of the Supreme Court's Policies during Three Historical Periods

Period	Predominant area on agenda	Extent of activism	Content of policy
1890s to 1930s	Economic regulation	Variable, increasing over time	Mixed, primarily conservative
1937 to 1969	Economic regulation, then civil liberties	Initially low, then increasing, very high in 1960s	Generally liberal, very liberal in the 1960s
1969 to 2012	Civil liberties	High, declining in some respects after the 1970s	Initially moderate, then increasingly conservative

Note: Characterizations of each period are approximate and subject to disagreement. Extent of activism is gauged primarily by the striking down of government policies.

general public. The Court's relative insulation from external pressures distinguishes it from the other branches of government.

The Court's freedom is reflected in some of the positions that it takes in individual decisions. Political realities would not allow a legislature to support the right to burn the American flag as a form of political protest or to prohibit student-led prayers at football games. But the Court did make those decisions.[36]

More important, the Court has adopted some broad lines of policy that clearly conflicted with the majority view in the general public and elsewhere in government. To a considerable degree, it resisted the widespread support for regulation of business in the early twentieth century. Even more striking was the Court's expansion of the procedural rights of criminal defendants in the 1960s. No elected body, even an elected court, could have adopted so many rules favoring a segment of society that was so unpopular.

Influence from the Other Branches. The Court is not entirely free from external pressure. For one thing, Congress and the president have substantial powers over the Court and its decisions. The other branches frequently act to override Court decisions or to limit their impact. They seldom take action against the Court itself, but threats of such action—especially bills to limit the Court's jurisdiction—are common. The existence and use of these powers give the justices some incentive to avoid or minimize conflicts with the other branches.

It is difficult to ascertain the effect of this incentive on the Court's policies. On the whole, it appears, the justices have felt free to go their own way. But there are some specific episodes in which the other branches appeared to influence the course of Court policy. Examples include the Court's retreat from some of its expansions of civil liberties in the late 1950s and its refusal to decide whether American participation in the Vietnam War was unconstitutional.

More broadly, the Court has shown some caution about using judicial review to strike down significant national policies that enjoyed strong support in the other branches. It is noteworthy that the Court has struck down far more state laws than federal laws. The activism of the Warren Court in civil liberties was directed primarily at the states, and on the whole, that Court was sympathetic to the federal government.[37] Justices in the Rehnquist Court may have felt free to adopt new limitations on federal power because members of Congress during that period were largely sympathetic to those limitations.[38]

Societal Influence. It may be that the state of public opinion on particular issues exerts a subtle impact on justices. More important, however, are broader developments in society. Those developments affect justices' attitudes toward issues such as women's rights and terrorism, just as they reflect the attitudes of the public as a whole. They can also exert a direct influence on the Court.

One form of influence involves what can be called a requirement of minimum support: the Court is unlikely to take a sustained policy position that lacks significant support outside the Court, especially support from segments of society whose judgment is most important to its members. Justices may perceive that taking such positions would damage the Court's institutional position. More fundamentally, they may see positions with little support as unreasonable in themselves. Further, the Court acts on the cases that come to it. The justices cannot reshape their agenda without action by litigants and by the interest groups that support litigation. In turn, those groups develop from broad social movements.

These influences are reflected in the two most distinctive patterns in the Court's policies during the twentieth century. The Court's resistance to government regulation of the economy before 1937 may have had only minority support in society, but most of the business community and much of the legal community strongly approved that position. Corporations and their representatives engaged in a concerted litigation campaign, bringing to the Court a steady flow of litigation and strong legal arguments against government economic policies.

The Court's expansions of civil liberties from the 1940s to the 1970s also benefited from social support. If these expansions were not always popular, they had significant support within society as a whole and within political elite groups and the legal community.[39] Social changes and the work of organizations such as the National Association for the Advancement of Colored People (NAACP) and the American Civil Liberties Union (ACLU) allowed civil liberties to take a more prominent place on the Court's agenda and allowed the Court to broaden its interpretations of constitutional rights.[40]

To a degree, the Court's increased conservatism since the 1970s reflects changing attitudes in the general public and a growth in litigation by conservative groups. Yet there is probably too little support for the Court to fully reverse its earlier expansions of government regulatory power and protections for civil liberties. The Court has considerable freedom from societal opinion and social trends, but its freedom is not total.[41]

Policy Preferences and the Appointment Power

The freedom that justices do have generally allows them to make their own judgments about the issues they face. Those judgments are based in part on their assessments of cases in legal terms. But because the questions before the Court seldom have clear legal answers, justices' policy preferences are the primary basis for the positions they take.

The importance of policy preferences suggests that a great deal about the Court's policies can be explained simply and directly: during any given period in the Court's history, its policies have largely reflected the collective preferences of its members. Most of the justices who served from the 1890s through the early 1930s were political conservatives who questioned the desirability of government regulation of business enterprises. In contrast, the justices who came to the Court from the late 1930s through the mid-1960s were predominantly liberals who supported government management of the economy and, in most instances, broader protections of civil liberties.

For their part, with a few exceptions, the justices joining the Court since 1969 have been more conservative on civil liberties and economic issues than the justices of the preceding period. In 2007 Justice John Paul Stevens underlined how much the Court's membership has changed in ideological terms: "Including myself, every judge who's been appointed to the Court since Lewis Powell [selected in 1971] has been more conservative than his or her predecessor. Except maybe Justice Ginsburg. That's bound to have an effect on the court."[42]

An explanation of the Court's direction that focuses on the justices' policy preferences is not entirely satisfying, because it does not show why certain preferences predominated in the Court during particular periods. One reason is that some values were dominant in the nation during the periods in which justices were developing their attitudes. Another is that the justices came from backgrounds that instilled particular values in them. Most important, the higher-status backgrounds that predominated during most of the Court's history fostered sympathy for the views and interests of higher-status segments of society. Further, the prevailing ideology in elite segments of the legal profession shapes the views of its members, including future Supreme Court justices. The most direct source of the Court's collective preferences, however, is the decisions that presidents make in appointing justices.

Indeed, the predominant pattern of Supreme Court policy at any given time tends to reflect the identities of appointing presidents. If a series of appointments is made by conservative presidents, the Court is likely to become a conservative body. And because vacancies occur in the Court with some frequency—on average, once every two years—most presidents can affect the Court's direction significantly.

Robert Dahl argued that for this reason "the policy views dominant on the Court are never for long out of line with the policy views dominant among the lawmaking majorities of the United States."[43] In Dahl's judgment, the president's power to make appointments, with Senate confirmation of nominees, limits the number of times that the Court overturns major federal statutes: justices generally have the same views about policy as members of Congress and the president, so they seldom upset the policies of these branches. I think there is much to Dahl's argument. But because of several complicating factors, the appointment power produces only imperfect control by "lawmaking majorities."

One factor is time lag. Most justices serve for many years, so the Court usually reflects the views of past presidents and Senates more than those of the current president and Senate. The lag varies in length, chiefly because presidents have differing opportunities to make appointments. Richard Nixon selected four justices during his six years in office, but Bill Clinton and George W. Bush each chose only two justices in eight years. Jimmy Carter did even worse. The absence of vacancies during his term, combined with his failed reelection bid in 1980, made him the only president to serve at least four years without appointing any justices. In turn, it meant that every appointment to the Court between 1969 and 1992 was made by a Republican president.

Further, a president's influence on the Court depends on its ideological configuration and on which members leave it, as well as the number of appointments. Barack Obama appointed two new justices in his first two years in office. But each replaced one of the Court's most liberal justices, so the two appointments had little impact on the Court's ideological position.

Another complicating factor is the deviation of justices from presidential expectations. Presidents usually get most of what they want from their appointees, but that is not a certainty. The unprecedented liberalism of the Court in the 1960s resulted largely from Dwight Eisenhower's miscalculations in nominating Earl Warren and William Brennan. The Rehnquist Court was not as conservative as it could have been because Sandra Day O'Connor, Anthony Kennedy, and especially David Souter diverged from the expectations of the Republican presidents who chose them.

The role of chance in shaping the Court's general direction also deserves emphasis. Chance plays a part in the timing of Court vacancies and in the performance of justices relative to their appointers' expectations. For that matter, the identity of the president who fills vacancies in the Court sometimes reflects chance. The close electoral victories of John Kennedy in 1960 and Richard Nixon in 1968 were hardly inevitable. The election of George W. Bush in 2000 was even closer. The Kennedy and Nixon appointments had a major impact on the Court's policies, and Bush's appointments also affected those policies.

The policy orientations of the Supreme Court between the 1890s and the 1960s reflected the existence of strong lawmaking majorities during two periods: the conservative Republican governments that dominated much of the period from the Civil War to the Great Depression and the twelve-year tenure of Franklin Roosevelt that was accompanied by heavily Democratic Senates. These orientations also reflected patterns of resignations and deaths, unexpected behavior on the part of justices, and other factors that were a good deal less systematic. And if these factors had operated differently since 1969, the current Court might be less conservative— or even more so—than the one that actually exists. The forces that shape the Court's policy positions, like so much about the Court, operate in complex ways.

Conclusion

In this chapter I have examined several issues relating to the Supreme Court's policy outputs. A few conclusions merit emphasis.

First, in some periods the Court's policymaking has had fairly clear themes. During the first part of the twentieth century, the dominant theme was scrutiny of government economic policies. Later in that century the primary theme was scrutiny of policies and practices that impinged on individual liberties. In each instance the theme was evident in both the Court's agenda and the content of its decisions.

Second, these themes and the Court's work as a whole reflect both the justices' policy preferences and the influence of the Court's environment. The Court's policies are largely what its members would like them to be. But the Court is subject to some external influences that shape its policies in direct and indirect ways. And the president's appointment power creates a link between the justices' policy preferences and their political environment.

Finally, the Court's role as a policymaker, significant thought it is, has major limits. The Court gives considerable attention to some areas of policy but scarcely touches others. Some critical matters, such as foreign policy, are left almost entirely to the other branches of government. Even in the areas to which the Court gives the most attention, it seldom disturbs the basic features of national policy.

To a considerable degree, the significance of the Supreme Court as a policymaker depends on the impact of its decisions, the subject of Chapter 6. After examining the effect of the Court's decisions, I can make a more comprehensive assessment of the Court's role in the policymaking process.

NOTES

1. The discussion of agenda change in this section is drawn in part from Richard L. Pacelle, Jr., *The Transformation of the Supreme Court's Agenda from the New Deal to the Reagan Administration* (Boulder, CO: Westview Press, 1991); Richard L. Pacelle, Jr., "The Dynamics and Determinants of Agenda Change in the Rehnquist Court," in *Contemplating Courts*, ed. Lee Epstein (Washington, DC: CQ Press, 1995), 251–274; and Drew Noble Lanier, *Of Time and Judicial Behavior: United States Supreme Court Agenda-Setting and Decision-Making, 1888–1997* (Selinsgrove, PA: Susquehanna University Press, 2003), chap. 3. Numbers of cases in broad policy areas and involving particular issues were calculated from data collected and presented by Pacelle in his publications and from data in The Supreme Court Database, http://scdb.wustl.edu/.

2. These and other data in this paragraph are taken from Pacelle, *Transformation of the Supreme Court's Agenda*, 56–57. The civil liberties category includes cases classified by Pacelle as due process, substantive rights, and equality.

3. *Florida v. Department of Health and Human Services* (2012); *U.S. Department of Health and Human Services v. Florida* (2012); *National Federation of Independent Business v. Sebelius* (2012).

4. Because of ambiguities, different people have counted different numbers of federal and state laws that the Supreme Court struck down. The numbers presented in this chapter are based on data in Congressional Research Service, *The Constitution of the United States of America: Analysis and Interpretation, 2002 Edition* and *2008 Supplement* (Washington, DC: Government Printing Office, 2004, 2008), with my updating for 2009–2011. There are some errors and inconsistencies in the Congressional Research Service data, but the broad patterns shown in Table 5-2 are clearly accurate.

5. Linda Camp Keith, *The U.S. Supreme Court and the Judicial Review of Congress* (New York: Peter Lang, 2008), 26.

6. The distinctions made in the paragraphs that follow are drawn chiefly from Robert A. Dahl, "Decision-Making in a Democracy: The Supreme

Court as a National Policy-Maker," *Journal of Public Law* 6 (Fall 1957): 279–295.

7. Among these decisions were *United States v. Butler* (1936) and *Schechter Poultry Corp. v. United States* (1935).

8. See Keith E. Whittington, *Political Foundations of Judicial Supremacy: The Supreme Court and Constitutional Leadership in U.S. History* (Princeton, NJ: Princeton University Press, 2007).

9. The decisions were *McConnell v. Federal Election Commission* (2003); *Federal Election Commission v. Wisconsin Right to Life, Inc.* (2007); *Davis v. Federal Election Commission* (2008); and *Citizens United v. Federal Election Commission* (2010).

10. The cases were *Bullcoming v. New Mexico* (2011) and *Turner v. Rogers* (2011), respectively.

11. Robert Scigliano, "The Presidency and the Judiciary," in *The Presidency and the Political System*, 3d ed., ed. Michael Nelson (Washington, DC: CQ Press, 1990), 471–499; David A. Yalof, "The Presidency and the Judiciary," in *The Presidency and the Political System*, 9th ed., ed. Michael Nelson (Washington, DC: CQ Press, 2010), 456–459.

12. The decisions were *Rasul v. Bush* (2004); *Hamdi v. Rumsfeld* (2004); *Hamdan v. Rumsfeld* (2006); and *Boumediene v. Bush* (2008).

13. See, for example, *Desert Palace, Inc. v. Costa* (2003).

14. *Griggs v. Duke Power Co.* (1971).

15. *Meritor Savings Bank v. Vinson* (1986); *Burlington Industries v. Ellerth* (1998).

16. *Wal-Mart Stores, Inc. v. Dukes* (2011).

17. Sandra L. Wood, Linda Camp Keith, Drew Noble Lanier, and Ayo Ogundele, "The Supreme Court, 1888–1940: An Empirical Overview," *Social Science History* 22 (Summer 1998): 215–216; William G. Ross, *A Muted Fury: Populists, Progressives, and Labor Unions Confront the Courts, 1890–1937* (Princeton, NJ: Princeton University Press, 1994).

18. To obtain these figures and others that are presented later in the chapter, I categorized decisions that struck down laws according to whether they pertained to economics, civil liberties, or other subjects. The criteria that I used were necessarily arbitrary; other criteria would have resulted in somewhat different totals.

19. *Santa Clara County v. Southern Pacific Railroad Co.* (1886).

20. James W. Ely Jr., *Railroads and American Law* (Lawrence: University Press of Kansas, 2001); Richard C. Cortner, *The Iron Horse and the Constitution: The Railroads and the Transformation of the Fourteenth Amendment* (Westport, CT: Greenwood Press, 1993).

21. Benjamin Twiss, *Lawyers and the Constitution* (Princeton, NJ: Princeton University Press, 1942).

22. This discussion draws from John Braeman, *Before the Civil Rights Revolution: The Old Court and Individual Rights* (Westport, CT: Greenwood Press, 1988).

23. *Twining v. New Jersey* (1908).

24. See, for example, *Schenck v. United States* (1917). See also David Rabban, *Free Speech in Its Forgotten Years* (New York: Cambridge University Press, 1997).

25. Henry Steele Commager, "Judicial Review and Democracy," *Virginia Quarterly Review* 19 (Summer 1943): 428. The possible exception was *Wing v. United States* (1896).

26. Robert H. Jackson, *The Struggle for Judicial Supremacy* (New York: Knopf, 1941), 187.
27. William E. Leuchtenburg, *The Supreme Court Reborn: The Constitutional Revolution in the Age of Roosevelt* (New York: Oxford University Press, 1995), 235.
28. *United States v. Cardiff* (1952).
29. Ken Alexander, *San Francisco Examiner*, December 14, 1967, 42.
30. *Miller v. California* (1973).
31. The percentages of liberal decisions are based on analysis of data in The Supreme Court Database, http://scdb.wustl.edu/. Economic cases are those in issue areas 7–8. The unit of analysis is the case citation.
32. The decisions were *Bruesewitz v. Wyeth* (2011); *AT&T Mobility LLC v. Concepcion* (2011); and *PLIVA, Inc. v. Mensing* (2011).
33. The Court's decisions and rules of procedure affecting access to courts are discussed in Paul D. Carrington, "Politics and Civil Procedure Rulemaking: Reflections on Experience," *Duke Law Journal* 60 (December 2010): 597–667.
34. The decisions were *Brown v. Entertainment Merchants Association* (2011) and *Sorrell v. IMS Health Inc.* (2011), respectively.
35. Adam Liptak, "Justices Offer Receptive Ear to Business Interests," *New York Times*, December 18, 2010, A1; David L. Franklin, "What Kind of Business-Friendly Court? Explaining the Chamber of Commerce's Success at the Roberts Court," *Santa Clara Law Review* 49 (2009): 1019–1061; Constitutional Accountability Center, "Big Wins for Big Business: Themes and Statistics in the Supreme Court 2010-2011 Business Cases," Issue Brief No. 6, June 28, 2011, http://www.theusconstitution.org/issue/corporations.
36. *Texas v. Johnson* (1989); *Santa Fe Independent School District v. Doe* (2000).
37. Lucas A. Powe Jr., *The Warren Court and American Politics* (Cambridge, MA: Harvard University Press, 2000).
38. See Keith E. Whittington, "Taking What They Give Us: Explaining the Court's Federalism Offensive," *Duke Law Journal* 51 (2001): 477–520.
39. See Powe, *Warren Court and American Politics*, 485–501.
40. Charles R. Epp, *The Rights Revolution: Lawyers, Activists, and Supreme Courts in Comparative Perspective* (Chicago: University of Chicago Press, 1998), chaps. 3 and 4.
41. See John R. Howard, *The Shifting Wind: The Supreme Court and Civil Rights from Reconstruction to Brown* (Albany: State University of New York Press, 1999).
42. Jeffrey Rosen, "The Dissenter," *New York Times Magazine*, September 23, 2007, 52–53.
43. Dahl, "Decision-Making in a Democracy," 285.

Chapter 6

The Court's Impact

I n January 2010 the Supreme Court decided *Citizens United v. Federal Election Commission.* By a 5–4 vote, the Court overruled two of its prior decisions and struck down the limits on independent spending by corporations in campaigns for federal offices that were established by the Bipartisan Campaign Reform Act of 2002.

The decision drew immediate criticism from proponents of limits on campaign spending, primarily Democrats. President Obama issued a statement attacking the decision that day, and he continued his attack at his State of the Union address a week later while six justices sat in the audience. Obama sought legislation to reduce the effects of the *Citizens United* decision, but with no success.

Opponents of restrictions on campaign funding, who had won several other victories in the Supreme Court, sought to expand on *Citizens United* with new legal challenges to federal and state restrictions. Over the next two years, some lower courts upheld certain restrictions. Most notably, in December 2011, the Montana Supreme Court upheld the state's limits on campaign spending by corporations. The Montana court tried to distinguish the state law from the federal law that the court had overturned in *Citizens United*, but the Supreme Court summarily reversed the Montana decision in June 2012. Other lower courts expanded on *Citizens United* by striking down additional limits on campaign spending. Most important was a decision by the federal court of appeals for the District of Columbia, one that invalidated federal limits on the amount of money individuals could contribute to an independent group that spends money in campaigns.[1]

The 2010 congressional elections featured levels of spending by independent groups that were far higher than in 2006. There was another large jump in independent spending in 2012, which featured the rise of

"SuperPACs" that spent large sums on behalf of candidates in the campaigns for the Republican presidential nomination and the fall campaigns for president and Congress. The Court's decision has been widely viewed as the source of these changes, and indeed *Citizens United* made a considerable difference. Beyond its direct legal effects, the Court's ruling implicitly reassured corporate executives and other potential donors that there was no legal risk in making large contributions to independent campaign groups.[2] But lower-court rulings and actions by the Federal Election Commission also played a part, and ultimately it was decisions by donors to political campaigns that made the difference. *Citizens United* was just a part, albeit a key part, of a broader set of developments that helped to transform campaign politics in 2010 and 2012.

The aftermath of *Citizens United* underlines the impact that Supreme Court decisions can have. But that aftermath also makes it clear that the Court is only one participant in the processes that shape public policy on an issue and the impact of that policy on American life. In the case of *Citizens United*, those processes have reinforced and extended the effects of the Court's legal ruling. Similar processes have instead limited or even negated the effects of some other major Court decisions.

This chapter examines the impact of Supreme Court decisions and the forces that shape their impact. I begin by looking at what happens to litigants in the Court. In the remainder of the chapter I discuss the broader effects of the Court's policies: their implementation by judges and administrators, the responses of legislatures and chief executives, and their effects on society as a whole.

Outcomes for the Parties

Whatever else it does, a Supreme Court decision affects the parties in the case. But the Court's ruling does not always determine the final outcome for the two sides. Indeed, a great deal can happen to the parties after the Court rules in their case.

If the Court affirms a lower-court decision, that decision usually becomes final. If the Court reverses, modifies, or vacates a decision, it almost always remands (sends back) the case to the lower court for "further proceedings consistent with this opinion" or similar language. When it remands a case, the Court sometimes gives the lower court little leeway on what to do, and in that situation the judges on that court almost always follow the Supreme Court's lead. But often the lower court has wide discretion on how to apply the Court's ruling, and the party that wins in the Court may end up the ultimate loser. Such a result is especially common when the Court overturns a criminal conviction on procedural grounds.

Presidential candidate Mitt Romney at a Pennsylvania campaign office in April 2012. The Court's decision in *Citizens United v. Federal Election Commission* was a catalyst for major changes in campaign spending practices in 2010 and 2012.

The defendant is often retried after correction of the procedural problem, and the retrial sometimes produces a second conviction.

One example of a litigant who won in the Supreme Court but later lost in a lower court is Jeffrey Skilling, former chief executive officer of Enron Corporation. The Court ruled in 2010 that the lower federal courts had misinterpreted a criminal statute that was one basis for Skilling's conspiracy conviction. The Court remanded the case to the court of appeals to determine whether that error had been harmless. The court of appeals ruled that it *was* harmless and reinstated the conviction.[3]

Sometimes the parties settle a case after the Court's decision, with that decision providing leverage for the side that it favored. In some other cases the Court's decision is one event in a continuing battle in court. The Court ruled in *Wal-Mart Stores v. Dukes* (2011) that a national class action suit claiming sex discrimination in Wal-Mart's employment practices could not proceed. Narrower lawsuits were then filed against Wal-Mart, lawsuits that were likely to take many years to resolve. The range of paths that cases can take after a Supreme Court ruling is illustrated by the aftermath of *Cavazos v. Smith* (2011), in which California governor Jerry Brown commuted a defendant's sentence and thereby freed her from prison five months after the Court had ruled against her challenge to her conviction.[4]

Implementation of Supreme Court Policies

More important than the outcome of a case for the litigants are the broader effects of the legal rules that the Court lays down in its opinions. Like statutes or presidential orders, these rules have to be implemented by administrators and judges. Judges are obliged to apply the Court's interpretations of the law whenever they are relevant to a case. Similarly, administrators such as cabinet officers and police officers are expected to follow Court-created rules that are relevant to their work.

The responses of judges and administrators to the Court's rules of law can be examined in terms of their compliance or noncompliance with these rules. But the Court's decisions may evoke responses ranging from complete rejection to enthusiastic acceptance and extension, and the concept of compliance does not capture all the possible variations.

The Effectiveness of Implementation

When judges and administrators address issues on which the Supreme Court has ruled, most of the time they readily apply the Court's ruling. They often do so even when that requires them to depart from policy positions they had adopted before the Court's decision. In 2009, for instance, a federal court of appeals held that certain statements to the police by a criminal defendant could not be used in court. But two years later it reversed its position in the case because of an intervening Supreme Court decision.[5] These actions typically get little attention because they accord with most people's assumption that judges and administrators will follow the Court's lead and carry out its decisions fully.

Contrary to this assumption, however, implementation of the Court's policies is often quite imperfect. For Supreme Court decisions, like congressional statutes, the record of implementation is mixed. Some Court rulings are carried out more effectively than others, and specific decisions often are implemented better in some places or situations than in others.

Implementation of the Court's decisions is most successful in lower courts, especially appellate courts. When the Court announces a new rule of law, judges generally do their best to follow its lead. And when a series of decisions indicates that the Court has changed its position in a field of policy, lower courts tend to follow the new trend. For this reason, Court decisions that require only action by lower courts tend to be carried out more effectively than decisions that involve other policymakers.[6]

But even appellate judges sometimes diverge from the Court's rulings. Seldom do they explicitly refuse to follow the Court's decisions. More common is what might be called implicit noncompliance, in which a court purports to follow the Supreme Court's lead but actually evades the implications of the Court's ruling. To take one example, the Court ruled in *Boumediene v. Bush* (2008) that prisoners at the Guantánamo Bay Naval Station had a right to seek their release through writs of habeas corpus. The federal court of appeals for the District of Columbia (the circuit where Guantánamo prisoners had to bring their cases) then adopted standards that made it exceedingly difficult for prisoners to win their cases. The dissenting judge in a 2011 case complained that "it is hard to see what is left of the Supreme Court's command in *Boumediene* that habeas review be 'meaningful.'"[7]

The Court enjoys considerable success in getting compliance from administrative bodies, especially at the federal level.[8] Yet implementation problems are more common among administrators than among judges. For instance, a series of Court decisions since 1962 has limited organized religious observances in public schools, but many schools have maintained the prohibited practices or modified them only marginally.[9] And there has been widespread noncompliance with the Supreme Court's ruling in *Brady v. Maryland* (1963) that prosecutors must provide the defense with evidence that favors the defendant and that is relevant to the issue of guilt or innocence. The violations of *Brady* by the New Orleans district attorney's office over many years have been especially visible.[10]

Two Case Studies of Implementation

The implementation process can be illuminated with two case studies. School desegregation and police investigations highlight the difficulties of implementation and the variation in its success.

School Desegregation. Before the Supreme Court's 1954 decision in *Brown v. Board of Education*, separate schools for black and white students existed throughout the Deep South and in most districts of border states such as Oklahoma and Maryland. The Court's decision required that these dual school systems be eliminated. In the border states there was considerable compliance with the Court's ruling within a few years. In contrast, policies in the Deep South changed very slowly. As late as 1964–1965, there was no Deep South state in which even 10 percent of the black students went to school with any white students, a minimal definition of desegregation.[11]

Judges and school officials in the Deep South responded to the *Brown* decision in an atmosphere that was hostile to desegregation. Most white citizens were strongly opposed to desegregation. The opinions of black citizens had only a limited impact, in part because a large proportion of them were prevented from voting. Throughout the South, public officials encouraged resistance to the Supreme Court.

Because of this political atmosphere and their own opposition to *Brown,* most school administrators did everything possible to preserve segregation. Those administrators who wanted to comply with the Court's ruling were deterred from doing so by pressure from state officials and local citizens.

In places where the schools did not comply on their own, parents could file suits in the federal district courts to challenge the continuation of segregated systems. In many districts no suits were ever brought, in part because of fear of retaliation.

Even where suits were brought, their success was limited. In its second decision in *Brown* in 1955, the Supreme Court gave federal district judges great freedom to determine the appropriate schedule for desegregation in a school district. Many judges themselves disagreed with the *Brown* decision, and all felt local pressure against *Brown*. As a result, few judges demanded speedy desegregation of schools, and some actively resisted desegregation. Some judges did support the Court wholeheartedly, but they found it difficult to overcome delaying tactics by school administrators and elected officials.

After a long period of resistance, officials in the southern states began to comply. In the second decade after *Brown*, most dual school systems in the South were finally dismantled. Although school segregation was not eliminated altogether, the proportion of black students attending school with whites increased tremendously, as shown in Table 6-1.

The major impetus for this change came from Congress. The Civil Rights Act of 1964 allowed federal funds to be withheld from institutions that practiced racial discrimination. In carrying out that provision, President Johnson's administration required that schools make a "good-faith start" toward desegregation to receive federal aid. Faced with a threat

TABLE 6-1

Percentage of Black Elementary and Secondary Students Going to School with Any Whites, in Eleven Southern States, 1954–1973

School year	Percentage	School year	Percentage
1954–1955	0.001	1964–1965	2.25
1956–1957	0.14	1966–1967	15.9
1958–1959	0.13	1968–1969	32.0
1960–1961	0.16	1970–1971	85.6
1962–1963	0.45	1972–1973	91.3

Sources: For 1954–1967, Southern Education Reporting Service, *A Statistical Summary, State by State, of School Segregation-Desegregation in the Southern and Border Area from 1954 to the Present* (Nashville, TN: Southern Education Reporting Service, 1967); for 1968–1973, U.S. Bureau of the Census, Statistical Abstract of the United States (Washington, DC: Government Printing Office, 1971 and 1975).

Note: The states are Alabama, Arkansas, Florida, Georgia, Louisiana, Mississippi, North Carolina, South Carolina, Tennessee, Texas, and Virginia.

to important financial interests, school officials felt some compulsion to go along. The 1964 act also allowed the Justice Department to bring desegregation suits where local residents were unable to do so, and this provision greatly increased the potential for litigation against school districts that refused to change their policies. The Court reinforced the congressional action with decisions in 1968 and 1969 that demanded effective desegregation without further delay.[12]

In the 1970s the Court turned its attention to the North. In many northern cities, housing patterns and school board policies had combined to create a situation in which white and nonwhite students generally went to different schools. In a Denver case, *Keyes v. School District No. 1* (1973), the Court held that segregation caused by government in such cities violated the Fourteenth Amendment and required a remedy. In a line of decisions over the next decade, the Court spelled out rules with which to identify segregation that violated the Constitution and to devise remedies for that segregation.

Federal district judges in the North supported the Court more than their southern counterparts did. Many ordered sweeping remedies for segregation in the face of strong local opposition to those remedies, especially busing of students. One judge ordered the imposition of higher property taxes to pay for school improvements that might facilitate desegregation in Kansas City, Missouri. Another held a city in New York State and some of its council members in contempt for failing to approve new public housing for a similar purpose.[13] Ironically, the Court found some of these remedies *too* sweeping.

Few northern school districts took significant steps to eliminate segregation until they were faced with a court order or pressure from federal administrators. But most northern districts complied with desegregation orders. One reason was the willingness of some district judges to supervise school desegregation closely. Congress and some presidents took steps to limit northern desegregation, but their actions were mostly symbolic and had little impact.

Once desegregation plans were put in place, it was uncertain whether and when such plans could be terminated. In a pair of decisions in 1991 and 1992, the Court indicated that these plans need not remain permanent even if ending them would produce high levels of racial segregation within a school district.[14] With support for desegregation declining, many administrators have accepted this invitation and returned to systems in which students are assigned to schools based on where they reside.

In contrast, administrators in Seattle and Louisville designed school assignment plans to reduce segregation, and lower federal courts upheld those plans. But the Supreme Court struck down these plans in *Parents Involved v. Seattle School District No. 1* (2007) on the ground that they impermissibly took race into account. The ultimate impact of that ruling on school district policies remains uncertain.

Police Investigation. The Warren Court imposed substantial procedural requirements on two types of criminal investigation, issuing a landmark decision in each. For search and seizure, *Mapp v. Ohio* (1961) extended to the states the "exclusionary rule," under which evidence illegally seized by the police cannot be used against a defendant in court. The *Mapp* decision provided an incentive for police to follow rules for searches that the Court established in other decisions. For interrogation, *Miranda v. Arizona* (1966) required that suspects in custody be given certain rights and warnings notifying them of those rights before police questioned them if their statements were to be used as evidence in court.

Lower-court responses to *Mapp* and *Miranda* have been mixed. Some state supreme courts criticized the decisions and interpreted them narrowly. At the trial level many judges who sympathize with the police are reluctant to exclude evidence from trials on the basis of Supreme Court rules. But some lower-court judges have applied the Court's rulings vigorously, and the Court's rules on police searches and questioning of suspects have had considerable effect on the pattern of decisions in appellate courts.[15]

Although the basic rules of *Mapp* and *Miranda* remain standing, since the 1970s the Court has narrowed their protection of suspects in important respects. This is especially true of the exclusionary rule for illegal searches. *Davis v. United States* (2011) is the most recent in a series of decisions that has limited the reach of the exclusionary rule. Many lower courts have followed this new direction enthusiastically. In contrast, some state supreme courts that support the rulings of the 1960s have found a legitimate means to establish broader protections of procedural rights by declaring that certain rights denied by the Supreme Court under the U.S. Constitution are protected independently by state constitutions.

Inevitably, *Mapp* and *Miranda* were unpopular in the law enforcement community, because most police officers want maximum freedom for their investigative activities and resent court decisions that impose constraints on them. But they also want their evidence to stand up in court. The result has been a complex pattern of police behavior.

With regard to police questioning, the impact of *Miranda* on police practices has been complex.[16] It has become standard practice for police officers to issue the required warnings to suspects in most places. Perhaps the primary reason is that reading the warnings does not cause most suspects to invoke their rights. In part, this is because there is an inherently coercive atmosphere when police officers question suspects in custody, so that people tend to answer questions even after hearing the *Miranda* warnings. Further, officers have found ways to reduce the likelihood that suspects will invoke their rights and refuse to talk, such as treating the warnings as a formality with no meaning. And they can avoid providing the warnings by telling suspects they are free to go, so that *Miranda* does not apply.

The Court's narrowing of *Miranda* has also limited its practical impact. In some California police departments, for example, officers have told suspects who invoke their *Miranda* rights that they want to ask questions off the record and that nothing the suspect says can be used in court. What most suspects do not know is that under *Harris v. New York* (1971), statements obtained by officers who do not comply with *Miranda* can be used to discredit a defendant's testimony in court.[17] In *Berghuis v. Thompkins* (2010) and other decisions, the Court has said that suspects must explicitly invoke their rights; simply remaining silent for a lengthy period does not prevent officers from continuing to ask questions and ultimately getting answers that can be admitted in court.

This does not mean that *Miranda* had no impact on the results of police questioning. There is some evidence that confession rates went down after the Court's decision. But that impact probably declined over time as police officers adapted to the *Miranda* requirements.[18] To a considerable degree, police officers have learned to live with *Miranda*, complying at least partially with its requirements and continuing to get the information they seek from most suspects. Indeed, *Miranda* serves them well in one important respect. As one scholar put it, "If warnings were delivered by the police and a waiver was given or signed, it is almost impossible to persuade a judge that the resultant confession or admission is 'involuntary.'"[19] For this reason, although many officers still resent *Miranda*, police condemnation of the decision is far from universal.[20]

Before the *Mapp* decision, as one scholar put it, state and local law enforcement officers "*systematically* ignored the requirements of the Fourth Amendment because there was no reason to pay attention to it."[21] *Mapp* was intended to achieve greater compliance with rules for searches by providing a reason for compliance—potential exclusion of evidence from cases in court. To a degree, it has achieved this goal.[22] Faced with potential loss of evidence, many police departments changed their practices substantially. Most important, some made much greater use of search warrants.[23]

However, the available evidence indicates that compliance is far from perfect. One example is a study based on a sample of searches by a metropolitan police department in the early 1990s. The authors of the study concluded that at least 30 percent of the searches violated constitutional rules.[24]

Some noncompliance is inadvertent, reflecting the complexity and ambiguity of the rules that police are asked to follow in searches and seizures. Other noncompliance is intentional, resulting most fundamentally

A police search in New York City in 2011. The Supreme Court's decisions have had considerable impact on searches for evidence, but compliance with the legal rules for searches remains imperfect.

from the conflict that police officers often perceive: if they follow the applicable legal rules, they cannot obtain evidence they see as critical. Because violations of the rules for searches do not necessarily result in the exclusion of evidence, officers may resolve this conflict by violating those rules. Indeed, one scholar concluded that "for many police officers," the exclusionary rule "is not a significant influence when contemplating a search or seizure."[25]

Explaining the Implementation Process

It should be clear by now that the effectiveness of implementation for Supreme Court policies varies a great deal. That effectiveness depends on several conditions: communication of policies to relevant officials, the motivations of those officials to follow or resist the Court's policies, the Court's authority, and the sanctions it can use to deter noncompliance.

Communication. Judges and administrators can carry out Supreme Court decisions well only if they know what the Court wants them to do. The communication process begins with the Court's opinions. Ideally, an opinion would state the Court's legal rules with sufficient precision and specificity that an official who reads the opinion would know how to apply those rules to any other case or situation.

But opinions often fall far short of that ideal, primarily because it is very difficult to achieve. It would have been impossible to write the *Miranda* opinion in a way that made clear its application to all the situations and ways in which police officers question suspects. And sometimes the Court's decisions are murkier than they have to be. A 2006 decision on protection of wetlands under the Clean Water Act lacked a majority opinion and a clear position on the appropriate standards to apply, and judges continue to have difficulty in interpreting the decision.[26]

Ambiguous decisions provide officials with more room to reach judgments that accord with their own views. When officials are strongly opposed to a Court decision, ambiguity gives them leeway to avoid carrying out the Court's intent. For example, the Court's vague timetable for school desegregation gave southern judges and school administrators an excuse to delay desegregation.

The Supreme Court ruled in *District of Columbia v. Heller* (2008) that the Second Amendment protects gun ownership by individuals. The Court's opinion described some kinds of gun regulations that were likely to be acceptable, but it has not yet decided additional cases to build on that limited statement. In the meantime, lower courts have generally upheld regulations that were challenged, and that trend probably reflects a widespread belief among judges that some regulation is desirable. One federal court of appeals judge who had criticized the *Heller* decision wrote in a 2011 opinion that in the absence of "guidance" from the Supreme Court, he would not extend the ruling to cover gun regulation outside the home.[27]

Whether the Court's position on an issue is clear or ambiguous, its decisions must be transmitted to relevant judges and administrators. The communication of decisions is not usually automatic. Even judges seldom monitor the Supreme Court's output systematically to identify relevant decisions. Instead, decisions come to the attention of officials through other channels.

One channel is the mass media. A few Supreme Court decisions are sufficiently interesting to receive heavy publicity in newspapers and on television. But most decisions garner little or no coverage in the mass media, and what the media report is sometimes misleading.

Attorneys communicate decisions to some officials. Through their arguments in court proceedings and administrative hearings, lawyers bring favorable precedents to the attention of judges and administrators. Staff lawyers in administrative agencies often inform agency personnel of relevant decisions. But administrators such as teachers and public welfare workers usually lack that source of information.

Awareness of decisions is likely to fade over time. The Court's decision in *West Virginia Board of Education v. Barnette* (1943) prohibited public schools from requiring that students participate in flag salute ceremonies.

The decision received enormous publicity at the time, but occasional incidents in recent years make it clear that some teachers and school administrators do not know about that decision. A 2010 report by the New York Civil Liberties Union indicated that many school districts in the state asked students about their immigration status, despite the Court's decision in *Plyler v. Doe* (1982) prohibiting public schools from turning away students on the basis of that status.[28] In all likelihood, the school administrators who adopted those policies were unaware of the Court's decision.

Another channel of information is professional hierarchies. State trial judges often become aware of the Court's decisions when they are cited by state appellate courts. Police officers learn of decisions from department superiors. Here, too, there is considerable potential for misinformation, especially when the communicator disagrees with a decision. Some state supreme courts and most police officials conveyed negative views of liberal criminal justice decisions by the Warren Court when they informed their subordinates of those decisions.

Effective communication of decisions depends on the receivers as well as the channels of transmission. Legally trained officials are the most capable of understanding the Court's decisions and their implications. Police officers and other nonlawyers who work regularly with the law also have some advantage in interpreting decisions. On the whole, administrators who work outside the legal system have the greatest difficulty in interpreting what they learn about Supreme Court rulings.

These problems have an obvious impact. Policymakers who do not know of a decision cannot implement it, and those who misunderstand the Court's requirements will not follow them as intended. Successful implementation of the Court's policies requires both clarity in those policies and their effective transmission to the people who are responsible for carrying them out.

Motivations for Resistance. If policymakers know of a Supreme Court policy that is relevant to a choice they face, they must decide what to do with that policy. Officials are likely to carry out a Court policy faithfully if they think it is a desirable policy and that they will benefit from adopting it. But if that policy conflicts with their policy preferences or their self-interest, they may resist the Court's lead.

When judges fail to implement Supreme Court decisions fully, the most common reason is a conflict between those decisions and their policy preferences. After the Court adopts a new policy, lower-court judges may conclude that it has made a serious mistake. Those judges sometimes rebel against the Court's policy, although their rebellion is usually quiet.

Disagreement about judicial policy tends to follow ideological lines. For many years the federal Court of Appeals for the Ninth Circuit on the

West Coast has been the most liberal court of appeals, distinctly more liberal than the Supreme Court. As a result, it is relatively common for three-judge panels of the Ninth Circuit to take positions that diverge from those of the Supreme Court.

As with judges, the policy views of administrators affect their responses to decisions. The Court's decisions that prohibited some religious observances in public schools elicited strong disapproval from a great many teachers and school administrators, disapproval that largely explains the widespread continuation of the prohibited practices.[29]

Supreme Court policies conflict with officials' self-interest if they threaten existing practices that serve important purposes. Many trial judges who handle criminal cases feel considerable time pressure because of their heavy caseloads. As a result, they often fail to comply with decisions that would slow down their disposition of cases. There is also widespread noncompliance with the Court's 1990 decision that prohibited the hiring of low-level public employees on the basis of their partisan affiliation and political ties. That noncompliance is understandable, because elected officials have strong incentives to reward supporters with government jobs.[30]

Elected officials sometimes have good reason not to carry out highly unpopular decisions. In particular, judges' rulings in favor of criminal defendants may provide an issue to their opponents in election campaigns, and some judges have lost their positions as a result. The Texas Court of Criminal Appeals, the state's highest court for criminal cases, has deviated from some Supreme Court decisions expanding defendants' rights. One reason appears to be the electoral advantage of taking pro-prosecution positions.[31]

Because their positions are secure, federal judges might seem immune from these political concerns. But they too may wish to avoid incurring the public's wrath. Full adherence to *Brown v. Board of Education* would have made the lives of district judges considerably less pleasant because of the reactions of their friends and neighbors, and few judges were willing to pay that cost.[32] The negative reactions to a 2011 district court injunction in Texas against religious observances at a high school graduation included death threats as well as denunciations by Governor Rick Perry and presidential candidate Newt Gingrich,[33] and the prospect of such reactions may deter other judges from taking similar actions.

Differences in the implementation of Supreme Court policies result chiefly from differences in the policy preferences and self-interest of the implementers. Police departments tend to resist decisions that limit their powers but fully adhere to those that expand them. The Deep South and the border states responded differently to the *Brown* decision because attitudes toward race and segregation differed in the two regions.

The Court's Authority. In a 2007 opinion federal court of appeals Judge Timothy Tymkovich argued that a Supreme Court decision was entirely wrong as an interpretation of federal bankruptcy law. Having reached that conclusion, he asked, "What happens when the Supreme Court ignores the plain meaning of a statute?" His answer was clear: "As tempting as it would be to ignore the Supreme Court's interpretation of the text in favor of the actual text, that is not our role at the circuit court level."[34] Judge Tymkovich was accepting both the Supreme Court's authority to make conclusive judgments about the law and his own obligation to comply with the Court's decisions. This acceptance, broadly shared among judges and administrators, fosters faithful implementation of Supreme Court decisions.

The Court's authority is strongest for judges, who have been socialized to accept the leadership of higher courts and who benefit from acceptance of judicial authority. But on rare occasions a judge denies the Supreme Court's authority. An Alabama Supreme Court justice rebuked his colleagues "because they chose to passively accommodate—rather than actively resist—the unconstitutional opinion of five liberal justices on the U.S. Supreme Court."[35] More often, judges give narrow interpretations to Court decisions with which they disagree, thereby limiting the impact of those decisions while acknowledging the Court's authority. In some instances, these narrow interpretations seem inconsistent with the Court's decisions.

The Court's authority extends to administrators. To take one important example, some school officials have eliminated religious observances that they would prefer to maintain because they accept their duty to follow Supreme Court rulings.[36] On the whole, however, the Court's authority is weaker for administrators than for judges. Administrative bodies are somewhat removed from the judicial system and its norm of obedience to higher courts, and most administrators have not had the law school training that supports this norm. As a result, administrative officials find it easier to justify deviation from Supreme Court policies than judges do.

The Court's authority tends to decline as organizational distance from the Court increases. State trial judges typically orient themselves more closely to appellate courts in their state than to the Supreme Court, which is several steps away from them in the judicial hierarchy. For administrators at the grassroots level, both state courts and administrative superiors may seem far more relevant than the Supreme Court.

Sanctions for Disobedience. Alongside its authority, the Court has more concrete sanctions with which to secure effective implementation of its rulings. For judges, the most common sanction is reversal. If a judge does not follow an applicable Supreme Court policy, the losing litigant may appeal the case and secure a reversal of the judge's decision. This sanction is significant, chiefly because it suggests that a judge has erred. That suggestion is especially strong when the Court rebukes the lower court for its failure to follow its decisions, as it did to the West Virginia Supreme Court in a 2012 decision.[37]

In practice, however, the threat of reversal may not secure compliance. The primary reason is that reversal has its limits as a sanction. Judges who feel strongly about an issue may be willing to accept reversals on that issue as the price for following their personal convictions. The Court issues frequent reversals of decisions by the federal Court of Appeals for the Ninth Circuit, often when that court reaches liberal decisions that most of the justices perceive as inconsistent with the Court's legal doctrines. Indeed, Justice Ginsburg complained in one case that her colleagues had inappropriately taken a case and ruled against a criminal defendant "to teach the Ninth Circuit a lesson."[38] But some liberal judges on the Ninth Circuit continue to accept the risk of Supreme Court reversals as the price for adopting what they see as good policies.

For that matter, failure to follow the Supreme Court's lead does not always lead to reversal. The Court reviews a very small proportion of decisions by federal courts of appeals and state supreme courts. In part because the Court hears so few state cases, state supreme courts in particular enjoy a high level of autonomy from the Court's control.[39] Further, the great majority of judges are reviewed by a court other than the Supreme Court, and the reviewing court may share their opposition to the Court's policies.

For administrators, the most common sanction is a court order that directs compliance with a decision. If an agency fails to follow an applicable Supreme Court policy, someone who is injured by its failure may bring a lawsuit to compel compliance with the Court's decision. Administrative agencies find any suit unwelcome because of the trouble and expense it entails. A successful suit is even worse, because an order to comply with a Supreme Court rule puts an agency under judicial scrutiny and may embarrass agency officials. The agency may also be required to pay monetary damages to the person who brought the lawsuit.

But this sanction has weaknesses. Most important, it can be used only if people sue agencies, and often agency noncompliance does not lead to any lawsuits. Most school religious observances that violate the Court's decisions are not challenged in court, either because nobody in the community disagrees with those observances or because the negative consequences of bringing a lawsuit—including hostile reactions from people in the community—deter such challenges. If a lawsuit is threatened or actually brought, whether on school religion or another issue, agencies can usually change their practices in time to avoid serious costs. And sanctions lose some of their efficacy in situations in which noncompliance is difficult to ascertain.

Still, to follow a policy that conflicts with a Supreme Court ruling carries risks that officials usually prefer to avoid. This attitude helps to account for the frequency with which administrative organizations take the initiative to eliminate practices that the Court prohibits. Administrators whose actions require court enforcement such as some regulatory officials have even more reason to avoid noncompliance, since it may cost them judicial support.

Police practices in searches and seizures illustrate both the strength and the limitations of sanctions. Under *Mapp*, noncompliance with constitutional rules for searches prevents the use of evidence in court. Largely for this reason, officers frequently comply with rules they would prefer to ignore. Officers, however, seldom receive any personal sanctions for noncompliant practices that cause evidence to be thrown out. Moreover, illegal searches may not prevent convictions. Most defendants plead guilty, and by doing so they generally waive their right to challenge the legality of searches. Trial judges usually give the benefit of the doubt to police officers when searches are questioned. And evidence that is ruled illegal may not be needed for a conviction. Thus, police officers have an incentive to avoid illegal searches, but not so strong an incentive that they always try to follow the applicable rules.

This discussion points to two conditions that affect the implementation process. First, interest groups such as the American Civil Liberties Union (ACLU) help secure enforcement of Supreme Court decisions by challenging noncompliance. Second, the Court's decisions are easiest to enforce when the affected policymakers are small in number and highly visible. It is relatively simple for the Court to oversee the fifty state governments that must carry out its decisions on the drawing of legislative districts. It is far more difficult for the Court to oversee the day-to-day activities of all the police officers who investigate crimes.

In general, the sanctions available to the Court are fairly weak, so help from Congress and the president can make a great deal of difference when the Court faces widespread noncompliance. In enforcing school desegregation, that help was necessary.

Responses by Legislatures and Chief Executives

Congress, the president, and their state counterparts also respond regularly to Supreme Court decisions. Their responses shape the impact of the Court's decisions. Some responses by Congress and the president affect the Court itself.

Congress

Congressional responses to the Court's rulings take several forms. Within some limits, Congress can modify or override the Court's decisions. It also shapes the implementation of decisions, and it can act against individual justices or the Court as a whole.

Statutory Interpretation. In 2011, Congress enacted a statute called the Federal Courts Jurisdiction and Venue Clarification Act. As the title of the statute suggests, it was a technical and uncontroversial law. But among the provisions of the statute were some that ratified Supreme Court decisions by incorporating them into statutory law, a provision that resolved an ambiguity resulting from two of the Court's decisions, and one that partially overrode still another Court decision.[40]

As these actions indicate, in the statutory arena Congress is legally superior to the courts and thus can reshape the law after their decisions. Especially significant is congressional power to override Supreme Court decisions that interpret statutes by rewriting the law in a new statute. A high proportion of statutory decisions receive some congressional scrutiny, and proposals to override decisions are common. Most of these proposals fail, for the same reasons that most bills of any type fail: bills go through several decision points and can be killed at any of them, and there is usually a presumption in favor of the status quo. In recent years Democrats in Congress have sought to override an array of conservative decisions by the Court. But most of those efforts were doomed to failure because they lacked the degree of consensus necessary for enactment.

Still, overrides are sufficiently common to be a significant phenomenon. To take some recent examples, a 2011 law overrode a 2002 Supreme Court decision relating to federal court jurisdiction, a 2009 statute overrode a 2000 ruling that the federal Food and Drug Administration did not have power to regulate tobacco products, and a 2008 statute overrode four decisions interpreting the Americans with Disabilities Act.[41] A study of Supreme Court tax decisions from 1954 to 2004 found that Congress overrode at least 8 percent of them.[42] Most overrides come within a few years of the decisions that triggered them. In 2010 Congress overrode a decision *before* the Court issued it, because members correctly predicted a ruling that narrowed the right of individuals to bring lawsuits under the False Claims Act.[43]

Members of Congress themselves initiate some efforts to override decisions, but more often they respond to interest groups. Just as groups that are unsuccessful in Congress frequently turn to the courts for relief, groups whose interests suffer in the Supreme Court frequently turn to Congress. Sometimes the initiative comes from the Court itself. A dissenting justice may urge Congress to negate the decision in question. Justice Ginsburg did so in her dissent from a 2007 decision on pay discrimination, which Congress overrode two years later.[44] And occasionally, the Court's majority opinion invites members of Congress to override the Court's decision if they believe that the Court misinterpreted their intent or they think the Court's decision created an undesirable result.

Like other legislation, many successful overrides are enacted not as separate bills but as provisions of broader bills such as appropriations. The 2010 override of the anticipated Court decision on the False Claims Act came in the massive bill that restructured the nation's health care system. Members of Congress who vote for these broader bills sometimes do not know that they are overriding a Supreme Court decision.

Statutes that override the Court's decisions, like any other statutes, are subject to the Court's interpretation in later cases. Sometimes those interpretations read an override narrowly, limiting its impact on the law. This has been the case with some of the congressional overrides of decisions on employment discrimination.[45] Thus, neither institution necessarily has the last word on the issues that both address.

Constitutional Interpretation. When the Supreme Court strikes down a statute as unconstitutional, Congress can simply let the decision stand or choose from a wide range of responses. A study of decisions in which the Court struck down federal statutes between 1954 and 1997 found that about half the time Congress acted to restore at least a portion of the policy that the Court had invalidated.[46] All but one of those actions involved adoption of a new statute aimed at avoiding the constitutional problems the Court had found in its predecessor. One recent example came after the Supreme Court's decision in *United States v. Stevens* (2010), which struck down on First Amendment grounds a federal statute that made it illegal to make, sell, or possess certain kinds of material that depicted cruelty to animals. Later that year Congress enacted a narrower statute that was intended to meet the Court's objections to the earlier statute.

When Congress enacts such a statute, the Court often hears a case to determine whether the new statute avoids the constitutional problem it was designed to overcome. In recent years the Court has done so on two sets of laws regulating sexually oriented material. It upheld a statute to address issues relating to child pornography. But it reached inconclusive judgments in two cases involving challenges to a statute on children's exposure to sexually oriented material on the Internet, and then it denied certiorari after a court of appeals struck down the statute.[47]

On rules for criminal sentencing, the justices expected Congress to respond to a constitutional decision with a new statute. In *United States v. Booker* (2005), the Court held that the system of guidelines for sentencing that Congress had established was unconstitutional in part. The Court outlined a new sentencing system to address the constitutional problem but noted that "the ball now lies in Congress' court. The National Legislature is equipped to devise and install, long term, the sentencing system, compatible with the Constitution, that Congress judges best for the federal system of justice."[48] But Congress has not acted, because there has been insufficient consensus to enact a comprehensive change in sentencing rules. As a result, the federal courts continue to work with a sentencing system that had been expected to operate only temporarily.[49]

In situations in which constitutional decisions cannot be negated by statute, members of Congress often introduce resolutions to overturn them with constitutional amendments. These efforts seldom win the two-thirds majorities needed for Congress to propose an amendment. Congress has proposed an amendment that was aimed directly at Supreme Court decisions only five times. One of these, proposed in 1924 to give Congress the power to regulate child labor, was not ratified by the states. (A few amendments have indirectly negated Supreme Court decisions.) Since the child labor proposal, the only amendment that Congress has proposed to overturn a decision was the Twenty-Sixth Amendment, adopted in 1971. In *Oregon v. Mitchell* (1970), the Court had ruled that Congress could not regulate the voting age in elections to state office. Congress quickly proposed an amendment overturning the decision, and the states quickly ratified it.

The difficulty of the constitutional amendment route is illustrated by the repeated failure of efforts to overturn Supreme Court rulings by allowing criminal penalties for flag burning. In 1989 and 1990, the Supreme Court struck down state and federal statutes prohibiting flag burning on the ground that they punished people for political expression. Shortly after the 1989 decision, some members of Congress began working for a constitutional amendment to allow prohibition of flag desecration. Its passage might seem inevitable, because most members of Congress share an abhorrence of flag burning and because a member's vote against the amendment could provide an election opponent with a powerful issue. Indeed, the House approved flag desecration amendments in every Congress from 1995 to 2006, and in 2006 the Senate came within one vote of sending an amendment to the states. But the general reluctance to amend the Constitution was compounded by a special reluctance to limit the protections of the Bill of Rights. Those concerns were just enough to keep any anti-flag-burning amendment from getting through Congress.

Affecting the Implementation of Decisions. By passing legislation, Congress can influence the implementation of Supreme Court decisions by other institutions. Its most important tool is money. Congress can provide or fail to provide funds to carry out a decision. It can also affect responses to Court decisions by state and local governments through its control over federal grants to them. Congressional use of this latter power was critical to school desegregation in the Deep South.

In a 2001 education statute, Congress employed the same power in two different ways. The first was related to *Boy Scouts of America v. Dale* (2000), in which the Court held that the First Amendment allows the Boy Scouts to prohibit membership to gay men and boys. In response, some schools ended their ties with the Scouts. One provision of the 2001 law required that no federal funds be provided to schools that "deny equal access" to the Scouts or "discriminate against" them. Another provision required that schools receiving federal money allow "constitutionally protected prayer." By enacting this provision, Congress gave school districts an incentive to adopt narrow interpretations of the Court's limitations on school religious observances.[50]

When a Supreme Court decision requires Congress itself to comply with the decision, Congress generally does so. The legislative veto is a partial exception. In *Immigration and Naturalization Service v. Chadha* (1983), the Court indicated that any statutes allowing Congress as a whole, one house, or a committee to veto proposed actions by executive-branch agencies are invalid. After the decision, Congress eliminated legislative veto provisions from several statutes. But it has maintained others and adopted more than 1,000 new legislative veto provisions—most requiring that specific congressional committees approve action by administrative agencies. Congress does not use its veto power formally. Rather, veto provisions lead to informal accommodations between agencies and committees, accommodations that administrators accept as preferable to more stringent controls by Congress.[51]

Attacks on Justices and the Court. When members of Congress are unhappy with the Supreme Court's policies, they can attack the Court or the justices directly. The easiest way to do so is verbally, and members of Congress sometimes denounce the Court publicly. More concretely, Congress can take several types of formal action against the Court or its members.[52]

One type is reduction of the Court's jurisdiction. The Constitution allows Congress to alter the Court's appellate jurisdiction and the jurisdiction of other federal courts through legislation, although some scholars argue that there are limits to congressional power over the Court's jurisdiction. Apart from such limits, if members of Congress are unhappy with the Court's decisions in a field of policy, they can eliminate the Court's appellate jurisdiction in that field.

For a variety of reasons, Congress frequently changes the jurisdiction of the Supreme Court alone or the federal courts in general. Members of Congress often propose to limit jurisdiction in order to keep the Court from addressing a particular issue or to blunt the impact of its decisions, and in a few instances those proposals have been successful. In 1869 Congress withdrew the Court's right to hear appeals in habeas corpus actions in order to prevent the Court from deciding a pending challenge to the post–Civil War Reconstruction legislation. In *Ex parte McCardle* (1869), the Court ruled that Congress had acted properly. In 1932 Congress withdrew the federal courts' power to hear certain kinds of cases in labor law, partly in reaction to Supreme Court decisions that were perceived as antagonistic to labor unions.[53]

Other types of actions have also been proposed with some frequency. Among them are constitutional amendments to limit the justices' terms and amendments or statutes to limit the Court's judicial review of legislation under the Constitution. There have also been occasional threats to impeach justices whose decisions displease members of Congress or to use its budget power by limiting Court resources or refusing to increase the justices' salaries. (The Constitution prohibits Congress from reducing justices' salaries.)

Proposals to attack the Court in these and other ways have been more common in some eras than in others. The activism of the Court in support of civil liberties since the 1950s has led to high rates of anti-Court proposals during several periods in this era. The early twenty-first century is one of those periods. Despite the Court's relative conservatism in this period, most of the proposals to take action against the Court have continued to come from congressional conservatives.[54]

In light of the range of congressional powers over the Court and the frequency with which members of Congress threaten to use them, it is striking how little Congress has actually employed its powers during the past century. Of the many actions that members of Congress contemplated using against the conservative Court in the early part of the twentieth century, culminating in Franklin Roosevelt's Court-packing plan, almost none were carried out.[55] None of the attacks on the Court for its civil libertarian decisions since the 1950s have resulted in any concrete action, though in one instance (in 1964 and 1965), congressional unhappiness with the Court resulted in the enactment of salary increases for the justices that were lower than those for all other federal judges.[56] Why has Congress been so hesitant to use its powers, even at times when most members are unhappy about the Court's direction?

Several factors help to explain this hesitancy.[57] First, there are always some members of Congress who agree with the Court's policies and lead its defense. The means available to block legislation give defenders of the

Court tools to prevent the enactment of measures they oppose. Second, serious forms of attack against the Court, such as impeachment and reducing its jurisdiction, seem illegitimate to many people, even members of Congress who strongly disagree with the Court's decisions. Finally, when threatened with serious attack, the Court occasionally retreats to reduce the impetus for congressional action. For these reasons, the congressional bark at the Supreme Court has been a good deal worse than its bite.

The President

Presidents affect the use of congressional power over the Court, and they may also act on their own to shape the outcomes of decisions.

Influencing Congressional Response. The president can influence congressional responses to the Supreme Court by taking a position on proposals for action. Sometimes it is the president who first proposes anti-Court action. The most noteworthy example in the past century was Franklin Roosevelt's Court-packing plan.

Since the 1960s, conservative presidents have encouraged efforts in Congress to limit or overturn some of the Court's liberal rulings on civil liberties. For example, George H. W. Bush led the effort to overturn the Court's flag-burning decisions in 1989 and 1990, and George W. Bush supported a constitutional amendment to prohibit flag desecration. Bill Clinton supported legislation in response to conservative decisions on regulation of tobacco and prohibition of guns in and around schools. As a presidential candidate, Barack Obama championed an effort to override *Ledbetter v. Goodyear Tire & Rubber Co.* (2007), which set a tight time limit on lawsuits for discrimination in pay under the Civil Rights Act of 1964. Within two weeks of his inauguration, he signed an override bill.

Using Executive Power. As chief executive, the president can shape the implementation of Supreme Court decisions. Most directly, presidents help to determine how the executive branch carries out decisions that require agencies to change their policies. One example was *Massachusetts v. Environmental Protection Agency* (2007). The Court ruled that the Clean Air Act required the Environmental Protection Agency (EPA) to regulate emissions of pollutants from automobiles unless the agency determined that those emissions did not contribute to climate change or it provided a "reasoned explanation" for deciding not to make a judgment about that issue. The EPA responded a few months later by producing a report that supported regulation of emissions. White House officials refused to open the e-mail message containing the report, and they persuaded the EPA to issue a second report that was less favorable to regulation. In contrast, in the Obama administration the EPA used the decision as a basis for strong rules on greenhouse gases, which the administration favored.[58]

Presidents also decide whether to support the Court with the power of the federal government when decisions encounter open resistance from state and local officials. The most coercive form of federal power is deployment of the military. In 1957, when a combination of state interference and mob action prevented court-ordered desegregation of the schools in Little Rock, Arkansas, President Dwight Eisenhower abandoned his earlier position against the use of federal troops to enforce *Brown v. Board of Education*. In 1962 President John Kennedy used federal troops to enforce desegregation at the University of Mississippi.

Presidents can also employ litigation and their control over federal funds, and the Johnson administration used both mechanisms vigorously to break down segregated school systems in the Deep South. President George W. Bush reinforced a Supreme Court decision allowing drug tests of public school students who participated in extracurricular activities by using federal monetary grants to encourage drug testing in schools.[59]

Compliance with Decisions. Occasionally, a Supreme Court decision requires compliance by the president, either as a party in the case or—more often—as head of the executive branch. Some presidents and commentators have argued that the president need not obey an order of the Supreme Court, on the ground that the Court is a coequal body rather than a legal superior. During his campaign for the Republican presidential nomination in 2012, Newt Gingrich made that argument emphatically.[60] In any case, presidents would seem sufficiently powerful to disobey the Court with impunity.

In reality, their position is not that strong. The president's political power is based largely on the ability to obtain support from other policymakers. In turn, this ability depends in part on perceptions of the president's legitimacy. Because disobedience of the Court would threaten this legitimacy, presidents feel some pressure to comply with the Court's decisions.

This conclusion is supported by presidential responses to two highly visible Court orders. In *Youngstown Sheet and Tube Co. v. Sawyer* (1952), the Court ruled that President Harry Truman had acted illegally during the Korean War when he seized steel mills to keep them operating if a threatened strike took place. The Court ordered an end to the seizure, and Truman immediately complied.

Even more striking is *United States v. Nixon* (1974). During the investigation of the Watergate scandal, President Richard Nixon withheld recordings of certain conversations in his offices that were sought by special prosecutor Leon Jaworski. In July 1974 the Supreme Court ruled unanimously that Nixon must yield the tapes.

In oral argument before the Court, the president's lawyer had indicated that Nixon might not comply with an adverse decision. But he did comply. At the least, this compliance speeded Nixon's departure from office. The content of the tapes provided strong evidence of presidential misdeeds, and opposition to impeachment evaporated. Fifteen days after the Court's ruling, Nixon announced his resignation.

In light of that result, why did Nixon comply with the Court order? He apparently did not realize how damaging the evidence in the tapes actually was. Perhaps more important, noncompliance would have fatally damaged his remaining legitimacy. For many members of Congress, noncompliance in itself would have constituted an impeachable offense, one on which there would be no dispute about the evidence. Under the circumstances, compliance may have been the better of two unattractive choices.

State Legislatures and Governors

State governments have no direct power over the Supreme Court as an institution. But like Congress and the president, state legislatures and governors can influence the impact of the Court's decisions. They do so most often through their responses to decisions that strike down a state statute directly or to a ruling that a similar law from another state is unconstitutional.

Like Congress, state and local legislatures sometimes respond to such a decision by doing nothing, leaving an unconstitutional statute on the books. That inaction creates a problem only if the statute is actually enforced. There have been occasional arrests under laws against desecrating the flag despite the Supreme Court's decision in *Texas v. Johnson* (1989), which invalidated those statutes. In a 2009 Missouri case, the prosecutor dropped the desecration charge he had filed only when he was alerted to the *Johnson* decision.[61]

President Richard Nixon and members of his family departing from Washington, DC, after his resignation from office in 1974. The Supreme Court's decision in *United States v. Nixon* ensured that Nixon would leave the presidency.

When legislatures respond to a decision striking down a statute with a new statute, they sometimes adopt a measure that clearly fails to comply with the decision. Such action is usually a means to express opposition to the decision. This has been true of some statutes to restore religious observances in public schools that the Court had ruled unconstitutional.

More often, legislators try to craft a new statute that will limit or negate the effects of a decision while adhering to its dictates. For instance, the Supreme Court's decision in *McDonald v. Chicago* (2010) effectively struck down a Chicago ordinance that generally prohibited the ownership of handguns. Four days later the Chicago city council adopted a new law regulating guns that its members hoped the courts would accept.[62] States have responded in similar ways to decisions on issues such as state regulation of sales by out-of-state wineries and protests at funerals.[63] Laws of this type are frequently challenged in court on the ground that they do not actually comply with the Supreme Court's rulings.

One of the most consequential responses to a constitutional decision by state legislatures concerned capital punishment. After the Court struck down existing death penalty laws in *Furman v. Georgia* (1972), by 1975 thirty-one states wrote new laws that were designed to avoid arbitrary use of capital punishment and thus meet the objections raised by the pivotal justices in *Furman*.[64] In a series of decisions that followed, the Court upheld some of the new statutes and overturned others. States whose laws were rejected by the Court then adopted the forms that the Court had found acceptable.

Like presidents, governors can influence both legislative responses to the Court's decisions and the implementation of those decisions. Southern governors helped to block school desegregation in the 1950s and 1960s through their efforts to stir up resistance. Some governors have played a similar role in opposition to the Court's limitations on religious observances in public schools.

Legislatures, governors, and their local counterparts sometimes must do more than eliminate or modify unconstitutional statutes in order to put Supreme Court decisions into effect. *Gideon v. Wainwright* (1963) and later decisions required that indigent criminal defendants be provided with legal counsel. The Court's decisions spurred state and local governments to increase their commitment to provide attorneys for indigent defendants. This commitment has been reflected in much higher levels of funding—more than $5 billion by state and local governments in 2008[65]—and low-income defendants are now in a far better position than they were prior to 1963. But funding of counsel has often been inadequate, and studies of the quality of indigent defense in states and local areas regularly report serious deficiencies.

A quite different situation arises when the Supreme Court has held that a right is unprotected by the Constitution. State governments do not need to take any action in response to such a decision, but occasionally legislatures act to protect such a right under state law. In *Kelo v. City of New London* (2005), the Court upheld broad government power to take private property with compensation through eminent domain. *Kelo* evoked a strong negative reaction, and within eighteen months two-thirds of the states had enacted legislation to limit the use of eminent domain by local governments.[66] Their action was fully consistent with *Kelo*, since such a decision leaves the states free to protect rights that the U.S. Constitution does not.

Two Policy Areas

Responses to the Court's decisions by the other branches of government can be examined more closely by looking at two areas in which the Court and other policymakers interact. One involves a long-standing issue in which the Court's decisions have evoked a series of responses by the federal and state governments; the other involves a set of issues triggered by the federal government's efforts to attack terrorism.

Abortion. The Supreme Court's decision in *Roe v. Wade* (1973) initiated a process of interplay between the courts and the other branches of government that continues today. Legislatures and chief executives frequently adopt measures to limit abortion, opponents of these measures usually challenge them in court, and the other branches respond to favorable or unfavorable court decisions with new measures.

State legislatures have been the most active in responding to *Roe*. Across the country, legislators have enacted a variety of laws intended to reduce the number of abortions. These laws deal with matters such as the facilities in which abortions can be performed, waiting periods for women seeking abortion, and requirements for the consent of parents or husbands.

In the first fifteen years after *Roe*, the Supreme Court and lower federal courts generally struck down laws that limited access to abortion substantially, although the Court upheld prohibitions of government funding for abortion. The Court's decision in *Webster v. Reproductive Health Services* (1989) seemed to give states more room to restrict abortion, and one result was the enactment of laws in Louisiana and Utah that broadly prohibited abortion. When the Court largely upheld *Roe v. Wade* (1992) in *Planned Parenthood v. Casey* (1992), it was clear that it would strike down those prohibitions if a challenge reached the Court. However, states continued to enact laws that restricted abortion.

The appointment of Samuel Alito to succeed Sandra Day O'Connor in 2006 and the Court's decision upholding the prohibition of one method of abortion in *Gonzales v. Carhart* (2007) encouraged new state legislation restricting abortion, and Republican successes in state elections in 2010 increased support for restrictive legislation. State legislatures enacted an array of new laws in 2011 and 2012, including tighter regulations of abortion and general prohibitions of abortion after a certain point in pregnancies. Like the earlier restrictive laws, the new wave of laws spurred lawsuits challenging their validity.

At the federal level, many bills to overturn *Roe* with a constitutional amendment and to limit the Supreme Court's jurisdiction over abortion cases have been introduced but have not been adopted. But Congress has enacted some restrictions on abortion, including annual provisions limiting the use of federal Medicaid funds for abortion and other funding restrictions.

Chief executives have played an active role in this field. Governors in some states have encouraged restrictions on abortion, but other governors have prevented their enactment with vetoes. Similarly, presidents have influenced congressional policy on abortion. Presidents have also used their unilateral powers to shape federal policy on abortion. For example, President Reagan prohibited U.S. foreign aid to groups that use their own money in support of abortion, President Clinton repealed that prohibition, President George W. Bush reinstated it, and President Obama repealed it once again. Presidents have acted on other issues, such as the availability of abortion to members of the military. Because any legislation overturning such actions is subject to veto, presidents can effectively determine the rules on abortion in areas where they have the power to act.

Detainees at Guantánamo. After the terrorist attacks of 2001, the George W. Bush administration created a detention facility for suspected terrorists at the Guantánamo Bay Naval Station. Two sets of issues about the legal rights of detainees arose.

The first set of issues concerned the right of detainees to challenge their imprisonment. In *Rasul v. Bush* (2004) the Supreme Court ruled that federal courts had jurisdiction to hear challenges by detainees through habeas corpus suits. A week after the decision, the Defense Department created Combat Status Review Tribunals (CSRTs) to determine whether detainees were being properly held at Guantánamo. The CSRTs, staffed by military officers, were intended to provide an alternative to habeas corpus actions. The Bush administration's hope was that the federal courts would find the CSRTs an adequate substitute for habeas corpus.

Congress then enacted the Detainee Treatment Act of 2005, which prohibited federal courts from hearing habeas corpus suits brought by detainees. The only judicial review available to detainees would be limited scrutiny of CSRT decisions by the federal court of appeals in the District of Columbia. But in *Hamdan v. Rumsfeld* (2006) the Court ruled that the prohibition of habeas corpus actions did not apply to lawsuits that had been brought before the law was enacted.

Congress soon overrode that part of the *Hamdan* decision with the Military Commissions Act of 2006, which made the bar on habeas corpus actions retroactive. In *Boumediene v. Bush* (2008) the Court ruled that this provision of the Military Commissions Act was unconstitutional because detainees had the right to habeas corpus and the procedures in the Detainee Treatment Act were not an adequate substitute for it.

The second set of issues concerned the form of trials for Guantánamo detainees. In 2001 President Bush established military commissions to prosecute some detainees for criminal offenses. In *Hamdan v. Rumsfeld* the Supreme Court ruled that there was no legal authority for the president's action. The Military Commissions Act included a provision that authorized the commissions, and the commissions went into operation.

Congressional action in response to the Court's decisions on these two sets of issues reflected President Bush's strong advocacy of action and a degree of unhappiness with the Court's interventions on matters relating to national security. On the availability of habeas corpus, the Court's decisions eventually blunted action by the other branches. As discussed earlier, however, decisions of the federal court of appeals for the District of Columbia have greatly limited the impact of the *Boumediene* decision.

On the use of military commissions, Congress and President Bush overrode the Court's ruling against the use of commissions, and the override stands. After some hesitation, and under some pressure from Congress to avoid civilian trials of detainees, President Obama has continued the use of commission trials at Guantánamo under revised procedures. The course of events on both habeas corpus and the commissions provides a good illustration of the interplay between the Court and the other branches that occurs in many areas of policy.

Impact on Society

The impact of the Supreme Court on government policy is important, but the Court's impact on American society as a whole is even more important. How much difference does the Court make for life in the United States? Among scholars and commentators there is considerable disagreement about the extent of the Court's influence.[67]

A General View

The Supreme Court's impact on society is difficult to ascertain. Any effects of the Court's decisions operate in conjunction with the effects of actions by other policymakers, groups outside government, and broad social forces. As a result, judgments about the Court's impact are necessarily imperfect and subject to debate. But it is possible to identify some patterns in that impact.

The Court has a direct effect when it prevents government from taking an action that would have a broad effect on society. The Court's decisions in the early twentieth century that struck down minimum wage requirements and prohibitions of child labor affected large numbers of people in the period before changes in the Court's doctrines allowed these policies to be re-established. If the Court had invalidated most provisions of the federal health care law that was enacted in 2010, that decision would have prevented a reshaping of the medical system.

More often, decisions have a less direct impact. When the Court makes a ruling, it strengthens the legal position of some set of people or institutions, such as consumers, businesses in a particular industry, or state governments. In effect, it tells them that if they go to court or they are taken to court, they will be in a better position to win. If these beneficiaries of a ruling take advantage of the benefit by bringing legal claims or acting with less fear of legal claims by someone else, those choices can affect some activity in society.

One example is *National Labor Relations Board v. Mackay Radio & Telegraph Company* (1938). That decision allowed employers to hire new employees as permanent replacements for striking workers—in effect, saying that they could do so without fear of a challenge in the National Labor Relations Board or in federal court. For many years companies made little use of the decision. But employers increasingly did so in the 1980s, and in this way they helped to weaken the power of organized labor by deterring strikes and threats of strikes.

Another example is *Marquette National Bank v. First of Omaha Service Corp.* (1978), in which the Court held that the interest rates that banks charged were subject to regulation by the state in which a bank is "located." Banks moved their credit card operations to states that allowed them to charge high interest rates on credit card balances. This decision, extended by a 1996 decision on late-payment fees, resulted in a transfer of large sums of money from consumers to banks. One commentator has argued that the effects were even broader: by giving incentives to banks to profit from unpaid credit balances, the Court helped precipitate the economic downturn of 2008.[68]

These examples underline the complexity of the relationship between Supreme Court decisions and social realities. Even in the seemingly simple example of replacement workers, the Court's impact depended on the willingness of employers to make use of the right that the Court had given them. Their new willingness in the 1980s was triggered by President Reagan's 1981 decision to hire replacements for striking air traffic controllers who were federal employees. And, of course, Congress had enacted the statute that the Court interpreted in its 1938 decision and could have amended the statute if its members were unhappy with the decision.

The connection between the Court's 1978 decision on interest rates and the economic downturn of 2008 is considerably more difficult to trace, because so many factors may have contributed to the downturn. The same is true of some other possible effects of Court decisions. For instance, *Quill Corp. v. Heitkamp* (1992) exempted merchants from the duty to collect sales tax from consumers in states where the merchants lacked a physical presence. That decision helped to spur the growth of online retailers such as Amazon by giving them an advantage over regular stores that have to charge sales tax, but other advantages to consumers from shopping online may have been considerably more important.

As these examples suggest, the Court may contribute to significant changes in society when other forces work in the same direction. When those forces work against the Court, they limit its impact. For instance, when the Court establishes a new legal right, other policymakers may balk at providing that right, and people who would benefit from that right may refrain from asserting it. Some commentators have ascribed serious negative consequences to the Court's decisions limiting religious observances in public schools; one book pointed to increases in the incidence of social problems ranging from juvenile crime to corruption by public officials after the Court's key decisions in 1962 and 1963.[69] But compliance with those decisions has been far from complete, because of opposition from school personnel and the communities in which they work and because noncompliance usually goes unchallenged. This reality limits any effects of the Court's decisions on school religion, good or bad.

More broadly, the Court is only one participant in the processes that shape society. As a policymaker, it works alongside other courts and the other branches of government. In environmental policy, for instance, Congress sets the basic legal rules, administrative agencies elaborate on these rules and apply them to specific cases, and lower courts resolve most of the challenges to agency decisions. The Court's participation is limited to resolving a few of the legal questions that arise in the lower courts. Under these conditions the Court can hardly determine environmental policy by itself.

Moreover, forces outside government also have strong effects on societal conditions. The crime rate and the quality of education are affected by family socialization, the mass media, and the economy. Those forces are likely to exert a much stronger impact on the propensity to commit crimes or the performance of students than does any Supreme Court policy. This limitation is common to all public policies, no matter which branch issues them. But the Supreme Court is in an especially weak position, because it has little control over the behavior of the private sector and because it seldom makes comprehensive policy in a particular area.

These limitations should not be exaggerated. The Court can have considerable effect on phenomena such as labor relations and perhaps even the state of the economy. Its decisions influence the outcomes of elections to the other branches of government and thus indirectly affect what those branches do. But the Court's power should not be exaggerated. When commentators credit or blame the Court for broad social ills, as they sometimes do,[70] they may be losing sight of all the other institutions and forces that operate on society.

Two Areas of Court Activity

The Court's impact on society and the forces that shape this impact can be probed by looking at two areas of the Court's activity as a policymaker. Each of these areas illustrates the complexity of the relationship between Supreme Court decisions and social reality.

Abortion. Prior to the Court's 1973 decisions in *Roe v. Wade* and *Doe v. Bolton,* two-thirds of the states prohibited abortion altogether or allowed abortions only under quite limited circumstances, and abortion was basically unrestricted in only four states. With its 1973 decisions the Court disallowed nearly all significant legal restrictions on abortion. The most likely effect of the Court's decisions, then, was a very substantial increase in the rate of legal abortions.

Indeed, the number of legal abortions per year increased by about 150 percent between 1972 and 1979, and the number has remained near that high level ever since. Understandably, people who care about the abortion issue treat the Court as the source of the growth in the abortion rate. But the reality is more complicated, and it is impossible to determine the Court's impact with any precision.[71]

That complexity is suggested by Figure 6-1. As the Figure shows, the rate of increase in abortions was actually greater between 1969 and 1972, before *Roe v. Wade,* than it was afterward. That increase reflected changes in state laws before and during that period, as some states relaxed their general prohibitions of abortion and a few eliminated most restrictions. If the Court had never handed down *Roe,* the number of legal abortions likely would have continued to rise because of more changes in state laws and increasing abortion rates in the states that allowed abortion. But it is impossible to know with any certainty how state laws would have evolved and how abortion rates would have changed if the Court had not intervened.

FIGURE 6-1
Estimated Number of Legal Abortions and Related
Government Policy Actions, 1966–2008

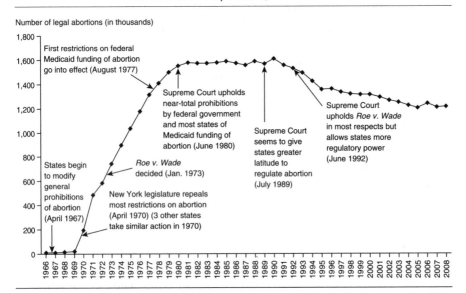

Number of legal abortions (in thousands)

First restrictions on federal Medicaid funding of abortion go into effect (August 1977)

Supreme Court upholds near-total prohibitions by federal government and most states of Medicaid funding of abortion (June 1980)

Supreme Court seems to give states greater latitude to regulate abortion (July 1989)

Supreme Court upholds *Roe v. Wade* in most respects but allows states more regulatory power (June 1992)

States begin to modify general prohibitions of abortion (April 1967)

Roe v. Wade decided (Jan. 1973)

New York legislature repeals most restrictions on abortion (April 1970) (3 other states take similar action in 1970)

Sources: Estimated number of abortions for 1966–1985 are taken from Gerald N. Rosenberg, *The Hollow Hope: Can Courts Bring about Social Change?* 2d ed. (Chicago: University of Chicago Press, 2008), 180; for 1986–2008, Rachel K. Jones and Kathryn Koolstra, "Abortion Incidence and Access to Services in the United States, 2008," *Perspectives on Sexual and Reproductive Health* 43 (March 2011): 43. Figures for some years are interpolated from figures for earlier and later years.

Since the Court decided *Roe v. Wade*, its impact has been shaped by policies of the other branches of government that were discussed earlier in the chapter. For instance, comparisons of states indicate that restrictions on Medicaid funding of abortion reduce the abortion rate and that requirements of parental consent or notification before abortions are performed reduce the rate for girls under eighteen.[72] Undoubtedly, the widespread policy of performing no abortions in government-run medical facilities has considerable impact.

Conditions other than government policy also affect the abortion rate.[73] First, the number of abortions largely depends on the number of unintended pregnancies and on women's choices to seek abortions. A second condition is the ability of women who want abortions to obtain them. Only a small minority of privately owned hospitals perform abortions. Urban areas generally have clinics that perform abortions, but many rural areas lack such clinics. The number of facilities that perform abortions has declined substantially in the past two decades. These patterns reflect the personal beliefs of medical personnel as well as the restrictive laws and pressures against providing abortions, ranging from disapproval in the local community to threatened and actual violence. The reduced number of facilities that perform abortions, in conjunction with growing state restrictions on abortion, helps to explain the lower numbers of abortions in recent years.

All this does not mean that the Supreme Court has had little effect on abortion in the United States. Almost surely, the Court has made considerable difference. But its impact is more limited and less certain than most people think.

Since the 1970s, abortion has been a pervasive national issue. Disagreements about abortion affect policy in areas ranging from the funding of health care to foreign aid as well as the politics of appointments to judgeships. Opposition to legalized abortion helped to spur a conservative movement based on "social issues." In turn, that movement strengthened the electoral position of the Republican Party by motivating voters and political activists to support Republican candidates.

The Supreme Court certainly was not the only source of the political changes that have been associated with the abortion debate.[74] Abortion was becoming a salient and divisive issue even before *Roe v. Wade,* and there would have been a conservative social movement even if abortion had not become a national issue. But *Roe* was one impetus for these developments, and the Court has remained a focus of the debate over abortion policy. The role is a reminder that the Court's impact can extend beyond the policy issues it addresses to the political process.

Racial Equality. In debates about the Supreme Court's impact, no issue receives as much attention as racial equality. The Warren Court of the 1950s and 1960s did a great deal to combat racial discrimination. It ruled against discrimination in education and voting, it upheld federal laws prohibiting discrimination, and it sought to protect the civil rights movement from legal attacks. To a degree, that line of policy extended back to the Court of the 1940s and forward to the Court of the 1970s. Implicitly, the Court was making a commitment to improve the status of black Americans. To what extent have the Court's policies achieved that goal?

That question has no clear answer, because this is a very complicated matter. To start with, the extent of change in the status of black Americans since the 1950s is ambiguous. The most dramatic progress has been political. Racial barriers to black voting in the South were overcome. Partly as a result, the number of black elected officials has grown substantially.[75] The social segregation of American life has broken down unevenly. Official segregation of public schools, the target of *Brown v. Board of Education,* was eliminated. But the level of actual school segregation remains high, and it has increased since the 1990s as active efforts to achieve integration have declined.[76] In the economic arena, reduced employment discrimination and growth in average levels of education have helped to improve the economic status of black Americans. But there remain substantial differences in economic well-being by race. In 2010, the median income of black households was 62 percent of the median for white households, and the poverty rate was nearly three times as high for black individuals as it was for whites.[77]

To the extent that we have come closer to racial equality, there is no reason to think that the Supreme Court was the primary source of that progress. Other relevant forces include the other branches of government, the mass media, and the civil rights movement. In some respects these sources are considerably more powerful than the Court.

The Court's relative weakness is clear in the areas in which it was most active from the 1940s to the 1970s, education and voting. *Brown v. Board of Education* spurred substantial desegregation in the border states, but in itself it was largely ineffective in the Deep South. The Court's decisions striking down devices to limit black voting in the Deep South probably had some impact, but the barriers to voting remained strong so long as the Court acted alone. Ultimately, it was enactment of the Civil Rights Act of 1964 and the Voting Rights Act of 1965 and their vigorous enforcement by the Lyndon Johnson administration that broke down official school segregation and made the right to vote effective in the South.

Because constitutional protections against discrimination apply to the private sector only to a limited degree, policies to attack housing and employment discrimination had to come primarily from the other branches. The most important government action on housing was the Fair Housing Act that Congress enacted in 1968. That statute may have contributed to the substantial decline in housing segregation since that time.[78] In contrast, the Court has not played a significant role in the field of housing.

By the 1960s many states had enacted laws against racial discrimination in employment. At the federal level Congress took the key action in attacking employment discrimination with the Civil Rights Act of 1964, and President Johnson issued an executive order in 1965 (still in force) prohibiting discrimination by employers that do work for the federal government. In the 1970s and early 1980s, the Court generally gave broad interpretations to the laws against employment discrimination, interpretations that strengthened those laws. Some evidence indicates that these laws and their state counterparts have improved the economic status of black citizens.[79] The Court's decisions probably strengthened the effects of the federal laws, but in all likelihood its impact was marginal.

Perhaps the Court played a key indirect role in furthering racial equality. As some observers see it, its early civil rights decisions—especially

Brown v. Board of Education—helped to spur passage of federal legislation and served as a catalyst for the civil rights movement. The development of a mass civil rights movement in the South was probably inevitable, and the Supreme Court was hardly the major force contributing to it. But the Court may have speeded the movement's growth. Its decisions in education and other areas created hope for change and established rights to be vindicated by political action. And *Brown* served as a symbol that helped to spur litigation campaigns by other social movements.[80]

The series of civil rights laws adopted from 1957 on also may owe something to the Court. In education and voting, the Court initiated government action against discrimination and helped to create expectations that Congress and the executive branch were pressed to fulfill. It is true that congressional action was most directly responsible for bringing about school desegregation in the Deep South. But if the Court had not issued the *Brown* decision, Congress might have had less impetus to act against segregation.

Overall, the Supreme Court has had little direct impact on discrimination in the private sector. Even in the public sector, it has been weak in the enforcement of rights. But the Court helped to initiate and support the processes of change, and its members probably can take some credit for the country's progress toward racial equality. Although the Court's impact has been more limited than many people had hoped, the Court *has* contributed to significant social change.

Conclusion: The Court, Public Policy, and Society

It is now possible to reach some tentative conclusions about the role of the Supreme Court as a public policymaker. There are fundamental limits on that role, but the Court is still quite important.

The most obvious limit is that the Court decides relatively few public policy questions. One effect is that the Court can be only a minor participant in fields such as foreign policy, in which it seldom addresses major issues. Even in its areas of specialization, the Court intervenes only in limited ways. It makes decisions on a small sample of the issues that affect freedom of expression and the rights of criminal defendants, to take two examples.

The justices are not always shy about intervening on major issues of public policy, and the Court often reaches decisions that mandate significant changes in government policy. The impact of these decisions, however, is mediated and frequently reduced by the actions of other institutions and individuals. A ruling that public schools must eliminate organized prayers does not guarantee that those observances will disappear. Over the past three decades Congress has overridden a good many of the Court's decisions interpreting federal civil rights laws.

These limitations must be balanced against the Court's strengths. Certainly, a great many Supreme Court decisions have significant effects. The Court's decisions influence business practices and the outcomes of conflicts between economic groups such as labor and management. It affects the state of civil liberties through its rulings on an array of constitutional issues. Decisions on capital punishment are literally a matter of life and death for some people.

In recent years, the Court's impact on the political process has been especially clear. Its decision in *Bush v. Gore* resolved a presidential election. Its rulings on the drawing of legislative districts have affected the balance between the major political parties. And the limitations it has imposed on regulation of campaign finance in *Citizens United* and other decisions have helped to transform the funding of presidential and congressional campaigns.

The Court also shapes political and social change. Its partial opposition to government regulation of private business in an earlier era was ultimately overcome, but the Court slowed a fundamental change in the role of government. Although *Roe v. Wade* was not as consequential as most people think, it *has* been the focus of a major national debate and struggle for four decades. The Court's decisions have not brought about racial equality, even in conjunction with other forces, but they have helped to spur changes in race relations.

As the examples of abortion and civil rights suggest, the Court is perhaps most important in creating conditions for action by others. Its decisions help to put issues on the national agenda so that other policymakers and the general public consider them. The Court is not highly effective in enforcing rights, but it often legitimates efforts to achieve rights. By doing so, it provides an impetus for people to take legal and political action. Its decisions affect the positions of interest groups and social movements, strengthening some and weakening others.

The Supreme Court, then, is neither all-powerful nor inconsequential. Rather, it is one of many institutions that shape American society in significant ways. That is a more limited role than some have claimed for the Court. But the role that the Court does play is an extraordinary one for a single small body that possesses little tangible power. In this sense, perhaps more than any other, the Supreme Court is a remarkable institution.

NOTES

1. The Montana decision was *Western Tradition Partnership v. Attorney General* (Mont. Sup. Ct. 2011). The federal court of appeals decision was *Speechnow.org v. Federal Election Commission* (DC Cir. 2010).
2. The effects of the *Citizens United* decision are discussed in Michael Luo, "Changes Have Money Talking Louder Than Ever in Midterm," *New York*

Times, October 8, 2010, A13, A17; and Richard L. Hasen, "The Supreme Court's Citizens United Decision Has Led to an Explosion of Campaign Spending," *Slate*, March 9, 2012, www.slate.com.

3. *Skilling v. United States* (2010); *United States v. Skilling* (5th Cir. 2011).
4. Carol J. Williams, "Woman Won't Be Sent Back to Prison," *Los Angeles Times*, April 7, 2012, AA1. The decision was *Cavazos v. Smith* (2011).
5. *United States v. Plugh* (2nd Cir. 2011). The Supreme Court decision was *Berghuis v. Thompkins* (2010).
6. Matthew E. K. Hall, *The Nature of Supreme Court Power* (New York: Cambridge University Press, 2011).
7. *Latif v. Obama*, 2011 U.S. App. LEXIS 22679, at 98 (DC Cir. 2011). See Mark Denbaugh et al., "No Hearing Habeas: DC Circuit Restricts Meaningful Review," Center for Policy & Research, Seton Hall University School of Law (2012), http://law.shu.edu/ProgramsCenters/PublicInt GovServ/policyresearch/Guantanamo-Reports.cfm.
8. James F. Spriggs II, "Explaining Federal Bureaucratic Compliance with Supreme Court Opinions," *Political Research Quarterly* 50 (September 1997): 577–578.
9. Kevin T. McGuire, "Public Schools, Religious Establishments, and the U.S. Supreme Court: An Examination of Policy Compliance," *American Politics Research* 37 (January 2009): 50–74; Erik Eckholm, "Battling Anew Over the Place of Religion in Public Schools," *New York Times*, December 28, 2011, A11, A15.
10. Rich Campbell Robertson and Adam Liptak, "Louisiana Prosecutors' Methods Raise Scrutiny Again," *New York Times*, November 3, 2011, A19; *Connick v. Thompson* (2011); *Smith v. Cain* (2012).
11. Harrell R. Rodgers Jr. and Charles S. Bullock III, *Law and Social Change: Civil Rights Laws and Their Consequences* (New York: McGraw-Hill, 1972), 75.
12. *Green v. School Board* (1968); *Alexander v. Holmes County Board of Education* (1969).
13. *Missouri v. Jenkins* (1990); *Spallone v. United States* (1989). On *Spallone*, see Lisa Belkin, *Show Me a Hero: A Tale of Murder, Suicide, Race, and Redemption* (Boston: Little, Brown, 1999).
14. *Board of Education v. Dowell* (1991); *Freeman v. Pitts* (1992).
15. Sara C. Benesh and Wendy L. Martinek, "Context and Compliance: A Comparison of State Supreme Courts and the Circuits," *Marquette Law Review* 93 (Winter 2009): 795–824.
16. This discussion is based in part on Richard A. Leo and K. Alexa Koenig, "The Gatehouses and Mansions: Fifty Years Later," *Annual Review of Law and Social Science* 6 (2010), 330–335.
17. See *Missouri v. Seibert*, 542 U.S. 600, 609–611 (2004).
18. Hall, *Nature of Supreme Court Power*, 68–71.
19. Steven B. Duke, "Does Miranda Protect the Innocent or the Guilty?" *Chapman Law Review* 10 (Spring 2007): 562.
20. Marvin Zalman and Brad W. Smith, "The Attitudes of Police Executives toward *Miranda* and Interrogation Policies," *Journal of Criminal Law and Criminology* 97 (2007): 873–942.
21. Jerome H. Skolnick, *Justice without Trial: Law Enforcement in Democratic Society*, 3d ed. (New York: Macmillan, 1994), 277, emphasis in original.
22. Evidence on the impact of *Mapp* is discussed in Hall, *Nature of Supreme Court Power*, 51–61.

23. Bradley C. Canon, "Is the Exclusionary Rule in Failing Health? Some New Data and a Plea against a Precipitous Conclusion," *Kentucky Law Journal* 62 (1974): 702–725; Myron W. Orfield Jr., "The Exclusionary Rule and Deterrence: An Empirical Study of Chicago Narcotics Officers," *University of Chicago Law Review* 54 (Summer 1987): 1024–1049; Craig D. Uchida and Timothy S. Bynum, "Search Warrants, Motions to Suppress and 'Lost Cases': The Effects of the Exclusionary Rule in Seven Jurisdictions," *Journal of Criminal Law and Criminology* 81 (Winter 1991): 1034–1066.

24. Jon B. Gould and Stephen D. Mastrofski, "Suspect Searches: Assessing Police Behavior under the U.S. Constitution," *Criminology and Public Policy* 3 (2004): 901–948.

25. Christopher Slobogin, "Why Liberals Should Chuck the Exclusionary Rule," *University of Illinois Law Review* 1999 (1999): 369.

26. Lawrence Hurley, "Supreme Court Murky Clean Water Act Ruling Created Legal Quagmire," *New York Times*, February 7, 2011.

27. *United States v. Masciandaro*, 638 F.3d 458, 475 (4th Cir. 2011). See J. Harvie Wilkinson III, "Of Guns, Abortions, and the Unraveling Rule of Law," *Virginia Law Review* 95 (April 2009): 253–323.

28. Nina Bernstein, "Despite Ruling, Many School Districts Ask for Immigration Papers," *New York Times*, July 23, 2010, A16.

29. See Kevin T. McGuire, "Public Schools, Religious Establishments, and the U.S. Supreme Court: An Examination of Policy Compliance," *American Politics Research* 37 (January 2009): 50–74. The first and most important decisions were *Engel v. Vitale* (1962) and *Abington School District v. Schempp* (1963).

30. The decision was *Rutan v. Republican Party of Illinois* (1976). See Ray Long, John Chase, and David Kidwell, "Hiring Law? What Hiring Law?" *Chicago Tribune*, September 17, 2006, sec. 1, 1, 16; and David Kocieniewski, "New Jersey's State Medical School Provides a Blatant Lesson in the Spoils System," *New York Times*, April 5, 2006, A20.

31. Cragg Hines, "Supremes to Texas Appeals Court: You Still Don't Get It," *Houston Chronicle*, November 21, 2004, 3; Michael Hall, "And Justice for Some," *Texas Monthly*, November 2004, 154–157, 259–263.

32. J. W. Peltason, *Fifty-Eight Lonely Men: Southern Federal Judges and School Desegregation* (Urbana: University of Illinois Press, 1971), 9.

33. Mark Walsh, "Federal Judge OKs School Prayer Settlement, Answers Critics," *The School Law Blog*, February 9, 2012, http://blogs.edweek.org/edweek/school_law/2012/02/federal_judge_oks_prayer_settl.html.

34. *Troff v. State of Utah*, 488 F.3d 1237, 1243 (10th Cir. 2007).

35. Tom Parker, "Alabama Justices Surrender to Judicial Activism," *Birmingham News*, January 1, 2006, 4B. The case was *Adams v. State* (Ala. 2005).

36. William K. Muir Jr., *Prayer in the Public Schools: Law and Attitude Change* (Chicago: University of Chicago Press, 1967); Richard Johnson, *The Dynamics of Compliance* (Evanston, IL: Northwestern University Press, 1967).

37. *Marmet Health Care Center v. Brown* (2012).

38. *Cavazos v. Smith*, 181 L. Ed. 2d 311, 322 (2011).

39. Jason Mazzone, "When the Supreme Court Is Not Supreme," *Northwestern University Law Review* 104 (Summer 2010): 979–1065.

40. *Federal Courts Jurisdiction and Venue Clarification Act of 2011*, Report of the Committee on the Judiciary, U.S. House of Representatives, 112th Cong., 1st Sess., Rep. No. 112-10 (2011).

41. The decisions were *Holmes Group v. Vornado Air Circulation Systems* (2002) (jurisdiction); *Food and Drug Administration v. Brown & Williamson Tobacco Corp.* (2000) (tobacco); and *Sutton v. United Airlines* (1999), *Murphy v. United Parcel Service* (1999), *Albertsons's v. Kirkingburg* (1999), and *Toyota Motor Manufacturing v. Williams* (2002) (disability).

42. Nancy Staudt, René Lindstädt, and Jason O'Connor, "Judicial Decisions as Legislation: Congressional Oversight of Supreme Court Tax Cases, 1954–2005," *New York University Law Review* 82 (November 2007): 1354.

43. The decision was *Graham County Soil and Water Conservation District v. United States ex rel. Wilson* (2010). See Joan Biskupic, "Supreme Court Restricts Whistle-Blower Lawsuits," *USA Today*, March 31, 2010, 7A.

44. *Ledbetter v. Goodyear Tire & Rubber Co.*, 550 U.S. 618, 660 (2007).

45. Deborah A. Widiss, "Shadow Precedents and the Separation of Powers: Statutory Interpretation of Congressional Overrides," *Notre Dame Law Review* 84 (January 2009): 511–583.

46. J. Mitchell Pickerill, *Constitutional Deliberation in Congress: The Impact of Judicial Review in a Separated System* (Durham, NC: Duke University Press, 2004), 42. This discussion draws from the Pickerill book.

47. The decision on child pornography was *United States v. Williams* (2008). The sequence of events on the Internet law is summarized in *American Civil Liberties Union v. Mukasey*, 534 F.3d 181, 184–186 (3d Cir. 2008). The Supreme Court decisions were *Ashcroft v. American Civil Liberties Union* (2002, 2004) and *Mukasey v. American Civil Liberties Union* (2009).

48. *United States v. Booker*, 543 U.S. 220, 265 (2005).

49. Linda Dale Hoffa, "How Likely Is Congress to Fix Federal Sentencing Laws?" *National Law Journal*, November 28, 2011, 24.

50. The provision on school religion is at 20 U.S.C. § 7904; the provision on the Boy Scouts is at 20 U.S.C. § 7905.

51. Louis Fisher, *On Appreciating Congress: The People's Branch* (Boulder, CO: Paradigm Publishers, 2010), 82–83; Hall, *Nature of Supreme Court Power*, 105–108.

52. This discussion draws much from the catalog and analyses of congressional action against the Court in Tom S. Clark, *The Limits of Judicial Independence* (New York: Cambridge University Press, 2011), chap. 2.

53. George I. Lovell, *Legislative Deferrals: Statutory Ambiguity, Judicial Power, and American Democracy* (New York: Cambridge University Press, 2003), 162.

54. Clark, *Limits of Judicial Independence*, 49–60. See Stephen M. Engel, *American Politicians Confront the Court: Opposition Politics and Changing Responses to Judicial Power* (New York: Cambridge University Press, 2011), chap. 7.

55. William G. Ross, *A Muted Fury: Populists, Progressives, and Labor Unions Confront the Courts, 1890–1937* (Princeton, NJ: Princeton University Press, 1994); Jeff Shesol, *Supreme Power: Franklin Roosevelt vs. the Supreme Court* (New York: W.W. Norton, 2010).

56. John R. Schmidhauser and Larry L. Berg, *The Supreme Court and Congress: Conflict and Interaction, 1945–1968* (New York: Free Press, 1972), 8–12.

57. See Charles Gardner Geyh, *When Courts and Congress Collide: The Struggle for Control of America's Judicial System* (Ann Arbor: University of Michigan Press, 2006).

58. Felicity Barringer, "White House Refused to Open E-Mail on Pollutants," *New York Times*, June 25, 2008, A15; Jenna Greene, "Air Assault," *National*

Law Journal, June 14, 2010, 1, 10. The quoted language is from p. 534 of the Court's opinion.

59. Donna Leinwand, "More Schools Test for Drugs," *USA Today,* July 12, 2006, 1A; "Conference Call Briefing . . . on the 2008 National Drug Control Strategy," Business Wire, March 1, 2008, www.businesswire.com. The decision was *Board of Education v. Earls* (2002).

60. David Savage, "Gingrich Might Scrap Certain Judges, Courts," *Los Angeles Times,* December 18, 2011, A20.

61. Lee Rudi Keller, "Cape Girardeau Man Released After Arrest for Flag Desecration," *Southeast Missourian,* October 25, 2009.

62. Abdon M. Pallasch, "Aldermen OK New Limits on Guns," *Chicago Sun Times,* July 3, 2010, 2.

63. The winery decision was *Granholm v. Heald* (2005); the funeral decision was *Snyder v. Phelps* (2011).

64. Lee Epstein and Joseph F. Kobylka, *The Supreme Court and Legal Change: Abortion and the Death Penalty* (Chapel Hill: University of North Carolina Press, 1992), 87.

65. Holly R. Stevens et al., *State, County and Local Expenditures for Indigent Defense Services, Fiscal 2008,* November 2010, 76, http://www.abanow.org/2011/06/aba-report-details-indigent-defense-services-throughout-the-u-s/.

66. David G. Savage, "Even a Supreme Court Loss Can Propel a Cause," *Los Angeles Times,* January 3, 2007, A10.

67. For two divergent views, see Gerald N. Rosenberg, *The Hollow Hope: Can Courts Bring about Social Change?* 2d ed. (Chicago: University of Chicago Press, 2008); and Hall, *Nature of Supreme Court Power.*

68. Thomas Geoghegan, "Infinite Debt: How Unlimited Interest Rates Destroyed the Economy," *Harper's Magazine,* April 2009, 31–39. The 1996 decision was *Smiley v. Citibank.*

69. David Barton, *America: To Pray or Not to Pray?* 5th ed. (Aledo, TX: WallBuilder Press, 1994).

70. One example is Rick Perry, *Fed Up! Our Fight to Save America from Washington* (New York: Little, Brown, 2010), chap. 6.

71. This discussion of abortion is based in part on Rosenberg, *The Hollow Hope,* 175–201; and Matthew E. Wetstein, "The Abortion Rate Paradox: The Impact of National Policy Change on Abortion Rates," *Social Science Quarterly* 76 (September 1995): 607–618.

72. Michael J. New, "Analyzing the Effect of Anti-Abortion U.S. State Legislation in the Post-*Casey* Era," *State Politics & Policy Quarterly* 11 (March 2011): 28–47.

73. See Rachel K. Jones and Kathryn Koolstra, "Abortion Incidence and Access to Services in the United States, 2008," *Perspectives on Sexual and Reproductive Health* 43 (March 2011): 41–50.

74. Linda Greenhouse and Reva B. Siegel, "Before (and After) *Roe v. Wade:* New Questions about Backlash," *Yale Law Journal* 120 (June 2011): 100–159.

75. Figures on the number of black elected officials from 1970 to 2002 (the most recent year for which data have been compiled) are in U.S. Census Bureau, *Statistical Abstract of the United States: 2010* (Washington, DC: Census Bureau, 2009), table 404.

76. Gary Orfield and Chungmei Lee, *Racial Transformation and the Changing Nature of Segregation* (Cambridge, MA: Civil Rights Project, Harvard University, 2006).

77. Carmen DeNavas-Walt, Bernadette D. Proctor, and Jessica C. Smith, U.S. Census Bureau, *Income, Poverty, and Health Insurance Coverage in the United States: 2010* (Washington, DC: Government Printing Office, 2011), 15, 33.

78. Edward Glaeser and Jacob Vigdor, "The End of the Segregated Century: Racial Separation in America's Neighborhoods, 1980–2010," *Civic Report* (Manhattan Institute) 66 (January 2012).

79. See William M. Carrington, Kristin McCue, and Brooks Pierce, "Using Establishment Size to Measure the Impact of Title VII and Affirmative Action," *Journal of Human Resources* 35 (Summer 2000): 503–523; and David Neumark and Wendy A. Stock, "The Labor Market Effects of Sex and Race Discrimination Laws," *Economic Inquiry* 44 (July 2006): 385–419.

80. David S. Meyer and Steven A. Boutcher, "Signals and Spillover: *Brown v Board of Education* and Other Social Movements," *Perspectives on Politics* 5 (March 2007): 81–93; Martha Minow, *In Brown's Wake: Legacies of America's Educational Landmark* (New York: Oxford University Press, 2010).

Glossary of Legal Terms

Affirm. In an appellate court, to reach a decision that agrees with the result reached in the case by the lower court.

Amicus curiae. "Friend of the court." A person, private group or institution, or government agency, not a party to a case, that participates in the case (usually through submission of a brief) at the invitation of the court or on its own initiative.

Appeal. In general, a case brought to a higher court for review. In the Supreme Court, a small number of cases are designated as appeals under federal law; formally, these must be heard by the Court.

Appellant. The party that appeals a lower-court decision to a higher court.

Appellee. A party to an appeal who wishes to have the lower-court decision upheld and who responds when the case is appealed.

Brief. A document submitted by counsel to a court setting out the facts of the case and the legal arguments in support of the party represented by the counsel.

Certiorari, Writ of. A writ issued by the Supreme Court, at its discretion, to order a lower court to send a case to the Supreme Court for review. Most cases come to the Court as petitions for writs of certiorari.

Civil cases. All legal cases other than criminal cases.

Class action. A lawsuit brought by one person or group on behalf of all persons in similar situations.

Concurring opinion. An opinion by a member of a court that agrees with the result reached by the court in the case but offers its own rationale for the decision.

Dicta. See Obiter dictum.

Discretionary jurisdiction. Jurisdiction that a court may accept or reject in particular cases. The Supreme Court has discretionary jurisdiction over most cases that come to it.

Dissenting opinion. An opinion by a member of a court that disagrees with the result reached by the court in the case.

Habeas corpus. "You have the body." A writ issued by a court to inquire whether a person is lawfully imprisoned or detained. The writ demands that the persons holding the prisoner justify the detention or release the prisoner.

Holding. In a majority opinion, the rule of law necessary to decide the case. That rule is binding in future cases.

In forma pauperis. "In the manner of a pauper." In the Supreme Court, cases brought in forma pauperis by indigent persons are exempt from the Court's usual fees and from some formal requirements.

Judicial review. Review of legislation or other government action to determine its consistency with the federal or state constitution; includes the power to strike down policies that are inconsistent with a constitutional provision. The Supreme Court reviews government action only under the federal Constitution, not state constitutions.

Jurisdiction. The power of a court to hear a case in question.

Litigants. The parties to a court case.

Majority opinion. An opinion in a case that is subscribed to by a majority of the judges who participated in the decision. Also known as the opinion of the court.

Mandamus. "We command." An order issued by a court that directs a lower court or other authority to perform a particular act.

Mandatory jurisdiction. Jurisdiction that a court must accept. Cases falling under a court's mandatory jurisdiction must be decided officially on their merits, although a court may avoid giving them full consideration.

Modify. In an appellate court, to reach a decision that disagrees in part with the result reached in the case by the lower court.

Moot. A moot case is one that has become hypothetical, so that a court need not decide it.

Obiter dictum. (Also called dictum [sing.] or dicta [pl.].) A statement in a court opinion that is not necessary to resolve the case before the court. Dicta are not binding in future cases.

Original jurisdiction. Jurisdiction as a trial court.

Per curiam. "By the court." An unsigned opinion of the court, often quite brief.

Petitioner. One who files a petition with a court seeking action or relief, such as a writ of certiorari.

Remand. To send back. When a case is remanded, it is sent back by a higher court to the court from which it came, for further action.

Respondent. The party in opposition to a petitioner or appellant, who answers the claims of that party.

Reverse. In an appellate court, to reach a decision that disagrees with the result reached in the case by the lower court.

Standing. A requirement that the party who files a lawsuit have a legal stake in the outcome.

Stare decisis. "Let the decision stand." The doctrine that principles of law established in earlier judicial decisions should be accepted as authoritative in subsequent similar cases.

Statute. A written law enacted by a legislature.

Stay. To halt or suspend further judicial proceedings. The Supreme Court sometimes issues a stay to suspend action in a lower court while the Supreme Court considers the case.

Vacate. To make void or annul. The Supreme Court sometimes vacates a lower-court decision, requiring the lower court to reconsider the case.

Writ. A written court order commanding the designated recipient to perform or not perform acts specified in the order.

Selected Bibliography

General

Cushman, Clare. *Courtwatchers: Eyewitness Accounts in Supreme Court History.* Lanham, MD: Rowman & Littlefield, 2011.

Epstein, Lee, Jeffrey A. Segal, Harold J. Spaeth, and Thomas G. Walker. *The Supreme Court Compendium: Data, Decisions, and Developments.* 4th ed. Washington, DC: CQ Press, 2007.

Lamb, Brian, Susan Swain, and Mark Farkas, eds. *The Supreme Court: A C-Span Book Featuring the Justices in Their Own Words.* New York: PublicAffairs, 2010.

Savage, David G. *Guide to the U.S. Supreme Court.* 5th ed. Washington, DC: CQ Press, 2010.

Chapter 1

Davis, Richard. *Justices and Journalists: The U.S. Supreme Court and the Media.* New York: Cambridge University Press, 2011.

Gibson, James L., and Gregory A. Caldeira. *Citizens, Courts, and Confirmations: Positivity Bias and the Judgments of the American People.* Princeton, NJ: Princeton University Press, 2009.

Hoekstra, Valerie J. *Public Reaction to Supreme Court Decisions.* New York: Cambridge University Press, 2003.

Peppers, Todd C., and Artemus Ward, eds. *In Chambers: Stories of Supreme Court Law Clerks and Their Justices.* Charlottesville: University of Virginia Press, 2012.

Perry, Barbara A. *The Priestly Tribe: The Supreme Court's Image in the American Mind.* Westport, CT: Praeger, 1999.

Slotnick, Elliot E., and Jennifer A. Segal. *Television News and the Supreme Court: All the News That's Fit to Air?* New York: Cambridge University Press, 1998.

Chapter 2

Abraham, Henry J. *Justices, Presidents, and Senators: A History of the U.S. Supreme Court Appointments from Washington to Bush II.* Rev. ed. Lanham, MD: Rowman & Littlefield, 2008.

Comiskey, Michael. *Seeking Justices: The Judging of Supreme Court Nominees.* Lawrence: University Press of Kansas, 2004.

McMahon, Kevin J. *Nixon's Court: His Challenge to Judicial Liberalism and Its Political Consequences.* Chicago: University of Chicago Press, 2011.

Nemacheck, Christine L. *Strategic Selection: Presidential Nomination of Supreme Court Justices from Herbert Hoover through George W. Bush.* Charlottesville: University of Virginia Press, 2007.

Ward, Artemus. *Deciding to Leave: The Politics of Retirement from the United States Supreme Court.* Albany: State University of New York Press, 2003.

Yalof, David Alistair. *Pursuit of Justices: Presidential Politics and the Selection of Supreme Court Nominees.* Chicago: University of Chicago Press, 1999.

Chapter 3

Baird, Vanessa A. *Answering the Call of the Court: How Justices and Litigants Set the Supreme Court Agenda.* Charlottesville: University of Virginia Press, 2007.

Collins, Paul M., Jr. *Friends of the Supreme Court: Interest Groups and Judicial Decision Making.* New York: Oxford University Press, 2008.

Lawrence, Susan E. *The Poor in Court: The Legal Services Program and Supreme Court Decision Making.* Princeton, NJ: Princeton University Press, 1990.

McGuire, Kevin T. *The Supreme Court Bar: Legal Elites in the Washington Community.* Charlottesville: University Press of Virginia, 1993.

Pacelle, Richard L., Jr. *Between Law and Politics: The Solicitor General and the Structuring of Civil Rights, Gender, and Reproductive Rights Litigation.* College Station: Texas A&M Press, 2003.

Sorauf, Frank J. *The Wall of Separation: The Constitutional Politics of Church and State.* Princeton, NJ: Princeton University Press, 1976.

Walker, Samuel. *In Defense of American Liberties: A History of the ACLU.* 2d ed. Carbondale: Southern Illinois University Press, 1999.

Chapter 4

Bailey, Michael A., and Forrest Maltzman. *The Constrained Court: Law, Politics, and the Decisions Justices Make.* Princeton, NJ: Princeton University Press, 2011.

Biskupic, Joan. *American Original: The Life and Constitution of Supreme Court Justice Antonin Scalia.* New York: Farrar, Strauss, & Giroux, 2009.

Brenner, Saul, and Joseph M. Whitmeyer. *Strategy on the United States Supreme Court.* New York: Cambridge University Press, 2009.

Clark, Tom S. *The Limits of Judicial Independence.* New York: Cambridge University Press, 2011.

Epstein, Lee, and Jack Knight. *The Choices Justices Make.* Washington, DC: CQ Press, 1998.

Friedman, Barry. *The Will of the People: How Public Opinion Has Influenced the Supreme Court and Shaped the Meaning of the Constitution.* New York: Farrar, Strauss, & Giroux, 2009.

Hansford, Thomas G., and James F. Spriggs II. *The Politics of Precedent on the U.S. Supreme Court.* Princeton, NJ: Princeton University Press, 2006.

Maltzman, Forrest, James F. Spriggs II, and Paul J. Wahlbeck. *Crafting Law on the Supreme Court: The Collegial Game.* New York: Cambridge University Press, 2000.

Maveety, Nancy. *Queen's Court: Judicial Power in the Rehnquist Era.* Lawrence: University Press of Kansas, 2008.

Pacelle, Richard L., Jr., Brett W. Curry, and Bryan W. Marshall. *Decision Making by the Modern Supreme Court.* New York: Cambridge University Press, 2011.

Segal, Jeffrey A., and Harold J. Spaeth. *The Supreme Court and the Attitudinal Model Revisited.* New York: Cambridge University Press, 2002.

Stevens, John Paul. *Five Chiefs: A Supreme Court Memoir.* New York: Little, Brown, 2011.

Chapter 5

Epp, Charles R. *The Rights Revolution: Lawyers, Activists, and Supreme Courts in Comparative Perspective.* Chicago: University of Chicago Press, 1998.

Kahn, Ronald, and Ken I. Kersch, eds. *The Supreme Court and American Political Development.* Lawrence: University Press of Kansas, 2006.

Keith, Linda Camp. *The U.S. Supreme Court and the Judicial Review of Congress.* New York: Peter Lang, 2008.

McCloskey, Robert G. *The American Supreme Court.* 5th ed., rev. Sanford Levinson. Chicago: University of Chicago Press, 2010.

Pacelle, Richard L., Jr. *The Transformation of the Supreme Court's Agenda: From the New Deal to the Reagan Administration.* Boulder, CO: Westview Press, 1991.

Whittington, Keith E. *Political Foundations of Judicial Supremacy: The Supreme Court and Constitutional Leadership in U.S. History.* Princeton, NJ: Princeton University Press, 2007.

Chapter 6

Canon, Bradley C., and Charles A. Johnson. *Judicial Policies: Implementation and Impact.* 2d ed. Washington, DC: CQ Press, 1999.

Geyh, Charles Gardner. *When Courts and Congress Collide: The Struggle for Control of America's Judicial System.* Ann Arbor: University of Michigan Press, 2006.

Hall, Matthew E. K. *The Nature of Supreme Court Power.* New York: Cambridge University Press, 2011.

Leo, Richard A. *Police Interrogation and American Justice.* Cambridge, MA: Harvard University Press, 2008.

Miller, Mark C. *The View of the Courts from the Hill: Interactions between Congress and the Federal Judiciary.* Charlottesville: University of Virginia Press, 2009.

Pickerill, J. Mitchell. *Constitutional Deliberation in Congress: The Impact of Judicial Review in a Separated System.* Durham, NC: Duke University Press, 2004.

Rosenberg, Gerald N. *The Hollow Hope: Can Courts Bring about Social Change?* 2d ed. Chicago: University of Chicago Press, 2008.

Shesol, Jeff. *Supreme Power: Franklin Roosevelt vs. the Supreme Court.* New York: W.W. Norton, 2010.

Sweet, Martin J. *Merely Judgment: Ignoring, Evading, and Trumping the Supreme Court.* Charlottesville: University of Virginia Press, 2010.

Sources on the Web

There are many sources on the Supreme Court on the World Wide Web. Some of the most useful ones are listed here; several of these websites have links to other useful sites. Access to each of these websites is available without charge.

Many colleges and universities subscribe to the LexisNexis Academic database, which provides access to all published court decisions as well as articles in newspapers, law reviews, and other sources. The database includes the text of briefs submitted to the Supreme Court in cases with oral arguments.

As is true of websites in general, the content of these sites can change over time, and websites sometimes disappear altogether. However, most of the sites listed below have been maintained for many years.

Supreme Court of the United States (www.supremecourtus.gov/). This is the Court's official website. The site includes the Court's rules and the calendar for oral arguments in the current term. The website also includes the docket sheets for each case that comes to the Court, sheets that list all the briefs filed and the actions taken by the Court. The site provides transcripts of oral arguments and briefs submitted by the parties in cases accepted for argument as well as the Court's opinions.

SCOTUSBlog (www.scotusblog.com). This site is the most extensive source of information about the Court. Postings provide a great deal of information and analysis on cases that the Court has accepted since the 2007 term as well as selective information on cases filed in the Court. The site also includes reports on oral arguments, the Court's decisions, statistics on the Court's work, and news and commentary on the Court. The postings are arranged chronologically, but a search function can be used to call up all postings on a particular case.

FindLaw (www.findlaw.com/casecode/supreme.html/). This website includes a database of Supreme Court decisions from 1893 to early 2005 and separate files of decisions by year since 2005. Under "Supreme Court Link Index" and "Findlaw Supreme Court Center" the site has links to a wide range of other sites, including those of several media organizations.

Legal Information Institute (www.law.cornell.edu/supct/). The law school at Cornell University provides this website, which includes collections of Supreme Court decisions and other kinds of information about the Court, as well as links to other sites. Connected with the website is a free e-mail subscription service that sends previews of cases prior to oral argument and syllabi of the Court's decisions on the same day they are handed down. Those syllabi are linked to the text of the opinions in the case.

The Oyez Project (www.oyez.org). This site, housed at IIT Chicago–Kent College of Law, provides several types of information about the Supreme Court, including extensive information about the justices through the Court's history. The most distinctive feature is a collection of audiotapes and transcripts of oral arguments and announcements of decisions in the Court.

Office of the Solicitor General (www.usdoj.gov/osg/). This website provides information on the solicitor general's office and on the Court. The site includes a file of briefs filed by the solicitor general's office in the Supreme Court. The "Help/Glossary" file (under "Briefs") provides information about technical matters related to the Court, such as jurisdiction and the assignment of docket numbers to cases.

The Constitution of the United States of America: Analysis and Interpretation (www.gpoaccess.gov/constitution/browse.html). (This publication is one of the entries at that site.) For many years the Congressional Research Service of the Library of Congress has compiled a highly detailed summary of the Supreme Court's interpretations of each provision of the Constitution, along with citations of the relevant cases. Also included are lists of all federal, state, and local statutes that the Court has declared unconstitutional and all Supreme Court decisions overruled by subsequent decisions. Editions of this compilation and supplements to those editions since 1992 are available at this site. Under "Supreme Court Nomination Hearings," the same site includes transcripts of the confirmation hearings for justices appointed since 1975.

Case Index

Case titles normally are followed by case citations. These begin with the volume of the reporter in which the case appears, for example, 374 in the first case listed below. This is followed by the abbreviated name of the reporter; "U.S." is the United States Reports, the official reporter of Supreme Court decisions. The last part of the citation is the page on which the case begins (203 in the first case below). There is some delay before cases are published in the United States Reports; recent Supreme Court decisions therefore are cited to unofficial reporters. In this text, the Lawyers' Edition (L. Ed. 2d) is the unofficial reporter used for that purpose. Lower court decisions have their own reporters, including the Federal Reports (F.3d) for the federal courts of appeals and various regional reporters for decisions of state supreme courts. For lower courts, the year of the decision is preceded by a designation of the specific court—the circuit for the federal courts of appeals, the district for the federal district courts, and the state for state supreme courts.

Index